100 THINGS
KNICKS FANS
SHOULD KNOW & DO
BEFORE THEY DIE

Alan Hahn

Foreword by Walt Frazier

TRIUMPH
BOOKS

Library of Congress Cataloging-in-Publication Data

Hahn, Alan.
  100 things Knicks fans should know & do before they die / Alan Hahn.
  p. cm.
  One hundred things Knicks fans should know and do before they die
  ISBN 978-1-60078-651-8
  1. New York Knickerbockers (Basketball team)—History. 2. New York Knickerbockers (Basketball team)—Miscellanea. I. Title. II. Title: One hundred things Knicks fans should know and do before they die.
  GV885.52.N4H34 2011
  796.323'64097471—dc23
                  2011020191

This book is available in quantity at special discounts for your group or organization. For further information, contact:

Triumph Books LLC
814 North Franklin Street
Chicago, Illinois 60610
(312) 337-0747
www.triumphbooks.com

Printed in U.S.A.
ISBN: 978-1-60078-651-8
Design by Patricia Frey
All photos courtesy of AP Images unless otherwised noted

To the Fixers, and the hope that someday soon we can add another championship chapter

New York has an abundance of everything, but there is—and always will be—only one basketball team.

—A.H.

Contents

Foreword

I'd say that the first thing that Knicks fans need to know and do before they die is go to a Knicks game! While I hope that, as a Knicks broadcaster, I can bring to the television audience a sense of "being there," of the dishin' and swishin', the swoopin' and hoopin'—and, on the best of Knick days—the spinnin' and winnin', there is nothing quite like being in Madison Square Garden when the Knicks are making a run, of coming from behind, say, to threaten to take the lead—or *taking* it.

I can still relate to those moments when I was a player and the crowd was really into it. You'd make a good play and then there's a timeout and you go back to the sideline and listen to the standing ovation. It made my blood jingle.

I had to laugh about a story told by the late Dick Schaap, a very fine sportswriter and broadcaster. It so happened that during the period when I was playing and we had those great teams, Dick had taken Bobby Fischer, the chess champion, to our game at the Garden, and he had never been to a basketball game. They had front-row seats. At one point, the crowd got very excited. Fischer looked back over his shoulder at the crowd, and in a very worried voice, said to Schaap, "Are they dangerous?"

Another important thing to know is the background information on some of the Knicks jerseys hanging from the Garden rafters, which represent the retired numbers of what the Garden calls "legendary Knicks." I'd have to first bring attention to the guys I played with when we won the only two Knick NBA titles—Earl the Pearl, Dick Barnett, Jerry Lucas, Dave DeBusschere, Dollar Bill Bradley, Willis Reed, our coach Red Holzman, and, well, Clyde, too. If you can go back and get videos of some of our games, you'd see the ultimate in teamwork and terrific defense: guys helping each other out. You'd have to say that it started with our coach. On defense: "See the ball and see your man." On offense: "Hit the open man." Sounds easy, but you'd be surprised how many pros ignore it.

Of course, Red knew how to handle situations, and often with a sense of humor. He was once in a restaurant with a few people and someone at another table recognized him and sent over a bottle of wine. When Red learned who had sent it, he nodded in appreciation. Shortly after, Red called over the waiter and said he wanted to reciprocate and send a bottle of wine to that table. The waiter complied, but it happened that the people at that table had finished dinner and were getting up to leave, which is when the bottle of wine arrived. "Red," said the man who had sent the original bottle of wine, "you sent over a bottle of wine when we're leaving." And Red said, "That's why I'm the coach."

Another jersey in the rafters is that of Dick McGuire, my first coach with the Knicks and one of the great ball handlers in basketball history, as well as a great defensive player. It was said about Dick that he not only held one guy he was guarding to just two shots, he held him to just two passes as well!

But this is just for starters. You'll find many more examples as you read this book, some of which I may even do before the final buzzer sounds for me.

—Walt Frazier

1 **The Garden**

This is the mecca—so when you enter for the first time, embrace that moment of hesitation as you gaze up at the famed copper-spoked ceiling. Yes, you're supposed to be in awe.

There is a reason why it is called "the World's Most Famous Arena." It has hosted some of the greatest events in sports and entertainment, from Frazier and Ali to John Lennon and Elton John, and, of course, the Stanley Cup Finals.

But when it comes to basketball, this is the game's biggest stage. This is where all of the greats come to make their mark before the most discerning fans in the world.

"This is the mecca of basketball," NBA MVP LeBron James has said about the Garden. "A lot of things have happened in this building. There is great history, and the fans have seen a lot. This is, like Kobe [Bryant] said, the last building that's still alive...I honestly feel like you go on stage rather than on a basketball court."

"There's no way," he added, "that this could be just another building."

It's not just a building or even a location. It's a landmark venue that, in New York, has been simply known as the Garden for well over a century. It has been in four different locations around Manhattan since the first Madison Square Garden was opened in 1874. That first location actually was an open-air venue located at Madison Square (Madison Avenue and 26th Street), with 28-foot walls surrounding it on all sides.

But it wasn't called Madison Square Garden. It was actually first known as Barnum's Monster Classical and Geological

Hippodrome. P.T. Barnum, the legendary showman and the Garden's first owner, must have been a man beside himself with humility.

The name didn't stick (thankfully) once it was auctioned to a bandmaster named Patrick S. Gilmore, who renamed it Gilmore's Garden. Why "Garden?" During that period, *garden* was a term used to describe a gathering place. There was no NBA—there wasn't even basketball yet (Dr. James Naismith wouldn't invent the game until 1891)—so this Garden was better known for boxing matches, horse shows, and other exhibitions.

The Garden changed owners a few times before railroad tycoon William Vanderbilt took over in 1878 and renamed it Madison Square Garden on May 31, 1879. It lasted until 1889, when it was demolished and replaced with a new venue that included an 8,000-seat arena, a 1,500-seat concert hall, a 1,200-seat theater, and the world's largest indoor swimming pool. (Yes, a pool!)

This was the architectural brainchild of the great Stanford White, who, as fate would have it, was murdered on his prized venue's rooftop garden by a jealous husband who learned of his wife's affair with White.

The Garden's glory years at Madison Square ended in 1925 (the New York Life Insurance building, its gold pyramidal gilded roof well known in the famous Manhattan skyline, has since held the place), but the name was carried over to the new location on the west side at 49th Street and Eighth Avenue.

This next version of the Garden, known now as the Old Garden, was an 18,000-seat arena that opened in November 1925 with a six-day bicycle race. This was promoter Tex Rickard's dream. He's the founding father of the NHL's New York Rangers, who have been a cotenant of the Knicks since this Garden opened.

With its famous classic marquee glowing MADISON SQ GARDEN and listing the events in block letters, it is there on 49th and Eighth where the Knicks first called the Garden home and basketball—especially the college game—became the main showcase. The Knicks played their first game at MSG on November 11, 1946, a 78–68 loss to the Chicago Stags. The last game came February 10, 1968, a 115–97 win over Philadelphia.

The current Garden opened February 11, 1968, eight years after it was originally proposed by then-Garden president Irving Mitchell Felt, and at yet another location: over Penn Station in the area between 33rd and 31st Streets and Seventh and Eighth Avenues.

The place is a treasured New York landmark, but truth be told, this "new" Garden was met with some heavy resistance when the plans were originally introduced. Though it was the president of the Pennsylvania Railroad, which owned Penn Station, who sold the "air rights" to construction above the station to make up for a deficit of over $70 million from the 1950s, the city came under fire for allowing the destruction of another New York landmark in Penn Station's classic street-level concourse with its majestic Corinthian columns and archways.

Penn Station would remain as a major commuter hub but as only a subterranean structure. The Long Island Rail Road concourse still maintains most of the Romanesque architecture from its pre-Garden days.

When Penn Station was demolished, an editorial in the *New York Times* called it a "monumental act of vandalism against one of the largest and finest landmarks of its age of Roman elegance." The outrage spurred a move by the city to enact architectural preservation statutes to protect other buildings from meeting the same fate.

Coincidentally, when the current Garden started to show its age at the turn of the 21st century, one of the first proposals was to build a new one across the street on Eighth Avenue at the U.S. Postal Service building and then build a new Penn Station concourse back where the Garden stands. But after battling with

New York City over various financially related matters, the Garden corporation decided the better plan would be to invest over $800 million into a major renovation of the current arena.

This project, which is being paid for with private funding, will see complete rebuilding of the entire arena—with expanded concourses, event-level and lower-level suites, a new upper-bowl seating area with significantly improved sightlines, two sky bridges that suspend over the playing surface, and a new and expanded Seventh Avenue entrance. The rebuild, which is being labeled as a "transformation," is expected to be completed by the 2013–14 season.

The beauty of this project is that the team will continue to call the Garden home for many years to come. In fact, as of 2012, this current Garden is 44 years old, making it the longest tenure of any of the previous Gardens.

It is here where that famous "Garden buzz" developed during the Knicks' championship era from 1968 to 1973 and where "celebrity row"—the front row of seats right on the court across from the team benches—became the famous place to be seen.

It is here where the crowd doesn't cheer, it roars. And it is here where the noise isn't just heard, it's felt.

Phil Jackson, who played many games at the Garden as a member of the championship-era Knicks, recalled in a *New York Times* story in February 2011 a night as coach of the Bulls in one of their many battles with the Knicks in the 1990s, when, during a timeout, he turned to his assistants and asked, "Do you feel this floor moving up and down, or am I crazy?"

Jackson then grinned and said, "So when they say 'The place is jumping,' it literally is."

2 What Is a Knickerbocker?

The NBA is loaded with nicknames that just don't fit the location. What lakes do you know of in Los Angeles? What jazz do you hear in Utah? Grizzlies in Memphis? Hornets in New Orleans?

Of the 30 teams in the league, Knicks may be the most curious of all and yet, with some research, you'll find the name may make the greatest historic connection.

So what is a Knick? Our explanation begins almost 150 years before the team was born. Knickerbockers started to become synonymous with New Yorkers in 1809, when the best-selling book, *A History of New York-From the Beginning of the World to the End of the Dutch Dynasty*, was released. It was a satirical work, with fiction mingled in with facts, written by the pseudonymous Diedrich Knickerbocker.

The book was actually written by Washington Irving, the famous New York–based author who penned short-story classics such as "The Legend of Sleepy Hollow" and "Rip Van Winkle"— and, as a slight to New York politicians, also was one of the first to use the word *Gotham*, which translates to "Goat's Town."

Knickerbocker was a character Irving created as an enjoyable older gentleman who left behind writings at the Columbian Hotel on Mulberry Street. Irving actually first introduced the character in small classified ads he posted in New York newspapers before the book was released. For instance, according to the *New York Times* archives, there was an ad in the *Evening Post* that asked for information about "a small, elderly gentleman in an old black coat and cocked hat" who had disappeared from the Columbian Hotel and left behind "a very curious kind of written book."

It was a brilliant way to create intrigue for a work that became the first best seller in the city's rich literary history. In fact, some people today view Irving's effort as an early example of the type of viral marketing we see today on the Internet.

Irving came up with the name using history as his foundation. The word *knickerbocker* was actually a label that was derived from the early Dutch colonists, who in the early 17th century began settling in the area that is now known as New York City. The Dutch colonists were recognizable for their short pants, or knickers.

The Dutch settlers, of course, bought Manhattan Island from the Lenape Indians for trade goods that amounted to about $1,000 in modern currency (sure, a bargain, but consider how much they had to spend in renovations!). The island was originally named New Amsterdam, but once the British took over in 1664, it was renamed New York, after the English Duke of York. For a brief period between November 1673 and November 1674, the Dutch reclaimed the city and gave it a third name: New Orange.

By 1785 New York City had emerged as the capital of the new United States. Through the 19th century, the city grew quickly and was the epicenter of not only great industrial and cultural development, but also many political battles and civil unrest.

The first use of Knickerbockers as a team name, according to the New York Knicks archives, was in 1845, when a Manhattan-based baseball team—the first organized team in baseball history—was called the Knickerbocker Nine. Casey Stengel actually made reference to this team when he was named manager of the expansion New York Mets in 1961. "It's great to be back as the manager of the Knickerbockers," the beloved "Old Perfessor" said at the time.

The Dutch translation of *Diedrich* is "father," and Irving's book not only created a nickname for a city's habitants, it spawned a beloved character, "Father Knickerbocker," who a century later showed up in political cartoons as an icon who took up causes for the people of New York, especially when it came to countering the rampant political corruption at the turn of the 20th century.

Knickerbocker became a commonly used term in relation to New York, including the hit Broadway musical *Knickerbocker Holiday* (1938), which starred Walter Huston, a famous stage actor of his time. Coincidentally, the stage version of this musical—it went to screen in 1944—included Washington Irving as a prominent character.

So how does all of this relate to a basketball team?

Ned Irish, who helped found the Knicks (and the NBA) in the 1940s, was originally a sportswriter in New York, and from his journalism background came an appreciation for Father Knickerbocker and all things New York.

"The name came out of a hat," Irish's right-hand man, Fred Podesta, told Leonard Lewin of the *New York Post* in 1994. "We were sitting in the office one day—Irish, [team publicist] Lester Scott, and a few others on the staff. We each put a name in the hat. And when we pulled them out, most of them were "Knickerbockers."...It soon was shortened to Knicks."

There is a legend, however, that Irish wanted the name all along. So either fate was on his side or the strong-willed founder got what he wanted.

The Greatest Generation

The road to greatness started with failure. The Knicks had just been finished off by the dominant though aging Celtics dynasty in the 1969 Eastern Finals. And in the cramped, almost medieval visiting-team locker room at the old Boston Garden, a steely determination was born.

"Everyone was talking championship, because we felt we were on par with the Celtics," Walt Frazier said in Dennis D'Agostino's wonderful book, *Garden Glory: An Oral History of the New York Knicks*.

"We weren't in awe of them anymore," Frazier said. "So we were all talking, 'Hey, this could be the year.' The confidence level was tremendous."

"We knew at that moment that we were the best," Bill Bradley said. "Or, at least, we thought we were the best, and we couldn't wait to get to training camp the next year."

We're not spoiling any ending by revealing that the Knicks went on to win their first NBA championship that following season in 1969–70 and then won another in 1972–73. It would be known as the "championship era" in franchise history, a proud period of time in which Madison Square Garden was still a spanking-new venue and the Knicks were the toast of the NBA and a team widely appreciated in basketball for their unselfish, intelligent style of play.

"We were not the biggest or the fastest," Frazier told NBA.com at a 30th anniversary celebration of the '73 championship team. "But we were the smartest. And we were the best."

The Knicks had come close before, in the early days of the NBA. They reached the NBA Finals in three straight seasons from 1951 to 1953 but lost in '51 to the Rochester Royals and in consecutive years to the Minneapolis Lakers in '52 and '53.

Then, after three more playoff appearances, came the first of two dark eras in franchise history, when the team failed to make the playoffs in nine of 10 seasons from 1957 to 1966. Pretty amazing, if you consider that the NBA only had nine teams during that time and six of them qualified for the playoffs each year.

The Knicks renaissance didn't happen overnight. It was built the old-fashioned way: incrementally over time and through smart moves in the draft.

The first building block of the championship era was put into place in 1964, when a bruising 6'10" forward/center with a soft touch from Grambling by the name of Willis Reed was drafted in the second round. In the following year, Bradley, a collegiate superstar from Princeton, was the team's No. 1 pick in the territorial draft. Bradley, however, didn't arrive until 1967 because he opted to spend two years at Oxford as a Rhodes Scholar. Frazier also came in '67, as a first-round pick out of Southern Illinois. (And, no, there was no such thing as Clyde at that point.)

In between the draft gems were a few shrewd trades, including a deal on October 14, 1965, that sent scoring forward Bob Boozer to the Lakers for sharp-shooting perimeter threat Dick Barnett. And, of course, the final piece of the puzzle, when Dave DeBusschere was acquired from the Detroit Pistons for Walt Bellamy and Howard Komives on December 19, 1968.

And in the midst was an unheralded yet significant decision made on December 27, 1967, after the Knicks lost to Seattle the night before and fell to 15–22 early in the season. Longtime scout Red Holzman, who essentially played a major role in putting the team together, was promoted to head coach. He replaced Dick McGuire, who simply switched jobs with Holzman, which would prove to have great long-term success for both. After years of failure, the Knicks seemed to get everything right.

The team, in its 24th season, won its first title on May 8, 1970, with a 113–99 win over the Los Angeles Lakers in an epic Game 7 at Madison Square Garden. The game produced one of the NBA's most legendary moments, when an injured Reed famously limped out onto the court during pregame warm-ups and sent the crowd into a frenzy.

That championship was part of a wild time in New York sports, as the New York Jets won the Super Bowl in January 1969, the New York Mets won the World Series in October 1969, and the Knicks followed with an NBA championship that following spring.

The five-season span from 1968 to 1973 was a great run for the Knicks, who reached at least the Eastern Conference Finals in each season and appeared in the NBA Finals in three of the five. Holzman and McGuire continued to tinker with the roster along the way, with the most significant addition being Knicks nemesis Earl "the Pearl" Monroe, who was acquired from the rival Baltimore Bullets on November 10, 1971, for Mike Riordan and Dave Stallworth to add yet another star to the marquee lineup that already was adored by the city.

Despite Monroe's arrival, the Knicks lost in the Finals to the Lakers in 1971–72 but then exacted revenge in '73 with their second title, which was clinched in a 102–93 win over the Lakers in Game 5 at the L.A. Forum.

Reed, who was named Finals MVP for the second time, joyfully skipped off the Forum court with the game ball tucked under his arm. It was the best of times for a franchise that has, to date, savored only those two championships in more than six decades.

"We personified 'team,'" Frazier said in a February 2011 interview with *Vanity Fair*. "You can't mention Frazier without Reed, without Bradley, without DeBusschere."

And you can't talk about the Knicks without mentioning any of them.

4 The Legend of Clyde

Walt Frazier strolled by the court at Staples Center in Los Angeles, and everyone stopped and stared. It wasn't his trademark sideburns and goatee, a ubiquitous grin, or his statuesque posture. It wasn't the fact that we were in the presence of, as broadcaster Gus Johnson always put it, a "living legend."

It was the suit.

Frazier has been known for his threads for almost as long as he has been known for his game. Most days he's a walking time machine, a man who goes by the coolest nickname in sports, "Clyde," who didn't allow the ever-changing fashion trends to affect his own personal style. He had a look, and that look, at least on him, was timeless. On this night it was a leopard-print suit—a suit he had made out of material from a couch he saw at a furniture store (no, seriously)—that motivated me to snap a photo and make Frazier a worldwide trending topic on Twitter. Talk about generations colliding.

"You made me famous again," Frazier said when we met at the Garden a few days later.

Hardly. If you know the Knicks, you know Frazier. No matter what generation you're from, every fan can connect with the very approachable franchise icon—either as the dynamic Hall of Fame guard who was a key member of two championship teams in New York or as the smooth-talking, quick-rhyming analyst on Knicks broadcasts for the last two decades.

Frazier arrived in 1967 as the team's first-round pick out of Southern Illinois after he led the Salukis to the '67 NIT championship (which was played at the Garden). Frazier wasn't an instant

Walt Frazier had unimpeachable skills on the basketball court, but in this photo taken on the New York City subway wearing his "Clyde" Borsalino, he shows off his secret weapon: swagger.

hit, nor was he anything like the magnetic, stylish Clyde personality that later developed.

He was a shy, wide-eyed, and almost introverted rookie from Atlanta who initially wondered if he could make it at the NBA level. What helped was that he wasn't the only rookie that season. Bill Bradley, who was drafted two years prior, had joined the Knicks that year after a two-year stint at Oxford. Bradley's collegiate fame preceded him, and most of the attention was on him.

To quell frustration over his early struggles, Frazier started buying stylish clothes. "I'd go out and dress up, then go back to my room and look in the mirror and say, 'Well, at least I still look good,'" Frazier told D'Agostino in *Garden Glory*.

It was while shopping in Baltimore that season that Frazier discovered a brown velour Borsalino hat with a wide brim. The first time he wore it, his teammates laughed. Later that year, the movie *Bonnie and Clyde* hit theaters and was a hit. Warren Beatty, who played Clyde Barrow in the movie, wore a wide-brimmed hat, and suddenly the style became popular.

It's also how Frazier's nickname came to be. Team trainer Danny Whelan is credited with first associating him with the moniker.

Frazier bought himself a Rolls Royce that he promptly labeled it the Clydemobile, and in 1969 longtime Garden photographer George Kalinsky took the famous photo of Frazier that became a cultural icon after appearing in the pages of *Newsweek*.

Then came the Puma Clydes in 1973. Frazier was one of the first NBA players to have his own signature shoe; it's still popular today.

Clyde was a stylish, photogenic character off the court and a gangster on defense on it. Willis Reed may have been the backbone of the championship era, but Frazier was the catalyst. And while Reed was named the MVP of the 1970 Finals and gets all the attention for his legendary presence in Game 7, few recall that Frazier had one of the greatest performances in Finals history, with 36 points and 19 assists, to lead the Knicks to their first title.

"David Lee came to me one day and goes, 'Hey man, did you have 36 points and 19 rebounds in a game once?'" Frazier said.

Frazier was a seven-time All-Star who was named to the All-NBA first team four times in his career. He played 10 seasons with the Knicks before he was traded to the Cleveland Cavaliers on October 7, 1977, as the team was looking to rebuild. Two years later, his No. 10 became the second number in Knicks franchise history to be officially retired.

Frazier currently is the Knicks' all-time leader in career assists (4,791) and ranks second behind Patrick Ewing in several other categories, including scoring (14,617), games played (759), minutes played (28,995), field goals made (5,736) and attempted (11,669), and free throws made (3,145) and attempted (4,017).

Named one of the 50 Greatest Players in NBA History, Frazier was enshrined into the Basketball Hall of Fame in 1987 and two years later began his broadcasting career as the Knicks radio analyst. He moved to television in 1997.

Clyde put the "color" in color commentary, with catchphrases such as "dishin' and swishin'," "posting and toasting," "wheeling and dealing," and "zest and finesse" and terminology such as describing a player as "percolating" or "vexing" or, if the player is a rookie, he may be a "precocious neophyte." His wide-ranging, often comically improvisational use of the English language stems from a dedication to literally study the dictionary in an effort to improve his vocabulary.

Frazier is an institution on MSG Network, the Knicks' home broadcast network. He attacks the job with the same fervor he did an opponent on the court.

"I pride myself on trying to be good in bad games, because anybody can do good games," Frazier once told me. "But try to keep people interested in a bad game."

5 The Frozen Envelope

Of the many legends in Knicks history, there is none more historic and controversial than the story of the 1985 NBA Draft Lottery, the first of its kind, and how the Knicks wound up with the best player in the draft: Patrick Ewing.

"Oh God, I can't believe it," the NBA commissioner said to himself when he realized the Knicks had won. "Now everyone's going to want to know how I did it."

Theories abound, but before we present the cases that have been made against the league, let's first consider the history of the NBA lottery process and the bizarre bingo-style system that was employed. (Look, it was 1985, and clearly George Orwell overshot the technology age by a decade. At that point, the Commodore 64 computer was only good for flight simulators and strip poker.)

In the early years of the NBA, the draft order was set by reversing the order of the final standings, so the team with the worst record would get the first pick and so on. In 1966 a little more intrigue was added to the process with a coin flip between the teams with the two worst records in a season. The winner would get the first pick.

That system was used, believe it or not, until 1984 (and you wonder why the use of video-replay technology doesn't have a greater role in getting calls right in today's game). Before the lottery, teams would tank games just to get into that coin-flip tandem.

So in order to counter that, or maybe give more teams reason to tank (the Rockets were the final "winners" when they threw just enough games to earn the right to draft Hakeem Olajuwon), the league instituted a lottery-style system in 1985 that initially seemed almost as primitive as the coin flip. We're talking about a large, round hopper made of clear plastic and large envelopes with plac-ards inside that had the logo of each team.

To add to the drama, because David Stern loves a good show, the drawing was televised live on CBS, and representatives from each lottery team would be seated on a dais. Nothing like a national audi-ence capturing your look of failure when your team, after tossing games late in the season, comes up sixth. Hey Sacramento, welcome your new NBA team and their first-round pick, Joe Kleine!

Crickets.

While Kleine became a serviceable (a nice way to say he didn't suck) NBA center, and the '85 draft did produce Hall of Fame talent in Chris Mullin (seventh overall, Golden State Warriors), Karl Malone (13th overall, Utah Jazz), and Joe Dumars (18th overall, Detroit Pistons). There were also other very talented players such as Wayman Tisdale (second overall, Indiana Pacers), Xavier McDaniel (fourth overall, Seattle Supersonics), Detlef Schrempf (eighth overall, Dallas Mavericks), Charles Oakley (ninth overall, Cleveland Cavaliers), Joe Dumars (18th overall, Detroit Pistons), and Terry Porter (24th overall, Portland Trail Blazers), the grand prize that year was Ewing, who at Georgetown dominated the college game so much he had drawn Bill Russell comparisons and expectations of being the NBA's next great center. If your team wasn't named Lakers or Celtics, you had no reason to even try to win that year. One could argue that there was a better chance to win the lottery—and the rights to a franchise player like Ewing—than the NBA championship.

"I remember my heart beating out of my chest," Stan Kasten, who was general manager of the Atlanta Hawks at the time, told me in 2008. "It was as big of a buildup and intense a time as maybe I've ever had in my career."

Kasten would see Stern reveal the Hawks as the fifth to pick. Three draws from the hopper later, Stern pulled out one of the two remaining envelopes and opened it to reveal the logo of the Indiana Pacers. Dave DeBusschere, who was general manager of the Knicks at the time, rose up from his seat on the dais and pounded the table.

DeBusschere brought with him one item for luck—a horseshoe from harness-racing champion On the Road Again—and a Knicks jersey with Ewing's name and No. 33 already stitched on. It's as if he knew something.

It's as if the NBA, with stars in all of the biggest cities—Magic Johnson in Los Angeles, Michael Jordan in Chicago, Larry Bird in Boston—wanted to plant a superstar in its largest and arguably most important market.

It didn't take long for cries of a conspiracy to rise up from among the losers that day. The prevailing theory is that the league froze the envelope with the Knicks logo inside so that Stern could tell by feel which one he should leave for last.

"Someone should try and freeze an envelope and see if they can really pick the right one out," former NBA deputy commissioner Russ Granik told Darren Rovell in a May 16, 2002, story on ESPN.com. "I don't think anyone has ever tested it to see if it would work. But if people want to believe in the conspiracy, they don't want to think about those details."

Another theory arose in 2007 when ESPN's Bill Simmons followed up on an observation made by a reader. After watching video of the '85 draft lottery—which can be easily found on YouTube—Simmons insists that the accountant from Ernst & Whinney who deposited the seven envelopes into the hopper banged one against the side to crease the corner.

"So you're telling me that, out of seven envelopes in that glass drum, during a lottery when the NBA desperately needed the most ballyhooed college center in 15 years to save the league's marquee franchise, the commissioner coincidentally pulled out the enveloped with a giant crease in the corner that happened to have the Knicks logo in it?" Simmons wrote on April 19, 2007. "This is the Zapruder film of sports tapes, isn't it?"

The Knicks, of course, chose Ewing in the draft on June 18, 1985, and a 15-year career began. It led to a renaissance for the franchise, which was one of the league's elite teams through the 1990s despite never winning a championship.

The league stayed with the hopper for four more seasons until it changed to a weighted system in 1990. The Knicks have been in the lottery nine times since 1985 and have yet to win again. Perhaps, with the league so afraid of further allegations, there's a conspiracy theory involved in this as well?

6 The Captain

After years of being the doormat of the NBA, Willis Reed signaled the end of the days the Knicks would be pushed around when he literally took on the Lakers. But this wasn't that magical night of the legendary Game 7 of the 1970 NBA Finals.

This came October 18, 1966, in the second game of what would become the eighth-straight losing season. Reed was a burly 6'10" forward in his third NBA season and his first as team captain. He was a second-round pick, a battler who was a fighter literally from his first day of school as an only child growing up in rural Bernice, Louisiana.

And Rudy LaRusso was getting on his nerves.

The two lined up along the lane for a free throw at the old Garden on 49th Street and battled for rebounding position. Reed—accidentally or not—tripped LaRusso, who quickly took offense. The 6'7" forward, a five-time All-Star who came from Brooklyn, threw a punch at Reed just as Lakers center Darrall Imhoff had grabbed Reed in a bear hug, which left him defenseless. (Imhoff, by the way, was a former Knicks center who you'll read about later for his role in another historic night in Knicks history.)

Suddenly, a one-man melee resulted, as Reed pounded Imhoff and then went after LaRusso, who ran to the Lakers bench. A 6'9" rookie named John Block came at him, fists raised, but Reed dropped him with a hammer that sent Block toppling backward. He took out five of his teammates as he fell.

"They said I should be banned," Reed said in the October 31, 1977, issue of *Sports Illustrated*. "All I got was an ejection and a small fine, nothing like what they give out now. You know what would happen if someone did all that today?"

Willis Reed, shown here triumphant after the Knicks vanquished the Lakers for the 1973 championship, is one of the greatest in team history.

This was no Malice at the Palace, however. No fans were involved. This was a straight-up, old-school basketball brawl that, at the time, wasn't completely absent from the NBA game. More important, this was Reed giving clear indication that the days of punking the Knicks were over.

"You started to realize that, 'Hey, we've got a warrior here,'" Knicks forward Johnny Green said in *Garden Glory*.

That's usually how it starts. You get that one player who can walk the walk, and others begin to follow in lockstep. Reed was the foundation of what became the championship era.

Though generously listed at 6'10", Reed had always believed himself to be a center. He was strong enough to defend the imposing big men such as his idol, Bill Russell, and the indomitable Wilt Chamberlain, and yet he had the finesse to score against them. Reed had a soft midrange jumper and an insatiable appetite for rebounds.

And, yes, he was tough.

"He wouldn't crack," Hall of Famer Wes Unseld, a Reed rival from the Baltimore Bullets, once said in an NBA Entertainment video, *Classic Confrontations*. "I knew [playing against him] was going to be a job. I would try to make him quit, but I knew Willis Reed was not a quitter."

There was no greater evidence of this, of course, than that unforgettable Game 7 in 1970, when Reed took an injection of cortisone in his thigh and limped out onto the new Garden court to a roar from the crowd. (We'll have more on this later.) Fittingly, Reed had intimidated the Lakers once again.

That night culminated in the Knicks' first NBA championship and completed a first in league history: the MVP sweep. Reed earned MVP honors for the regular season, the All-Star Game, and the Finals. It wasn't until 27 years later that the feat was accomplished again, by Michael Jordan.

Reed added a second Finals MVP (again against the Lakers) and a second championship in 1973 but didn't make it through the following season. On November 2, 1973, while playing against—who else?—the Lakers in Los Angeles, Reed felt something snap in his knee.

He played just 19 games that season. Knee troubles actually began in 1971–72, when Reed played just 11 games and missed the playoffs as a result of issues in both of his knees. Years of pounding, of torquing and twisting and battling, had taken their toll.

On October 21, 1976, on a night the Knicks opened the season hosting, naturally, the Lakers, Reed's No. 19 was the first retired in franchise history. He was inducted into the Basketball Hall of Fame in 1982 and was named among the game's 50 Greatest Players.

The championship era came to an obvious close with his retirement, and the Knicks had their first losing season in eight years in '74–'75 and then failed to make the playoffs over the following two seasons.

Reed briefly replaced Red Holzman as head coach for the 1977–78 season as the Knicks tried to quickly rebuild. With new stars such as Bob McAdoo, Reed guided the Knicks to a 43–39 finish that season and the team reached the second round of the playoffs—though they were dominated by the 76ers in a four-game sweep.

Reed was also out in front on the emotional decision to trade his longtime teammate, Walt Frazier, before the 1977–78 season. His influence didn't last, however, as the following year, former New York Jets owner and Meadowlands Complex developer Sonny Werblin took over Madison Square Garden. Just 14 games into the 1978–79 season, he fired Reed and sent Holzman back to the bench.

Reed later coached at the collegiate level, as head coach at Creighton University (1981–85), and returned to the NBA as an assistant coach with the Sacramento Kings and Atlanta Hawks. In

February 1988 he was named head coach of the Nets, and after a 33–77 record, it was abundantly clear that coaching was not his forte.

But Reed did have an eye for talent and for managing personalities. He moved into the Nets front office in 1989 and built the laughingstock franchise into a playoff team in the early 1990s. He was less involved later on as the Nets developed into a championship contender in the early 2000s.

So he returned "home" to the Knicks organization in 2003–04 as an adviser to then–general manager Scott Layden but moved back to his native Louisiana in 2004 as an executive with the New Orleans Hornets. He retired three years later and, as he turns 70 years old, still closely follows his beloved Knicks with just one wish remaining.

"I'm just hoping before I pass to the great beyond," Reed said in February 2010, "we can have another championship."

7 "It Was Time to Go"

This book will be loaded with moments to savor, moments that will last a lifetime, moments that will leave you insatiable for more details and nostalgic for the past.

But among the most significant facts Knicks fans need to know and understand before they die is that Patrick Ewing wanted out. And the Knicks, regrettably, obliged their aging superstar in a move that would prove to be the first crack in the epic crumbling of the franchise.

It was, as Ewing's agent David Falk called it, "a mutual mistake."

Years later, with his belly swollen, his knees creaking, and flecks of gray in his hair, Ewing admitted his mistake when he told the sold-out Garden crowd, "If I had to do it over, I wouldn't want to play anywhere but in New York."

But in the off-season before the 2000–01 season, which would have been his 16th with the franchise, Ewing wanted to be anywhere but New York. He had reached the NBA Finals twice but had to agonize as a spectator in 1999, when an Achilles tendon tear ended his season after the first round. The team won without him, which hadn't ever before been possible, but now they were younger, faster, and more athletic.

And New York—especially its harsh, critical media—had finally broken his will. Ewing arrived in 1985 as the prize of the historic, inaugural (and, as you've already learned, controversial) NBA Draft Lottery. As a college superstar, he was sheltered by the intimidating John Thompson at Georgetown, where Hoya Paranoia kept him safe from incessant questions from reporters. But once he became a Knick, Ewing quickly learned the challenges of dealing with the media on a daily basis.

One time early in his career, after the Knicks endured losing records in his first three seasons, a reporter approached him and said, "Patrick, now that you're an expert on losing..."

Ewing, who was never one for small talk with reporters, interrupted him, "No."

"No what?" the reporter replied.

"I'm not an expert on losing," Ewing snapped back.

After some early struggles, especially with coach Hubie Brown, Ewing's game blossomed on the court once Mark Jackson arrived as the perfect setup man and then Charles Oakley came in to be his bodyguard. To his teammates and opponents, Ewing was a respected warrior. He brought the lunchpail every game. He was the Hoya Destroya, the Madison Square Guardian.

He sweat buckets and played with an effort New Yorkers could appreciate and a scowl of a man who had no time for strangers as he stomped through a crowded subway station to catch his train.

But as much as fans could relate, they demanded more. On the ice, Mark Messier was an icon with the New York Rangers. He was already a superstar when he arrived in 1991 and embraced the city and the fans with a beaming smile. And when they booed him at the end of the 1993 season, Messier sucked it up and admitted his faults and set out a year later to win the city its first Stanley Cup in 54 years.

Ewing grew into an All-Star right before the eyes of these same fans, but unlike the gregarious Messier, he remained very introverted and was mostly ornery with the media. Fans also had a hard time embracing Ewing completely, mainly because he made so many bold promises and year after year failed to come through with the hardware.

He came close, yes. He took them to Game 7 of the 1994 NBA Finals the same week that Messier brought home the Cup. But Ewing's Knicks couldn't make it a two-team ticker-tape parade. The following year, he missed a last-second finger roll in Game 7 of the Eastern Conference semifinals against the Indiana Pacers. What's of course forgotten in the disappointment of that series is that Ewing got the Knicks to Game 7 with the winning jumper with 1.8 seconds left in Game 5, with the Pacers holding a 3–1 series lead.

The Knicks remained an elite team through the late 1990s, as the franchise tried in vain to assemble the right kind of talent around Ewing while he was still in his prime. But the Knicks couldn't get beyond the second round in four straight seasons, until 1999. There was always another star in his way, another star who got it done more than he could, whether it was Michael Jordan, Reggie Miller, or even Tim Hardaway.

And then came the NBA lockout in 1998, which shortened the season to 50 games. Ewing, who was president of the NBA players' union, spent most of his time in a suit at labor meetings and not in high-tops on the basketball court. He gained weight and was unprepared for the rigors of a truncated season, which included, at times, three games in three nights and little time to get ready.

Though he missed out on most of the '99 run to the Finals against the San Antonio Spurs—the Knicks certainly could have used him against Tim Duncan and David Robinson—Ewing made one last playoff push with the Knicks in 2000. He was back in the Eastern Conference Finals for the third time in his career (we're not counting 1999, considering he was injured), mainly because he helped the Knicks knock off the Miami Heat in another epic seven-game series.

But he walked off the court as a Knick for the last time on June 2, 2000, in a 93–80 loss to the Pacers in a playoff Game 6 at the Garden. He had 18 points and 12 rebounds in the loss, but fans were divided as to whether the franchise—with the younger bodies of Allan Houston, Latrell Sprewell, and Marcus Camby—were better off without him.

Ewing was entering the final year of his contract in 2000–01 and decided he didn't want to negotiate an extension. The Knicks could have held onto the 38-year-old center for one more season and saved themselves $14 million in salary-cap space for the following summer, but management folded to Ewing's demands to be traded.

Even Jeff Van Gundy, who coddled Ewing almost as much as Thompson did at Georgetown, tried to talk Ewing out of leaving. But his mind was made up.

"It became clear he was looking for a change," Layden told reporters at the time of the trade. "And when he requested a trade, we respected his request."

"It was time to go," Ewing said in *Garden Glory*.

On September 20, 2000, the Knicks traded Ewing in a four-team, 12-player deal that brought in Glen Rice and Luc Longley, among others, and sent Ewing to the Seattle Supersonics. He played one more season, with the Orlando Magic, before he retired in 2002.

Rather than hold firm and let Ewing walk at the end of the 2000–01 season to save the team cap space, the trade was a weak attempt by Layden at getting value for the aging All-Star. What it did, however, was start a 10-year trend that kept the franchise buried in salary-cap hell and luxury tax payments with no chance to rebuild with free agency.

But what was really lost in that trade couldn't be explained with numbers. "You could see the void in the identity of what it is to be a Knick," Allan Houston once told me. "I think that's what kind of really left with that era: the identity of a Knick. You look at Patrick, that's what he brought and that's the thing—and you can talk about so many other variables—but that's what I see that is still looking to get back."

Ewing has since gotten into coaching, most recently as an assistant with the Magic. The Knicks never called him to interview for the vacant head coach position when Isiah Thomas was demoted after the 2007–08 season, which once again created some controversy. But Ewing's No. 33 was retired by the franchise in February 2003 and his son, Patrick Jr., has twice been invited to training camp.

And, perhaps most important, Ewing now receives a warm welcome from the Garden crowd every time he returns. The feeling is mutual again. But this time there's no mistake.

"Regardless of whatever uniform he wore," longtime friend and teammate Herb Williams said, "he'll always be remembered as a Knick. He will always be a Knick at heart."

The First NBA Game

Most New Yorkers talk as if the game was invented right here in the rugged streets of this city. But Dr. James Naismith invented the game in Springfield, Massachusetts.

And Naismith was Canadian, so it was fitting that the first-ever NBA game was played in Naismith's home province of Ontario. But we New Yorkers can at least claim some role among the game's pioneers, because the Knicks played in that inaugural game. And won it.

The game, just like the league, looked a lot different back then, and we don't just mean the really short shorts and funny-looking two-handed set shots. First of all, it wasn't yet called the National Basketball Association, but instead it was the Basketball Association of America. The BAA was formed with 11 teams in 1946.

Walter Brown, who owned the old Boston Garden, spearheaded the formation of this professional basketball league to create another event to host at his arena when his NHL team, the Boston Bruins, weren't playing.

Ned Irish turned Madison Square Garden into a gold mine by organizing college basketball doubleheaders that drew large crowds. Irish was against the idea of a pro basketball league mainly because the Garden was already packed with events. But with cities such as Boston, Chicago, and Detroit committed, the league begged Irish to include a team to play at the Garden. When someone else stepped up with an offer to field a team and rent the Garden when it was available and play elsewhere when it was not, Irish finally relented, paid the $10,000 franchise fee—what a bargain!—and agreed to create a team to play at the Garden.

The entire league was supposed to open on the same night, November 2, a Saturday, but there was already a hitch in the schedule (which became a routine issue for the fledgling league). The Knicks were scheduled to play the Toronto Huskies at Maple Leaf Gardens, but the NHL's Toronto Maple Leafs had a game that night. So the Knicks-Huskies game was moved to Friday, November 1, and as a result, it would be forever recognized as the first game in NBA history.

The Knicks began with a team loaded with New York talent, including coach Neil Cohalan, who was hired away from Manhattan College, and original Knicks players such as Sonny Hertzberg, Ozzie Schectman, and Ralph Kaplowitz.

When the Knicks took the train up to Toronto for the game, they went through customs. As legendary basketball writer Sam Goldaper described in a story for NBA.com, the customs agent apparently asked the players, "What are you?"

Cohalan replied, "We're the New York Knicks."

"We're familiar with the New York Rangers," the agent then said. "Are you anything like that?"

"They play hockey," Cohalan explained. "We play basketball."

And so began the long climb to what is now a multibillion-dollar league with some of the most famous athletes in the world.

The game didn't draw much interest in hockey-mad Toronto, though it didn't help that the Huskies had just one Canadian, Hank Biasatti (who would later quit to play Major League Baseball). The Huskies did have a promotion for the game: any fan who was taller than 6'8" George Nostrand could get in for free. At that time, anyone over 6'8" might have been asked to play.

Schectman, a 6'0" guard from Long Island University, scored the game's first basket, therefore etching himself into the history books as the player to score the first points in what is now the NBA.

"I scored on a two-handed underhand layup," Schectman told ESPN.com's Charley Rosen in a story posted March 4, 2008, "which was the standard chippy shot back then. I also remember being on the receiving end of a give-and-go, but I can't remember who I received the pass from."

The Knicks took an early 6–0 lead and led by as many as 25 points in the second quarter before going into halftime with a 37–29 lead. The Knicks actually trailed 48–44 in the third quarter before rallying in the fourth to put away a 68–66 victory. Leo Gottlieb led the Knicks with 14 points.

The Knicks finished 33–27 that season, which was good enough for third place in the Eastern Division and a playoff berth. They went on to beat the Cleveland Rebels in the first round but then were swept by the Philadelphia Warriors in the semifinals. The Warriors went on to beat the Chicago Stags to win the first-ever BAA championship.

The Huskies folded after one season and major-league basketball wouldn't return to Toronto again until 1995. The NBA began its 50th anniversary celebration by fittingly scheduling the Knicks and Raptors to open the 1996–97 season at the Air Canada Centre. The Knicks won 107–99.

The Knicks also opened the 2010–11 season in Toronto on October 27, 2010, with a 98–93 win. In the same city the franchise won it's very first game, it claimed win number 5,000.

By 1948 the BAA claimed victory against its rival league, the National Basketball League, when four teams from the NBL—including the Minneapolis Lakers and the game's biggest star, George Mikan—switched leagues. On August 3, 1949, the BAA agreed to merge with the NBL to form the National Basketball Association.

In that first season of the NBA, the Knicks went 40–28 and finished second in the Eastern Division under coach Joe Lapchick. The Knicks' first game with the NBA was, fittingly, also on November 1, another two-point win: 89–87 over the Chicago Stags.

9 Attending the NBA Draft... Just to Boo

It is an annual rite for Knicks fans, whether the team has a first-round pick or not. The NBA has made it easy for Knicks fans to voice their opinion, because since the draft became a public event in 1979, it has been held in New York City most of the time.

And most of the time, Knicks fans come to the same collective conclusion: Boo!

So when you go, wear a Knicks jersey and a menacing look. Mug for the camera and, by all means, bring a sign, because whichever network is televising the event—ESPN, TNT—they'll want to get you on camera.

The goal is to be extreme: either uncontrollably elated or completely beside yourself with disgust. There is no in-between. The NFL also holds their draft in the same city. And as notorious as Knicks fans are at the NBA Draft, you have a formidable rival in New York Jets fans, who have had just as much reason—or so they believe—to treat draft night like it's the Super Bowl.

The kick is up and it's...Kyle Brady over Warren Sapp?

Boo!

Madison Square Garden's theater, which has gone by several different names over the years—from the Felt Forum to the Paramount Theatre to its current name, the Theater at Madison Square Garden—has hosted the NBA Draft 22 times in 30 years. The 1996 draft was held in New Jersey's Meadowlands Arena, a close enough proximity to New York to call it a 23rd time the draft has been in New York.

And in that span, the Knicks have gotten it right on draft night a total of three times. One was obvious, of course: the only time the team has ever had the first overall pick in the draft event era was 1985. Fans were already wearing Patrick Ewing jerseys to the draft that night, so there was little suspense, just a cheer when it was made official.

For a franchise that has been in the lottery as often as it has over the years—especially recently—the Knicks have seen many draft blunders. Arguably the worst of them all came in 1999, when a St. John's star and a local product from Queensbridge named Ron Artest slipped all the way to the Knicks at No. 15.

That year the Knicks had yet to hire a general manager to replace the fired Ernie Grunfeld, so Grunfeld's former assistant, Ed Tapscott, was placed in charge of the draft. With Patrick Ewing in his twilight years, Tapscott thought the team needed to find a center to one day replace Ewing. Artest was a 6'8" forward and a rugged defender but not a center.

So Tapscott chose a 7'0" Frenchman named Frederick Weis, and Artest was crushed. The Knicks wound up hurt the most, of course, as Artest developed into an All-Star and one of the league's best defensive players. Weis never even made it to training camp.

The Knicks were spared the usual shower of angry boos that would have come with such an incorrigible decision because the draft that year was held at the MCI Center (now the Verizon Center) in Washington, D.C.—far enough away from the ire of most Knicks fans.

That draft was during a period in which the NBA took the draft on a league-wide tour. After holding it in New York from 1979 to 1991, the NBA made stops in Portland (1992), Detroit (1993), Indiana (1994), Toronto (1995), New Jersey (1996), Vancouver (1998), Washington (1999), and Minnesota (2000) before returning to New York, for good, in 2001. (The draft was moved to Newark's Prudential Center in 2011 to accommodate the construction schedule of the Garden's transformation project.)

Not Every Pick's a Winner

Sometimes the fans aren't always right on draft night. In the 2003 NBA Draft, the Garden theatre roared with delight when the Knicks were on the clock in the second round with the 30th pick in the draft. They had already selected power forward Michael Sweetney from Georgetown with the ninth overall pick, but the crowd now wanted them to take a gamble on a player who had a great deal of buzz around him going into the draft, seven-footer Maciej Lampe. The 19-year-old from Poland had been projected to be a lottery pick, but teams avoided him because he had a tricky and expensive buyout in his European contract. The Knicks made the plunge, the crowd was happy...and then Lampe never played. He was traded that January in the Stephon Marbury deal.

The Knicks didn't have a first-round pick in 2001, so they avoided any real backlash, aside from the usual reactions of, "Who?" when second-round picks Michael Wright (Arizona) and Eric Chenowith (Kansas) were selected. Neither made the team. But in 2002, the Theater exploded in anger when, with the seventh overall pick (the team's first lottery selection in 16 years), the Knicks chose a Brazilian big man named Maybyner Hilario.

They passed on players such as Chris Wilcox of the NCAA champion Maryland Terrapins and Caron Butler of UConn, two of the crowd favorites that night. They also, it should be noted, decided against taking a high school stud from Cypress Creek, Florida, by the name of Amare Stoudemire (there was no apostrophe yet).

Shortly after the pick, the four words everyone in attendance loves to hear came from the commissioner: "We have a trade."

Knicks general manager Scott Layden pulled off a major trade when he sent that draft pick, Hilario, along with Marcus Camby and Mark Jackson, to the Denver Nuggets in a four-player deal that returned All-Star power forward Antonio McDyess and Denver's first-round pick, guard Frank Williams.

You would think the fans would be happy with landing an explosive player such as McDyess, but instead, the deal prompted more boos and chants of, "Fire Layden!"

Of course McDyess would blow out his knee in a preseason game and miss the entire 2002–03 season. After 18 games in 2003–04, he was traded.

Oh, and Hilario? We know him today as Nene. He's developed into one of the NBA's toughest big men.

The trend seemed to continue well into the 2000s. In his trade for Eddy Curry in September 2005, Isiah Thomas agreed to give the Chicago Bulls the right to swap draft places with the Knicks in the 2006 and 2007 drafts. Thomas, feeling confident that the young Curry—a lottery pick himself—could lead the Knicks to the playoffs, decided not to protect either pick. So when the Knicks finished with the second-worst record in 2005–06, you can imagine the horror knowing the Bulls would gladly take that pick.

Now in Chicago's spot at No. 20, the Knicks selected a relative unknown from South Carolina named Renaldo Balkman, who most draft experts considered a second-round talent. Thomas insisted the Knicks were led to believe the Phoenix Suns, who sat at No. 21, would take Balkman if the Knicks didn't grab him. But ask anyone in Phoenix, and they'll tell you that wasn't the case.

There was little doubt no one at the Theater was buying it either, as boos once again rained down on the Knicks. Fans then started up a chorus of, "Fire Isiah," which became a choice selection at most home games over the next two seasons.

By taking Balkman, who has hardly proven himself to be a capable NBA rotation player, the Knicks passed on several quality late-round talents such as Rajon Rondo and Kyle Lowry.

Knicks fans have made it a habit, make that a tradition, of booing the pick. Wilson Chandler in 2007? Boo! Danilo Gallinari in 2008? Boo! Jordan Hill in 2009? Boo! Iman Shumpert in 2011? Boo!

No one is safe anymore.

Now if you go to the draft, don't go in with too much pessimism. There have been nights—very few, but there have been—when the Knicks got it right.

In 1996 Grunfeld managed to stockpile a few first-round picks with an effort to infuse some youth into what was an older team that every year went deep into the playoffs. The team had three first-rounders when the draft began that night at the Meadowlands in New Jersey. With the 18th overall pick, the Knicks chose Syracuse power forward John Wallace, and the crowd roared with approval. Kentucky's Walter McCarty was selected with the very next pick at No. 19, which drew more cheers. After the Cleveland Cavaliers interrupted the celebration by drafting Zydrunas Ilgauskas at No. 20, the Knicks were back on the clock at No. 21, and Mississippi State's Dontae' Jones was called up to join the Knicks' new triumvirate.

It was the first time the Knicks had made three first-round picks since 1979, when the team selected Bill Cartwright (No. 3), Larry Demic (No. 9), and Sly Williams (No. 21). As time went by, there was little doubt the Knicks fared much better in '79. Wallace never really broke through as a rotation player and bounced around with five teams in seven seasons, McCarty was traded to Boston the following season, and Jones never played a game for the Knicks.

Okay, but really, there were better nights than this.

One of the most satisfying drafts came in 1987, when the Knicks were on the clock at No. 18. The crowd loudly chanted for the hometown guy and a Brooklyn-born Knicks fan himself: Mark Jackson.

"We want Mark! We want Mark!"

Jackson starred at St. John's, and the New York crowd already loved him. The Knicks, like in 1999, were without a general manager, however, as Dave DeBusschere had been ousted. The draft decisions were left up to the one man left in the franchise who knew a thing or two about basketball and New York: Dick McGuire. The decision was made, Jackson's name was announced, and the crowd at the Theater got their wish.

It was a pretty good pick by the fans, too. Jackson went on to win the NBA's Rookie of the Year Award for the 1987–88 season.

But a year later, after Jackson took a smiling picture with the Rookie of the Year trophy at Manhattan's Tavern on the Green, they assembled again for another draft day. The Knicks had the 19th overall pick and selected another New York native, Rod Strickland.

Wait, another point guard?

Boo!

10 Seventh Heaven: Here Comes Willis!

Every franchise, very great team, has a defining moment. For the Knicks, it came May 8, 1970.

Most moments usually end with a big shot. This one *started* with one: a long needle and 200 cc's of a local anesthetic called mepivacaine (generally referred to as "carbocaine").

"It was a big needle," Willis Reed said in a story in the *NBA Encyclopedia*. "I saw that needle, and I said, 'Holy cow.' And then I just held on. I think I suffered more from the needle than the injury."

So technically it was Dr. James Parkes, the team physician at the time, who actually made the greatest shot in Knicks history.

This was the 1970 NBA Finals, of course. The Knicks had overcome the Bullets in a grueling seven-game first-round series, then dismissed Lew Alcindor and the young Bucks in five games in the second round to advance to their first championship series since 1953.

They faced the Lakers, an aging team loaded with Hall of Fame talent (the original Big Three: Elgin Baylor, Jerry West, and Wilt Chamberlain) that kept running into the Celtics dynasty and who saw this as a chance to finally win a title. But these were the days long before Magic Johnson arrived and Pat Riley directed the dazzling Showtime style of play.

These Lakers were slow and methodical; the Knicks were the run-and-gun team.

The series was tied after the first two games in New York and tied again after the teams split two games in Los Angeles. In Game 5 back at the Garden, the Knicks were trailing 25–15 when Reed got the ball at the foul line and made a move. Chamberlain stepped up to cut off Reed's path to the basket, so the Knicks center attempted to cut left—but his foot caught Chamberlain's size 19 sneakers and he collapsed to the court.

No foul was called, so the Lakers took possession and went down the floor while Reed rolled on the Garden hardwood in obvious, desperate pain. He tore his quadriceps muscle, one of the largest muscles in the body.

The Knicks came into the locker room at halftime not only down 13 points in a pivotal game in the series, but seeing Reed on the training table, they knew they were going to be without their captain.

After failed attempts to use backup center Nate Bowman against Chamberlain, the high-IQ Knickerbockers—led by Rhodes Scholar Bill Bradley—got together with Red Holzman and devised a plan: a 3-2 zone and the 6'6" Dave DeBusschere at center. (And you thought Mike D'Antoni is the only Knicks coach to ever believe in small-ball.)

The plan worked, as Chamberlain was pulled away from the basket on defense, which opened up a lot of shots for the up-tempo Knicks. On offense, the Lakers stubbornly tried to overwhelm the Knicks with the Chamberlain mismatch down low, but the relentless, swarming Knicks defense forced turnovers and bad shots. The Garden crowd was inspired by the effort, and the building became electric. The Lakers didn't have a chance in what became a 107–100 win for New York to take a 3–2 series lead.

Just one game to go for a title.

"The fifth game," DeBusschere says in the *NBA Encyclopedia*'s look back at the series, "was one of the greatest basketball games ever played."

But in Los Angeles, Game 6 was a disaster for the Knicks, as Reed was forced to sit out with the injury and Holzman, despite pleading from his players, wouldn't go back to the small-ball approach. Chamberlain completely dominated with 45 points and 27 rebounds in a 135–113 blowout win to tie the series at three games apiece.

Back to New York they went, and everyone wondered: *Would Willis play?*

"I knew I was going to try," Reed told D'Agostino in *Garden Glory*. "I knew I was going to go out there. I didn't know whether or not I was going to be successful. But I knew that the team needed me to be there after what Wilt had done to us in Game 6. There was no way they would have had any level of confidence if I didn't show up."

Two hours before that epic seventh game, Reed limped out to a quiet, deserted Garden court. The arena was mostly empty, other than some workers preparing the Garden for the biggest event in its young history. As Reed took a few shots from various spots on the court, an imposing figure was seen standing in the tunnel, watching with great interest.

It was Chamberlain.

A short while later, Reed was in the training room and DeBusschere came over. "Big guy," he said. "If you can give us just 20 minutes, we're going to win it. It's ours."

Phil Jackson, who was out for the season with his own injury and had taken up photography as a hobby, snapped a shot of Reed with the needle stuck in his leg as Dr. Parkes added more carbocaine.

"Man, it was a big needle," Reed told D'Agostino in *Garden Glory*. "So he would say to me, 'Willis, when this is all over I'll let you stick me with it.' I said, 'Okay, don't forget that!'"

Both teams were already on the court for the pregame warm-ups, and Reed had yet to emerge.

In a recorded version of game highlights, Marv Albert said, "The big question is, will Willis Reed play tonight? There is tremendous doubt."

Reed, in the training room, had made up his mind. "My decision was," he said, "if I could walk any way, I was going to play."

But first he had to get out on the court. There wasn't much time left before tip-off.

"I almost missed the start of the game," Reed told the *New York Times* in Parkes' obituary, which was published on December 15, 1999.

Mepivacaine works relatively quickly but does take some time to be effective. The Knicks had to stall until Reed was ready to go.

"When the injection was done," Reed told the *Times*, "we walked out and found that somehow the tip-off had been delayed until I got there."

Reed emerged from the tunnel in a white warm-up suit and gimped out with Dr. Parkes by his side. The Garden exploded.

Albert interrupted himself to announce, "And here comes Willis!"

Both teams paused to see what the commotion was all about. When the Lakers saw Reed, something was evident in their eyes.

"I knew we had them," Walt Frazier says with a gleam in his eye. Reed wasn't nearly as confident.

"When I got the standing ovation, everybody was saying, 'Everything's okay, the Captain is here,'" Reed said in an interview with MSG Network on February 23, 2010. "And I'm saying, 'This is a heck of a predicament. I've got to go out here and play Wilt, who just had a 47–25 game on us.'

"But I thought that being at home and if I could set screens for [Dick] Barnett and set screens for Bill Bradley, that we had a chance. I knew that the crowd was going to be our sixth man."

Spurred by Reed's mere presence—he still could hardly move—the Knicks rode a wave of emotion that was generated by the Garden crowd. And it only got louder as Reed hit the first shot of the game, a 15-footer from the elbow. Frazier hit him as he trailed the play, dragging his leg up the floor. Chamberlain was deep in the paint and never contested the shot.

On the next possession, Reed caught the ball on the right wing, faced up on Chamberlain, and drilled another jumper.

"When he appeared, we went to one plateau," Bradley said in an interview with NBA Entertainment. "When the Garden reacted, we went to another plateau. When he hit his first two shots, we were gone."

As it turned out, they were his only two baskets of the game. Frazier took over from there. Somewhat overshadowed by Reed's heroics is perhaps one of the greatest NBA Finals Game 7 performances in the history of the league. Frazier had 36 points and hit 12 of 17 from the field and all 12 of his free-throw attempts, and added 19 assists.

Reed was done at halftime, with just four points and three rebounds and smart use of four fouls, while bottling Chamberlain up.

The Knicks were ahead 69–42 at that point and cruised to an improbable 113–99 win for their first championship. The Big

Dipper finished with 21 points and made just 1 of 11 from the free-throw line. In a career of greatness, it is viewed as perhaps his greatest failure.

Meanwhile, the euphoria of winning the championship made the pain go away for Reed, at least for a little while. The team had postgame celebration at the Four Seasons Hotel in Manhattan.

"I was in pain when I was playing," Reed told D'Agostino in *Garden Glory*, "but once that carbocaine wore off, I tell you, it was *rough*."

11 Seventh Hell: That Will Never Go Away

John Starks was having the game of his life. Just four years removed from the decidedly minor-league World Basketball League circuit, here was the Tulsa native shredding Vernon Maxwell and Mario Elie for 27 points, with five three-pointers and eight assists in Game 6 of the NBA Finals against the Houston Rockets.

Starks was on fire and almost single-handedly gave the Knicks a chance to win the championship that night at the Summit in Houston with an explosive fourth quarter that saw him score 16 points, including his team's first 11 of the quarter. The ball was in his hands with 5.5 seconds left and the Knicks trailing by two when Patrick Ewing ran to him for a pick-and-roll. The Rockets switched, and suddenly Starks found himself guarded by seven-footer Hakeem Olajuwon.

With the seconds ticking down, Starks could have attempted a pass to Ewing, who was rolling unguarded into the paint. But instead he opted to ride his hot hand for one more shot and a chance to win it all, right in front of the Rockets bench.

But Olajuwon got a finger on the ball just as it released, and the ball fell short. The Knicks lost 86–84, which forced a Game 7 in Houston.

The Knicks still felt good about their chances. How could they not? Starks was absolutely destroying the Rockets shooting guards and had scored a total of 38 points in the fourth quarter of Games 4, 5, and 6. Ewing, who had played so well against Olajuwon in the middle games of the series back at the Garden, had a rare off-night in Game 6 with 17 points on just 6-of-20 shooting.

But Ewing didn't quite have that bounce-back game. He scored 17 again on 7-of-17 shooting, as Olajuwon outplayed him in the biggest game of their careers since they met in the 1984 NCAA Championship. (Ewing won that time.)

Meanwhile, Starks went from unconscious in Game 6 to unraveled in Game 7.

The Knicks, a team with success built on a foundation of defense and toughness, had struggled all season with shooting, with just a 46 percent season effort that was the lowest since 1985–86. Starks was a streaky shooter and scorer; he shot 42 percent during the season and 38.1 percent in the playoffs, which are very weak percentages for the shooting guard position.

But we're talking about a player the fans embraced because he had an intangible that is often immediately recognized—and appreciated—by New Yorkers: heart. And in some of the biggest moments of that Finals series, in three consecutive fourth quarters, Starks was a force under pressure.

But on this night, he went from being a force to forcing his shots. He took a team-high 18 of them, including 11 from three-point range, as if he was determined to shoot himself out of the untimely slump. Instead, he shot the Knicks out of a championship. He made just two shots in the entire game and none from three in one of the most devastating performances in NBA Finals history.

To make matters worse, Maxwell, who had struggled against Starks all series, came up big in the clutch this time, with a dagger three-pointer with 1:48 left to give the Rockets an 83–75 lead.

The Knicks trailed 84–78 with 52 seconds left—they still had a chance. And Starks kept shooting. He missed a three with 41 seconds left, another with 33 seconds left, and still another with 23 seconds left. Each one missed; the third was an air ball.

The Rockets prevailed 90–84 to win their first title.

The emotional guard's shoulders slumped and his eyes were glassy as reality set in during those last few seconds. It was a helpless feeling, one he once told me over a decade later he still couldn't shake.

"That always sticks with you and comes around at times," he said. "You may be watching a game, especially during the playoffs, where you're like, 'Man, if I would have done this or done that...' That will never go away," he said.

Starks isn't the only one who was haunted by that Game 7 loss. Pat Riley, the leader of the Lakers dynasty in the 1980s who came to New York in 1991 with the intention of getting the Knicks back on top and winning his fifth championship ring, opened up about his regrets years after the bitter loss.

Riley was heavily criticized for leaving veteran sharpshooter Rolando Blackman on the bench during most of that playoff run. Blackman, a career 34.4 percent shooter from three-point range, appeared in just six games in the 1994 playoffs and didn't play a single minute in the Finals.

Blackman, at age 34, retired after that season. Riley also left Doc Rivers, who had torn his knee earlier in the season, off the playoff roster. The Knicks basically had third-year guard Greg Anthony and second-year guard Hubert Davis as the backcourt reserves. Both played sparingly.

"I got caught up in the short rotation," Riley said when he finally returned to the Finals in 2006, this time with the Miami

Heat. "That's why we brought Rolando there. Immediately afterward, I knew. If we had played the two of them, but especially Ro, we would have won the championship."

Riley then added, "That's the biggest mistake I ever made."

Blackman, who faced Riley in that 2006 Finals series as an assistant coach with the Dallas Mavericks, said he has made his peace with Riley, but added, "Nobody says anything about the day. We've never talked about it."

Riley, of course, was in a tough situation. How could he give up on Starks after all the player had done to help get the Knicks that far? But a coach also has to believe in his entire team and, most especially, his veterans.

"The ironic thing is that he would have come through," Derek Harper said years later of Blackman. "That's what destroys him more than anything. Not only was he sitting over there and felt he should be out there, but he felt he could have added something for us in those games."

Especially in Game 7, when Starks couldn't find the rim and yet the Knicks were still somehow in the game.

"[Starks] needed to come out for a little bit to stop what was going on with him, he needed time," Blackman said. "But I don't want to be critical, because it's gone. It's passed. We still had other problems called Olajuwon."

Riley again talked about the game at his Hall of Fame induction in 2008. The class that year also included, fittingly, Ewing and Olajuwon.

"I always think I could have done something a little more," Riley told me that day. "I look back, and I always second-guess myself on that series."

As fate would have it, it would be the last real chance the Knicks would have at an NBA title in Ewing's career. The Knicks lost to the Indiana Pacers in the second round—this time it was Ewing who missed the critical shot—and Pat Riley left to run the

Heat. Starks was transitioned to the bench with the arrival of Allan Houston in 1996 and then traded for Latrell Sprewell in 1999.

He is back again with the franchise, this time with an executive position in charge of alumni relations and fan development. He's still beloved by the fans, who prefer to remember him for his unforgettable dunk over Michael Jordan and Horace Grant in the 1993 playoffs (more on this later) than the 16 misses that cost the Knicks a title.

Starks prefers that perspective as well.

"It's not something that will stop me from living," he once told me. "There are a lot of players that [get] destroyed over situations like that and really lose control of their lives and never regather themselves."

"You still have to keep it in perspective," Starks said. "It's a game, you play it to the best of your ability. You don't let it consume you. Unfortunately, I didn't do a good job in Game 7, and it wound up costing us."

# Sweetwater

The Brooklyn Dodgers had Jackie; the Knicks had Sweetwater. In the late 1940s, shortly after Jackie Robinson broke the color barrier in Major League Baseball by signing—and playing—with the Dodgers, other sports leagues became accountable to the call for equality among all men.

When the NBA began as the BAA in 1946, there was an unwritten rule that kept black players from being signed by the member teams. The BAA's rival league, the NBL, took a more progressive approach and included African American players on their rosters. In the 1942–43 season, in fact, the NBL had several African American players on teams such as the Toledo Jim White Chevrolets and Chicago Studebakers five years before Robinson signed with the Dodgers.

The decisions weren't really based on making a political stand, however. Both franchises were looking for bodies during a time when most of their current players were overseas fighting in World War II. Toledo barely made it a week into the season before the team folded. The Studebakers had the benefit of having several players from the famous Harlem Globetrotters, who happened to be working at their factory.

In 1948–49, after the Detroit Vagabond Kings folded, the NBL invited the New York Rens, a well-known, barnstorming all-black team from Harlem, to play that season out of Dayton, Ohio. Their name was changed to the Dayton Rens. Coincidentally, or not, the Rens—a dominating success in the sport since 1923, when Bob Douglas established the team from the Harlem Renaissance Casino and Ballroom—disbanded as a team after that season.

After the NBL and BAA merged to form the NBA in 1949, the Rens weren't absorbed into the NBA, which remained all-white. At least for one season, but after Robinson's arrival in Brooklyn, society's outlook on race was starting to change.

But there was serious resistance among the 11 teams that made up the new NBA in 1950. Some owners felt the move would ruin the league. Knicks owner Ned Irish, however, argued the contrary and, as some legends suggest, he threatened to pull the Knicks out of the league if the other teams didn't comply. The matter eventually went to a vote, and the result had the slimmest of margins, 6–5, in favor of including African American players in the league.

Red Auerbach played the part of Branch Rickey on April 25, 1950, by taking the first step in using the Boston Celtics' first pick

Sweetwater Clifton shows off some of his moves to coach Joe Lapchick.
(Getty Images)

in the second round to select Duquesne forward Chuck Cooper. The Washington Capitols also used a pick in that draft to select an African American player when they chose Earl Lloyd, a big man out of West Virginia State, with their ninth-round pick. Lloyd was the 100th player selected in a draft of 121.

Irish then worked out a deal with Abe Saperstein to bring a popular member of the Globetrotters to the Knicks: a 6'7" forward with gigantic hands named Nat "Sweetwater" Clifton. He became the first African American player to sign a contract with an NBA team.

Saperstein sold Clifton's rights for $12,500. Clifton got $2,500 out of the deal. Free agency hadn't been invented yet, either.

Lloyd would be the one to make history as the first African American to play in an NBA game, when the Capitols opened the season on October 31, 1950, before the Knicks and Celtics began their seasons.

Clifton, who made his debut on November 4, 1950, was clearly the most successful of the three pioneers, mainly because he came in as the oldest, at 28 years old, and most established. He had spent two years with the Rens and another three with the Globetrotters before he joined the Knicks. Clifton was already a well-known name in the game. He was a physical specimen, a forerunner of today's athletic wing players who can handle the ball and drive to the basket. And he could throw it down, too.

Clifton was mostly known for his funny nickname, "Sweetwater," or "Sweets" for short. With a kind, gentle disposition, you might think the nickname had something to do with his personality. Actually, it goes back to his childhood and a predilection for soda pop.

"You know," Clifton once explained in an interview, "sweet water."

In eight seasons in the NBA, seven with the Knicks, Clifton averaged 10 points and 8.2 rebounds per game. He was named to the All-Star team in 1956–57, when he averaged 10.7 points and

7.8 rebounds per game. His best scoring season came in 1954–55, when he topped out at 13.1 points per game, but he twice averaged a double-double. In 1951–52 he put up 10.6 points and 11.8 rebounds per game, and in 1952–53 he had 10.6 points and 10.9 rebounds per game.

During each of his first three seasons, Clifton and the Knicks reached the NBA Finals. But despite Clifton's talents—he was a tremendous ball handler and defender but wasn't considered to be a great shooter—Joe Lapchick's conservative, methodical offense was dominated by the likes of Vince Boryla, Max Zaslofsky, and Carl Braun.

Clifton, in fact, says one of the reasons why he wasn't a great scorer in the NBA was because he stayed within the team concept rather than freelance to display his talents the way he did with the Rens and Globetrotters.

"I played his system," Clifton once said in a televised interview for the 1970s-era show *Once a Star*. "I did what he wanted me to do."

But let's not suggest that there was any friction between Clifton and Lapchick. On the contrary, Lapchick welcomed Clifton with open arms, and Clifton had great respect for the coach.

"Joe was a great man," he once said. "He treated me nice and as a gentleman. I always gave Joe respect."

His teammates loved him, too. As was unfortunately a common situation in those days, Clifton's presence may have been appreciated in the locker room, but it wasn't always welcome on the road.

"There were two cities where we felt very bad for Sweets," Ray Lumpp, a member of those Finals teams, told D'Agostino in *Garden Glory*. "When we went to Indianapolis, we used to stay at the Claypool Hotel. Sweets wasn't allowed to stay there; he'd stay in the black area. When we went to Baltimore, we stayed at the Lord Baltimore Hotel. He wasn't allowed to stay there, either. He had to go to the other end of town.

"We felt very bad when we'd get off a plane and then take a cab or bus into town, and he couldn't stay with us. 'I'll see you at the game,' he'd always say. It never bothered him; it was just a fact of life back then. But all the guys felt bad that we could all play together on the court, but we couldn't sleep together. That was wrong. It had to be righted, and eventually it was."

Many years later, Clifton harbored no anger, no ill will. He only had good memories.

"I've had a good life," he said in the television interview. "Nobody mistreated me. I can't complain about anybody mistreating me. I'm pretty tough. I've been taking care of myself all my life. I don't let nobody run over me."

The Knicks did try to take care of him after his career ended. Gulf & Western, which later became the parent company of the team, even offered him a job at their Manhattan offices. But Clifton didn't want to live in New York City. His entire family— his mother, his children—was in Chicago and that's where he preferred to be. Until his death in 1990, Clifton lived in the house he bought with his first NBA contract in 1950.

And until his death, Clifton continued another personal tradition that started during his career. Players of his era didn't make enough money during the seven-month season to live comfortably for an entire year, so in the off-season, he found himself a job as a taxi driver. He enjoyed it enough to do well into his sixties, with many of his fares recognizing him.

He died at the wheel of his cab, parked near Chicago's Union Station, on August 31, 1990. The Knicks carry on his legacy with the Sweetwater Clifton Award, which honors New Yorkers who make a significant difference in the lives of others.

A movie about Clifton's life, which is an effort by well-known Hollywood filmmaker Martin Guigui is currently in production, with a cast that is expected to include James Caan (as Irish), Ed

Lauter (as Lapchick), and Wood Harris and Louis Gossett Jr. as the young and elder Clifton.

So once the movie hits the silver screen, make seeing it another thing to do before you die.

Get to Know Red

Don't let this man be just a name on a dusty banner that hangs from the Garden rafters. Don't allow yourself to go another day without knowing what the "613" represents beneath his name.

This is your coach. This is who Dave Checketts once called, "the most important man in the history of the New York Knicks franchise."

And he wasn't exaggerating.

The irony, however, is that Red Holzman wouldn't want you to think this way. To Red, no one individual was more important than the team. That wisdom was the foundation of two NBA championships.

"We made them realize that playing that way would be better for them, as individuals, as well as a team," Holzman said in an interview with the NBA for the league's 50th anniversary.

"Playing on their own is not going to do anybody any good… not even the guy who is doing well as an individual," he continued. "So I think that they were a very, very intelligent group—very, very smart basketball players and smart otherwise. They knew what it took and they were…unselfish people. They hit the open man, passed the ball, and helped each other defensively. That's what it takes. If you play as a team, you have a chance, especially if you have talented players, which we did have."

Read those words again: Hit the open man.

They should be written in block letters somewhere on a wall in the Knicks locker room. It is a simple phrase, yet it can be such a complex issue for most teams. For Red's boys, a highly intelligent group who prided themselves as thinkers who defined *team*, it wasn't difficult to understand.

"They wanted to play that way, too," Holzman said. "Yes, I think for a team to win, if you look back at the history in the NBA, most teams that won were unselfish; passed the ball; hit the open man; played good, hard defense; and took pride in their defense. That's where it all has to start, because that's hard work. That's when you have to be unselfish to work hard defensively."

Holzman seemed a natural as a coach, but the truth is, he never wanted the job.

Born in Brooklyn, William "Red" Holzman was a standout guard in high school and later went on to play at City College in New York City for legendary coach Nat Holman.

That "hit the open man" credo? It was a Holman philosophy within a motion offense that depended on crisp passing and moving without the ball. Sound familiar? It's the basic fundamental of Mike D'Antoni's famous Seven-Seconds-or-Less style of offense, too.

Royal Red

Before Red Holzman led the Knicks to their first (and only) two NBA championships as a coach, he beat them in their first NBA Finals appearance in 1951. Holzman was on the Rochester Royals team that defeated the Knicks in a wild seven-game battle that saw the Knicks force a Game 7 after Rochester went ahead 3–0 in the best-of-seven series. "Our fans at the Edgerton Park Arena were usually loud," Holzman said in his book, *Red on Red*, "but I never heard them roar like they did in that seventh game.... That was the greatest moment in the history of Rochester sports."

Holzman always credited Holman for his own basketball acumen. "A great teacher, a great coach," Holzman told Vic Ziegel of the *New York Daily News* in a February 13, 1995, story. "He helped me form my own opinions about basketball. I'll be indebted to him for teaching me the game. A lot of people are."

Holzman was also indebted to an old friend of his, Fuzzy Levane, for his career. Levane, a longtime scout with the Knicks, is the main reason why Holzman wound up with the Knicks in 1957. Levane was hired by the Knicks as their head coach and brought in Holzman, who had been coaching the Milwaukee/St. Louis Hawks, as his scout. Levane only lasted a season. Though the Knicks went through a terrible drought, Holzman kept his job, and by the early 1960s he started the building blocks for a team. It started with Willis Reed as a second-round pick in 1964, then Dick Van Arsdale the following year. Then came a trade for Dick Barnett and selecting Bill Bradley, Cazzie Russell, and Walt Frazier in the draft.

But while the talent was there, the direction was lacking. The Knicks went through two coaches in two years, with Harry Gallatin being replaced by another former Knick, Dick McGuire.

Then after a 15–22 start in 1967–68, in the season the team was preparing for the long-awaited move into the new Madison Square Garden, team owner Ned Irish told his longtime assistant, Fred Podesta, to make a coaching change. So rather than fire McGuire, he told Holzman that he was now the coach and McGuire would be the scout.

"I didn't want to coach," Holzman said in a videotaped interview for NBA Entertainment. "They said, 'There's nobody else. It's you. You've got the job.'"

It worked out brilliantly for both men, as McGuire remained with the franchise literally for the rest of his life as a scout and valued resource on determining talent. And within three years,

Holzman had the Knicks on top of the basketball world with a style of play that was appreciated by all who watched.

He also had a style all his own. He enjoyed banter with reporters but rarely gave any useful quotes. Perhaps one of the most retold Holzman lines is one he once used while trying to give perspective to Dave Checketts in the 1990s when the former Knicks president was lamenting a maddening player.

"He may be a putz," Holzman said, "but he's our putz."

His players adored him. Most of them, of course, knew they were in New York because he had brought them there. As the team's scout, he was usually the first person from the organization who they met. And in his understated way, he often left a lasting impression.

Phil Jackson recalled the time when Holzman went to Fargo, North Dakota, to sign Jackson, the team's second-round draft pick that year, to a contract. At the same time Holzman was there, New York City mayor John Lindsay was in Fargo to give a speech.

"Can you imagine, the mayor of New York is here and everybody knows it," Holzman said to Jackson. "And you're here getting signed and nobody knows it."

Little did anyone know, especially back then, but Jackson would become Holzman's most successful protégé. Jackson would eventually go on to join Holzman in the Basketball Hall of Fame as one of the game's all-time greatest coaches, with 11 NBA championships with two franchises, the Chicago Bulls and the Los Angeles Lakers.

"He is the reason why I am a coach, obviously," Jackson said during the 2009 NBA Finals, which became his 10th championship. "He told me I would be a coach. He said, 'You see the game.'"

Holzman coached the Knicks until 1977, when he was forced out and replaced with one of his own players, Willis Reed. But then he was brought back a year later, when Sonny Werblin took over the Garden and ordered the change. Holzman lasted three seasons after that but endured a difficult youth movement. There was one bright spot: the 50-win team in 1980–81 loaded with young talents such as Micheal Ray Richardson, Ray Williams, and Bill Cartwright. But they were swept out of the playoffs in the first round. The following year, the team went 33–49, and Holzman, at the age of 61, retired from coaching for good.

He was brought back into the organization by Checketts in June 1991 and remained a valued advisor until his death on November 13, 1998, when he succumbed to leukemia.

"People come up to me and say, 'Thank you for what happened,'" Holzman once said. "That's unusual for people to do that, but they're still doing it, and it makes me feel very good. It makes me realize that we did have something very, very special."

14 Attend an MLK Day Matinee

If you could attend one game a season and couldn't pick the opponent, the choice has to be to attend the annual Martin Luther King Jr. Day matinee at Madison Square Garden.

It is a tradition that began in 1987, a year after the holiday was first observed. The Knicks actually did play on the inaugural holiday, but the game was played at Philadelphia, with a 103–93 loss.

After that, the Knicks decided to make it their own special day at the Garden and have requested each year to host a game, preferably in the afternoon. Going into the 2012–13 season, on what is now known as the MLK Day Matinee, the Knicks have had amazing success. The team has won 18 of 26 games.

But not only is there a greater probability of seeing a Knicks win, there is also a chance, based on history, that something bizarre or controversial will happen.

Before we get into that, let's go back into history. Dr. King has very little connection to the Knicks, but the little that exists involves a story told by Cal Ramsey, a former NYU star who had a brief career in the NBA, including a seven-game stint with the Knicks in 1959–60, and later went on to become a beloved analyst for the Knicks in the 1970s.

After Ramsey's career ended in 1961, he became a teacher in the New York City school system, but he maintained a connection with several NBA stars, including the great Wilt Chamberlain.

In August 1963 Chamberlain invited Ramsey to join him on a trip to Washington, D.C., to attend the March on Washington for Jobs and Freedom. It was there, from the steps of the Lincoln Memorial on August 28, that King delivered his famous "I Have a Dream" speech in front of an estimated 200,000 that stood around the Reflecting Pool.

"[We] stood right in the middle of that crowd," Ramsey recalled in an interview with the *New York Daily News* in January 2009. "We didn't get any celebrity treatment, but then again, Wilt always loved being right in the middle of a crowd.

"It was hot and we heard a terrific speech. Then we came right back to New York."

Just shy of five years later, Dr. King was murdered at the Lorraine Hotel in Memphis, days after he delivered a hauntingly ominous speech:

"Like anybody, I would like to live a long life," King said. "Longevity has its place. But I'm not concerned about that now. I just want to do God's will. And He's allowed me to go up to the mountain. And I've looked over. And I've seen the promised land. I may not get there with you. But I want you to know tonight, that we, as a people, will get to the promised land!"

The Knicks championship-era team was still in its embryonic stage, but the social consciousness of the team, which became a widely respected trademark of that group, was already developed.

Phil Jackson, always an alternative thinker, was a rookie on the Knicks in 1967–68 and recalled the time.

"We were in the midst of a playoff series with Philadelphia," he told reporters in Los Angeles in January 2010. "We were disappointed those games were called off."

Jackson's recollection was a bit spotty here. Dr. King was killed on April 4. The 76ers eliminated the Knicks in the sixth game of their best-of-seven series on April 1. But we'll let him continue his thought:

"He made such a big impact on all of our lives," Jackson said of King. "I remember college students marched. That was a huge amount of energy involved in the nonviolent movement and that whole idea, the Gandhi experience."

Yes, nonviolence. The Knicks may have the intention to honor Dr. King's memory by playing on this day, but these games haven't always followed the nonviolent message.

Take, for instance, the game in 1993, when Charles Barkley was furious after no foul was called on Knicks forward Anthony Mason as Barkley missed a potential game-winning three-pointer with 12 seconds left. After the final buzzer sounded on a 106–103 Knicks win, Barkley got into a shouting match with referee Jim Clark, who, as he headed toward the tunnel to the locker-room area, shot back at the superstar, who was still on the court, "That's going to cost you money!"

Barkley was incensed by Clark's threat and jumped over the scorers' table, tripped and fell, and then got up to charge after the referee. Security guards had to restrain him as he continued to bark at Clark.

"When he said the part to me about money, I went off," Barkley told reporters that day. "Like he can control me with money. You can't control people with money. I thought he made bad calls all night, but when he said that thing about, 'It's going to cost you money,' like money can control me? Give me a break."

The following day, the NBA fined Barkley $10,000.

A break? How about a gash to the forehead?

There was an even more egregious disregard for King's message of nonviolence in 2001. As the Knicks were putting the finishing touches on a blowout win over the San Antonio Spurs, Danny Ferry and Marcus Camby jockeyed for rebounding position. As the two turned to head down the court, Ferry threw a backhand that caught Camby in the eye.

Ferry was immediately ejected by officials for the flagrant foul, but before he could leave the court, Camby, with a cut bleeding over his eye, charged after him. The 6'11" Camby, with a wingspan of over seven feet, raised his fist to deliver a roundhouse to the back of Ferry's head.

But Jeff Van Gundy had already stepped in to block his player, and instead of drilling Ferry, Camby missed and fell forward. Momentum caused him to knock heads with Van Gundy, who hit the floor and was now also bleeding.

And shouting angry expletives. But not about Ferry, but his own player.

Camby was suspended five games for his actions. Ferry? Got one game. Van Gundy got a shiner.

Punches weren't thrown in the 2008 game between the Knicks and Celtics, but both Quentin Richardson and Paul Pierce were ejected after the two carried on with trash talking and hard fouls that seemed to be a harbinger for a brawl.

Pierce and Richardson have a long history between them, which neither will discuss publicly. But in the third quarter of this game, after Richardson literally shoved Pierce to the baseline on consecutive drives, the officials had seen enough.

After he was tossed, Richardson barked at Pierce, "Back there," as in the locker-room area, where they could settle their differences. Pierce stayed by the Celtics bench and looked away while Richardson continued to point and challenge Pierce.

"Nonviolent!" Celtics forward James Posey yelled. "Nonviolent!"

That's Amar'e!

The date had been circled on the calendar of every Knicks fan for over two years: July 1, 2010. It was going to be the first time in 14 years that the franchise had enough salary-cap space to be major players in free agency.

And it just so happened that year included perhaps the greatest free-agency class in NBA history, headlined by two-time NBA MVP LeBron James.

Knicks fans endured an anxious courtship with James, who flirted just enough to keep New Yorkers swooning. The Knicks were first in line the morning of July 1, when the free-agency period officially began and James held meetings in Cleveland with those teams looking to recruit him.

But actually, it was at the first stroke after midnight on the East Coast, when Mike D'Antoni and an entourage from the Knicks franchise and Madison Square Garden, set up shop in a Los Angeles hotel. The Knicks took advantage of the time difference; it was still June 30, at 9:01 PM in California, when the free-agency period technically began.

Amar'e Stoudemire: No. 1 in New York.

The first call made wasn't to LeBron; it was to another of the high-profile free agents, Amar'e Stoudemire.

Mike D'Antoni and Stoudemire had some history. D'Antoni coached Stoudemire in Phoenix from 2004 to 2008 and the two shared great success over those seasons but yet also departed with some issues. While Steve Nash was annoyed with the Suns' decision to part ways with the popular coach, Stoudemire was critical for what he perceived as a lack of focus on defense by D'Antoni.

Anyone who paid even casual attention knew that LeBron was the Knicks' main target, but some in the media were suggesting that one of the top free agents the Knicks weren't interested in was Stoudemire. The suggestion that D'Antoni didn't want to coach him again was delivered as the reason.

So D'Antoni, desperate to not lose out on any of the top free agents, felt he needed to quickly clear the air with Stoudemire.

"I told him, 'What's out there about me not wanting you here, that's not true,'" D'Antoni told me that July. "I told him we absolutely wanted him."

Stoudemire appreciated the olive branch and agreed to come to New York for a formal visit that weekend. On the same Saturday the Knicks contingent was in Chicago to meet with free agents Dwyane Wade and Chris Bosh, Stoudemire arrived in New York City. Wearing a sport coat, a silk scarf, and a New York Yankees cap, he attended a Broadway show, *Rock of Ages*, which was produced by his agent, Happy Walters, and was immediately overwhelmed by the amount of fans who begged him to sign with the Knicks.

Stoudemire attended a Yankees game that weekend—where he again was met with pleading fans—and on Sunday morning he met with D'Antoni for brunch at the famous Jean-Georges Restaurant in the Trump International Hotel and Tower. The two had a candid conversation during which they hashed out their differences and found a common ground.

"It was just an opportunity to break the ice and get a feel for everything," D'Antoni said. "We just talked about how we could get it done here like we did in Phoenix."

Stoudemire had just reached the Western Conference Finals with the Suns that spring under coach Alvin Gentry, who was an assistant under D'Antoni in Phoenix. One could argue that D'Antoni, who had just endured two losing seasons in New York while the team made salary-dump trades to get under the cap, needed Stoudemire more than Stoudemire needed D'Antoni.

But Stoudemire wanted New York.

So the day after that Sunday brunch, during which D'Antoni made his earnest pitch, Stoudemire pulled a blue cap on his head, grinned, and said, "The Knicks are back." Outside of Madison Square Garden, his name glowed on the famous Seventh Avenue marquee.

"I've been thinking about New York since the 2002 draft," he said, when the Knicks—as you recall—passed on him to take Nene, who was moved in that Antonio McDyess trade.

The Knicks made up for that mistake by signing Stoudemire to a five-year, $99.7 million contract. It felt like a victory—especially later that week, after James chose to take his talents to South Beach—but it didn't come without some measure of risk.

Stoudemire was a five-time All-Star and four-time All-NBA selection but has a left knee that, in 2005, underwent microfracture surgery. The Knicks requested MRI results of the knee, which were taken before free agency by the Suns, who were concerned enough to offer Stoudemire a five-year, $96 million extension that did not come with a guarantee for the final two seasons.

The Knicks gave Stoudemire a fully guaranteed deal and considered it a calculated risk. After enduring two painful salary-dumping seasons, the team could ill afford to be shut out of the free-agency sweepstakes. Landing one star, they hoped, would attract others. The plan all along wasn't to just have one but multiple stars and follow the blueprint of the Boston Celtics, who won the 2008 NBA title after forming a Big Three by making trades for Kevin Garnett and Ray Allen to join Paul Pierce.

But when the 2010–11 season began, Stoudemire was the lone star and, with a swagger not seen in orange-and-blue in years, lifted the once-proud franchise on his shoulders. After a 3–8 start, Stoudemire led an incredible run that saw the Knicks win 13 of the next 14 games, including eight straight from November 28 to December 12.

During that stretch, Stoudemire scored 30 points or more in nine straight games, which was a franchise record. He played to chants of "MVP!" at the Garden and embraced his Gotham celebrity with a Times Square billboard and appearances on *The Late Show with David Letterman*, *Live with Regis and Kelly*, and even *Sesame Street*.

As the leading man of a Knicks revival that saw the franchise clinch its first playoff berth in seven years and record its first winning season in a decade, Stoudemire became everything the Knicks needed him to be.

"He put a lot of fears to rest," D'Antoni told the *Arizona Republic* on December 7, 2010. "The biggest thing is that he has not been daunted by being in New York. He looks at New York like a hurdle. Even when we were 3–8, he never backed down from the challenge. And that's helped everybody's bravado. That's given the team a broad pair of shoulders to jump on. It's made everyone feel that maybe we can get this thing done."

16 Know the Trent Tucker Rule

Because of its historic importance to the NBA game, this MLK Day moment deserves its own chapter. It was January 15, 1990, at the Garden, in a matinee between the Knicks and Bulls. From one-tenth of a second came a well-known rule that impacts the game—and strategy—to this very day.

This was still in the early days of the Knicks-Bulls rivalry from the early 1990s, the embryonic stages of Jordan's dominance over the Knicks. It was a tightly contested game, as usual, and with the score tied at 106, Jordan missed a three-pointer, which was rebounded by Charles Oakley with 4.6 seconds left.

After a timeout, Knicks coach Stu Jackson sent Rod Strickland and Trent Tucker, two of his best three-point shooters, into the game to pull the defense away from the middle and allow Mark Jackson to work for a final shot or pass to Patrick Ewing. But before Jackson could make a play, Scottie Pippen fouled him with :00.1 showing on the game clock.

The NBA had just introduced tenths of a second to the game clock, something regularly found in the European game, that season. Previous to this season, the clock would have read :00, though the buzzer would have yet to sound.

The Bulls had a foul to give, so the Knicks had to inbound the ball from the sideline. Bulls coach Phil Jackson, then a rookie head coach, figured the only play the Knicks had was a lob to Ewing for an alley-oop before the buzzer, so he set up a defense that keyed on the painted area and stopping the lob.

Mark Jackson had the lob in mind, too. Tucker's job was to run from the baseline under the basket as a decoy, to pull his defender out of the paint. But Jordan, who was guarding Tucker, dropped off Tucker as he left to anticipate the lob. Ewing had rolled to the basket looking for the alley-oop but was blanketed by Bill Cartwright, with Jordan waiting to spring for the lob.

With no clear play to Ewing, Jackson saw Tucker curling toward him and made the pass. Tucker caught it, squared, and fired just as the buzzer sounded. It swished through for the win.

"It's the greatest shot I ever made," Tucker said after the game. "I just caught the ball and flung it. When the ball left my hands, I knew it was on target. What I didn't know was whether it had the distance. When it went in, I thought to myself, *Not bad for a guy who was supposed to be a decoy on the play!*"

The Knicks ran off the court quickly as the Bulls tried to get the officials to wave off the basket. Afterward, Phil Jackson debated the human ability to complete a catch-and-shoot action within one-tenth of a second.

"A second or two, maybe," Jackson said. "But in one-tenth of a second, it can't be done. You can't shoot a shot in that time. The officials are still getting adjusted to the tenths of a second."

Jackson then simply labeled it as "a judgment call" and added that the Knicks "just got a friendly call, and let's leave it at that."

But the Bulls didn't just leave it at that. Two days later, the team filed a protest with the NBA office about the 109–106 loss. The Bulls said referee Ronnie Nunn, who called the basket good, made an error in judgment. After studying the replay, the Bulls countered that the shot attempt actually took two seconds.

The NBA spent two weeks reviewing, analyzing, and even debating the play. Among the league's top executives, only vice president of operations Rod Thorn believed the league should rule in favor of the Bulls. (Full disclosure: Thorn had previously served as general manager of the Bulls in the 1980s.) Thorn made a good case, arguing that European League studies showed such plays take at the very least three-tenths of a second to execute.

In the end, the league denied the protest and ruled the basket was good. In a statement from NBA commissioner David Stern, released by the league on January 31, 1990, Stern actually agreed that the shot did not get off in time. But the semantics of the Bulls' protest—blaming Nunn for the error—allowed the league to avoid the rare event of a do-over.

"The question before me is not whether Trent Tucker received Mark Jackson's pass and released his shot within one-tenth of second. Plainly, he did not," the statement said. "The question presented by Chicago's protest, rather, is whether the referees' failure to disallow Tucker's shot constitutes a sufficient basis for overturning the result of the game. The NBA has consistently denied protest based on errors in judgment by the game officials."

However, a result of the investigation and debate was a rule that the league adopted that day, which said that when there is less than three-tenths of a second on the game clock, any shot attempts other than an alley-oop or tip-in would be disallowed.

It would be over 26 years until such a play would be executed successfully under what is known around the league as "the Trent Tucker Rule." Coincidentally, it took place at Madison Square Garden.

It was December 20, 2006, and the Knicks were tied at 109 with the Charlotte Bobcats. Knicks guard Jamal Crawford had the inbound from the far sideline and, as the rule states, his only play was a lob at the basket. Isiah Thomas designed a play for David Lee to fake a pick for Eddy Curry at the top of the key and then cut back toward the rim. Crawford sent a lob toward the rim that was a bit long but needed to be get past 6'10" Emeka Okafor, who was defending Lee.

The 6'9" Lee was able to leap and reach it with his right hand—and his back to the backboard—and put just enough touch on the ball to redirect it into the basket just as the buzzer sounded. By rule, the clock doesn't start until the ball touches a player in play. After reviewing the play, the basket was allowed and the Knicks came away with the win.

It was the first time since the Trent Tucker Rule that a player had scored with less than three-tenths of a second on the clock.

Coincidentally, three players from that 1990 game were in attendance—Ewing, Oakley, and Jordan, who had just become the director of basketball operations for the Bobcats. So not only did the Knicks twice have game winners with one-tenth of a second left, but both times they did it to beat Jordan.

Double Nickels

The Trent Tucker Rule might have twice bitten Michael Jordan, but His Airness had many more nights on which he owned Madison Square Garden.

The game's ultimate showman always thrived on the game's biggest stage. It was as if he saved his best for those visits to New York, where the Garden crowd swooned as he was killing them softly with his song.

Jordan is a New Yorker by birth—he lived the first two years of his life in Brooklyn—and certainly felt at home from the moment he arrived in the NBA. In his Garden debut on November 8, 1984, Jordan recorded 33 points as he not only outdueled the great Bernard King but also stole the crowd from the Knicks.

The unforgettable highlight from that game came off a steal in the backcourt that saw him race in on the break, jump a good 10 feet from the basket, and cuff the ball for a cradle-dunk that brought the house down.

"I took off too far," a soft-spoken, polite Jordan told MSG Network's Jim Karvellas afterward, "and I barely made it."

In his third season, after missing most of the 1985–86 season with an ankle injury, Jordan returned to the Garden for yet another dazzling show in the season opener. He put up 50 points—a Garden record for an opponent—including 20 of 22 from the foul line, as Knicks guards Rory Sparrow and Gerald Wilkins had no chance in what became a 108–103 loss.

That was the season Hubie Brown experimented by playing Patrick Ewing at power forward next to Bill Cartwright at center. Ewing was miserable, and it showed in his 13-point, five-rebound effort.

It took a few years, but eventually both Jordan's Bulls and Ewing's Knicks emerged as Eastern Conference powers. They met in the playoffs four times in the five years spanning 1989 to 1993. The Knicks never beat the Bulls until Jordan left the NBA in shocking fashion before the 1993–94 season to embark on a baseball career. In the spring of 1994, when Jordan was made mortal by a minor-league curveball while playing with the Birmingham Barons, the Knicks beat the Bulls in the Eastern Conference semifinals.

Jordan returned to the NBA a year later with a simple declaration: "I'm back." His timing was curious. Sure, his claim was that he didn't want to get caught up in the ongoing baseball strike, which had wiped out the World Series in the previous fall. Word had gotten out that Jordan had been playing plenty of pickup basketball at his alma mater, the University of North Carolina. And he was looking like he was preparing himself for a comeback.

And so he did, on March 19, 1995, against the Indiana Pacers. Jordan was notably rusty, with 19 points on 7-of-28 shooting in a 103–96 Bulls loss. He steadily got back into the flow over the next four games, with 27 points in a win over Boston, 21 in a loss to Orlando, and then 32 in a win over Atlanta.

And wouldn't you know it, in the fifth game after his celebrated return, Jordan and the Bulls were scheduled to play at Madison Square Garden.

There were three days of anticipation for this game, on a Tuesday night in New York. Another sellout crowd and a Knicks team that had thought it exorcised the Bulls demons that previous spring. But that was while Michael was gone. As he said in his comeback press conference: He's baa-ack.

And with a vengeance. Jordan torched the Knicks for 35 points in the first half and had the Garden once again in a frenzy over his greatness. Jordan finished with 55 points, which Knicks superfan (and a Jordan pal from those popular Nike Air Jordan commercials) Spike Lee immediately dubbed "Double Nickels."

It was how the game would be forever remembered, as the Double Nickels Game.

The Knicks, however, had a chance to beat Jordan that night. Jordan's last points came on a jumper with 25.8 seconds left to give the Bulls a 111–109 lead. But John Starks, who was torched by Jordan throughout the game, drew a foul and hit two free throws with 14.6 seconds left to tie it at 111.

On the ensuing possession, Jordan had the ball at the top of the key and there was little debate as to who would be taking the final shot for the Bulls. Jordan crossed over, which sent Starks stumbling to the court. You know how basketball players refer to the "ankle-breaker"? Well, Starks literally sprained his ankle on that play—and as he pulled up for the shot, Ewing came over to contest.

That left Bulls center Bill Wennington wide open under the basket, and Jordan fed a pass around Ewing for a game-winning dunk by Wennington with 3.1 seconds left.

There would be no Trent Tucker heroics on this night, as Starks lost the ball on the final possession to cap the nightmare. Starks had just 14 points on 1-of-7 shooting from three-point range, but it was at the other end of the floor where he looked the most lost.

"I think he forgot how to play me," Jordan teased afterward.

"When he's on like that," Starks said, "it makes him double-tough."

That's double-*nickels* tough.

Jordan only faced the Knicks once more in the postseason—in 1996—though he did go on to win three more NBA titles. He would make two farewell visits to the Garden before his career came to a close.

The first time came on March 8, 1998, when Jordan announced his plans to retire for good. To make it special, he went into his closet and pulled out a pair of his very first Air Jordan sneakers— the famous red, white, and black high tops he wore for his Garden debut over 13 years prior.

He then delivered, fittingly, a vintage performance, with 42 points on 17-of-33 shooting. With stars such as Bruce Springsteen and Wayne Gretzky sitting along celebrity row, Jordan left what became a 102–89 blowout win to a standing ovation from the Garden crowd.

The shoes were saved for the memory and Jordan couldn't wait to take them off. Apparently, his foot had grown one full size since his rookie year, so the size 12½ original Air Jordan's were a bit tight.

"My feet are killing me," Jordan told NBC's Ahmad Rashad, one of his closest friends, after the game, "but it was fun."

The actual finale came five years later, almost to the day, with a 40-year-old Jordan wearing a Washington Wizards jersey. He was able to reach back for one more prolific scoring night, though his game was very much below the rim and perimeter-based at this point, with 39 points. He left the floor, however, with a 97–96 loss to the Knicks and the usual ovation from the New York crowd.

In an interview with NBC before that 1998 game, Jordan talked about his appreciation for the Garden and the New York fans. In his words, he gave clear indication that the respect over the years was mutual.

"It's always been a place where basketball enthusiasts could really notice a fake basketball player," he said. "If you're a real basketball player, they honor that, they show a respect for that. If you're just hype, you can't fool them, and they see it. And that's like stepping on a stage with an act."

And his was the greatest to ever play there.

# Wilt's 100

Michael Jordan may have owned the Garden—and the Knicks—with some prolific performances, but even Jordan never came close to matching the all-time greatest performance by a Knicks opponent.

It didn't happen at the Garden. In fact, it didn't even happen in an NBA arena. It happened in Hershey, Pennsylvania, on March 2, 1962, in a game that wasn't even televised.

Wilt Chamberlain was in his third NBA season and was already the league's most dominant player. Chamberlain didn't just occasionally score 50 points on a given night, he *averaged* 50 points a game that season.

Earlier in the season, on December 8, 1961, Chamberlain had 78 points against the Los Angeles Lakers, which broke Elgin Baylor's year-old league scoring record of 71, which Baylor achieved against the Knicks early in the 1960–61 season.

Chamberlain came close to challenging his own record a month later when he hit 73 points against the Chicago Packers. He wound up scoring over 60 points 13 times that season, including 67 against the Knicks on February 25, just a week before he would see New York again.

In fact, in the two games between, Chamberlain had 65 points against the St. Louis Hawks and 61 against the Packers.

For the Knicks, it was yet another lost season. Rookie coach Eddie Donovan's team arrived in Hershey with a 27–45 record and headed to a third-straight season without a playoff berth—so you can just imagine where their mind-set was at this point.

"We were pretty much playing the schedule out," Johnny Green told D'Agostino in *Garden Glory*, "and we took the bus down to Hershey."

One player, however, didn't make it out of his hotel room to the Hershey Sports Arena. That was 6'10" center Phil Jordon, who came down with a flu and was too sick to play by game time.

That left the Knicks with only one center, 6'10" Darrall Imhoff, to contend with the 7'2" Chamberlain. Cue the ominous music.

To further the Knicks' troubles, Imhoff got in early foul trouble, and Donovan was left to throw 6'9" rookie Cleveland Buckner, 6'6" Dave Budd, and 6'6" Willie Naulls on Chamberlain, which was like trying to cover a king-sized mattress with a handkerchief.

"Eddie kept shuttling guys in there," Green said. "Willie played him, I may have played him a little bit, the guy who sold popcorn may have played him. But Wilt simply had his way."

Chamberlain had 23 points in the first quarter and 41 by half-time. Certainly 100 was within reach. He had 28 in the third, to bring his total to 69, and the Hershey crowd started to buzz.

"After I got my third foul, I said to one of the officials, Willie Smith, 'Why don't you just give him 100 points, and we'll all go home?'" Imhoff told the *Los Angeles Times* in an October 13, 1999, story on Chamberlain. "Well, we did."

The Warriors got so caught up in the effort to get Chamberlain to 100 that, in a game they were *winning*, they actually started fouling the Knicks to stop the clock.

"That's not the way the game's supposed to be played," Richie Guerin told D'Agostino in *Garden Glory*. "To me, they made their minds up at halftime to see if they could get 100 points for Wilt.... There's no doubt in my mind that they made up their minds to do that. They made a little bit of a farce of the game. Even the officials got caught up in it a little bit.

"I tried to foul out," Guerin said. "I must have committed 10 fouls. But the refs said, 'Come on, Rich. If we gotta be out here, you gotta be out here.'"

The Knicks were annoyed, but there was nothing they could do to stop it. Well, there was one thing: fouling anyone but Chamberlain to keep him from scoring.

"The game was a farce in the last quarter," Chamberlain once said of the game (archived on Hoophall.com). "After I broke the record, the Knicks decided they didn't want someone to score 100 points against them. They started to do anything they could to prevent it. They'd foul my teammates intentionally so the ball wouldn't come to me. You should have seen Guy Rodgers. They couldn't even foul him, he was so fast."

Usually, fouling was the best kind of defense against Chamberlain, who was a notoriously bad free-throw shooter. It was the predecessor to the Hack-a-Shaq strategy often used against Shaquille O'Neal, who might be the closest to Chamberlain the NBA has seen of physically dominant centers.

But on this night, Chamberlain was even hitting his free throws. A career 51 percent shooter from the line (and a career-best 61.3 percent that season), Chamberlain hit 28 of 32 foul shots in the game.

But the 100th point was scored on a short jumper with 46 seconds left off a pass from Joe Ruklick. The game was stopped as fans raced onto the court to celebrate the amazing feat. Warriors publicity man Harvey Pollack found a blank sheet of paper and with a pen wrote "100" and had Chamberlain hold it up for a photo op for what is now one of the game's most famous images.

After a long delay, the game was officially finished, with Chamberlain standing in the middle of the court just waiting for the clock to expire. The final score was Warriors 169, Knicks 147. Guerin had 39 points, Buckner scored 33, and Naulls added 31 for the Knicks.

The Knicks were already embarrassed, but the kicker was they had to play Chamberlain and the Warriors again two days later at Madison Square Garden. Chamberlain even traveled to New York with a few Knicks players.

In New York, with the crowd buzzing about his 100-point game, Chamberlain tried to do it again. But this time Imhoff was able to avoid foul trouble and he "held" Chamberlain to 58 points.

That earned Imhoff a standing ovation from the Garden crowd.

19 The King of New York

Before Michael Jordan arrived in the NBA, or at least before he emerged as an unstoppable scoring machine, the league was dominated by small forwards. The 1980s were a golden age for the position, with high-scoring stars such as Larry Bird, Dominique Wilkins, Mark Aguirre, James Worthy, Adrian Dantley, and Alex English, to name a few.

Of all of them, Bird, who won three consecutive NBA MVPs from 1984 to 1986, was considered the best. But among his

Bernard King was a dominant force on the basketball court, respected but feared by his opponents.

peers, there was no one more respected—make that feared—than Bernard King.

"I have never feared anybody that I've played against—Bird, Magic, Dr. [J], Michael—and I respect and love all of those guys," Wilkins told John Hareas of NBA.com. "Bernard King is the only guy that ever scared the hell out of me."

Aguirre once told me that during his career, there were only three players that ever worried him as opponents: Bird, Worthy, and King.

When I asked Bird the same question, his reply was Jordan and Magic. Why not King?

"I didn't guard Bernard," Bird replied. "I had no chance guarding Bernard."

At 6'8" and 230 pounds, King was a brutal force on the low post and yet had a terrific midrange game with a powerful first step that made it difficult to guard him close. He was one of the league's most prolific scorers in the 1980s and is the only Knick to win the NBA scoring title (32.9 points per game in 1984–85). In just three-plus seasons for the Knicks, King averaged 26.5 points per game and shot a sizzling 54.3 percent from the field. He eclipsed the 40-point mark 23 times, had back-to-back 50-point performances in the 1983–84 season, and posted a franchise-record 60-point performance against the Nets on Christmas Day in 1984.

King came to the Knicks in 1982. It was a homecoming for King, who was raised in Brooklyn's Fort Greene neighborhood. After a brilliant career at Tennessee, King was drafted by the Nets—but they traded him during his rookie season. After battling alcohol abuse, he bounced from the Utah Jazz to the Golden State Warriors, where he got his career back on track as the NBA's Comeback Player of the Year.

His arrival on the Knicks, which coincided with Hubie Brown's first season, brought back the long-awaited return of the franchise as a playoff contender. And in the 1984 playoffs, he single-handedly led the Knicks to a five-game upset of the Detroit Pistons by averaging 42.6 points per game in the series. In the second round, he and the Knicks put a scare into Bird and the eventual champion Celtics, with a seven-game battle.

"Talk to any guy who's a scorer, and he'll tell you there are times when you go into a zone," King once told *Inside Sports*. "When I was averaging 30 points a game, I didn't have to think about anything. Everything is happening on a very instinctual level. On a particular night, no matter what you do, there's a feeling it's going to work. It's an incredible feeling. There's nothing like it."

But the following season, the Knicks were riddled with injuries to key players such as Bill Cartwright, Truck Robinson, and Marvin Webster, and King, despite leading the league in scoring, was doing just enough to keep the franchise in playoff contention. At 24–46 in late March, the team was fighting for one of the last playoff spots in the Eastern Conference. King, ever the fierce competitor who never gave up on a play, was chasing down Reggie Theus on a breakaway and, as he jumped to block the shot, he felt a pop. No, it wasn't really like a pop. As King often describes it, "I felt my knee shatter."

He tore the anterior cruciate ligament in his right knee, which these days is not nearly as devastating an injury as it was in the mid-1980s. Back then it was career-threatening. It would be two years before King would return to the court.

When he did, the Knicks were a much different team. After King's injury, the Knicks lost the last 12 games of the season. That was the first year the NBA held a draft lottery. (As you learned earlier in the book—so at this point you already know that Patrick Ewing was the selection.)

King played the final six games of the 1986–87 season and showed he had, in fact, made it all the way back. In those six games, he averaged 22.7 points. That year, however, the Knicks were again headed to the lottery and were looking for a new coach. King was excited about the prospect of teaming up with Ewing—because of injuries, the two never played together, despite being on the same roster for two seasons—but the Knicks had other ideas.

Rick Pitino, Brown's former assistant, came in from Providence College, and the goal was to go young. There was a fear that King's knee wouldn't be able to handle the rigors of an entire NBA season, so when he became a free agent that summer, he found his services no longer wanted in New York. He instead signed with the Washington Bullets.

He played four seasons in Washington, and his scoring steadily climbed back to among the league leaders as he transformed his game as primarily a post-up player. At the age of 34, he averaged 28.4 points per game and was again an All-Star. He needed another knee operation, which cost him the 1991–92 season, and returned for one more stint with the Nets in 1992–93 before he retired. King scored 19,655 career points, and his 22.5 points-per-game career average is 24th on the NBA's all-time list.

King never won an MVP, but he was selected as the NBA Player of the Year by the *Sporting News*, which based the award on a poll of NBA players. But, to date, he has yet to earn Hall of Fame consideration, which has many of his peers baffled.

"Bernard went toe-to-toe with every small forward in this league," Wilkins told NBA.com. "How many people do you know [who get] 50 on back-to-back nights? For whatever reason, people get overlooked, and I can't explain it. I don't know. But the funny thing is, his peers know. They know what Bernard King meant to this game. They know what he did to players in this game. People at the small forward position, guys did not want to play against Bernard King because they had to work too hard. He was relentless."

The Hall of Fame snub has irked King, but the respect of his contemporaries has its own value.

"I know that I have a trophy sitting in my office [that] was presented to me by the NBA [and] indicates that Bernard King was the most valuable player in the NBA for the 1983–84 season as voted by his peers," King told me. "And that's when only Magic Johnson, Larry Bird, Dr. J were in the league. So that means a great deal. I also know that there's no player in NBA history that was voted most valuable player in the league that's not in the Hall of Fame."

20 The City Game

"Basketball is the city game," Pete Axthelm begins his best-selling book, *The City Game*, which tells of the love affair between a sport and the city that embraced it as its own.

It fits New York well, with an up-tempo style based on a simple concept that is somehow elevated to an artistry, especially through a collective effort. And the fact that all you needed was a ball and a hoop—or something resembling a hoop, like a milk crate nailed to a telephone pole—made it fit the crowded city much better than the demands of a baseball diamond or a football field.

The game wasn't invented in New York, but it might have been perfected there. The growth of the game's popularity in the early 1900s can be traced to New York as early as 1905, 14 years after Dr. James Naismith took a soccer ball and instructed students at a YMCA in Springfield, Massachusetts, to toss it into a peach basket that hung from a railing 10 feet high above the gym's floor.

Columbia University, the oldest institution of higher learning in New York (and fifth oldest in the United States), had a very good team that went by the nickname "the Blue and White Five."

In 1905 teams from a pair of Midwestern colleges, the University of Minnesota and the University of Wisconsin, traveled to the Morningside Heights campus to challenge Columbia's well-known group. Columbia beat both teams, but from those games came the idea of forming an intercollegiate tournament.

In 1938 the National Invitation Tournament was created by—get this—a group of sportswriters (See? We're not all that bad). Members of the Metropolitan Basketball Writers Association, which was basically a bunch of New York City–based scribes, formed the tournament. It was played, of course, in New York.

Everyone has heard of the Harlem Globetrotters; the barnstorming team has entertained crowds with their showman style since 1927. But despite the name, the Globetrotters were really not from Harlem. In fact, they originated in Chicago.

But Barnumesque owner Abe Saperstein felt using Harlem, the tradition-rich section of Manhattan well known as the epicenter of African American culture, would be a catchier name as a home city for his group. Truth be told, the Globetrotters didn't actually play a game in Harlem until 1968.

But while the Globetrotters weren't a real New York team (they were even made up of players from Chicago), one of the most successful franchises in basketball history was formed in New York—and legitimately based out of Harlem—in 1923. The Harlem Renaissance Big Five, later known as the Rens were formed by Robert "Bob" Douglas as part of a deal with the Harlem Renaissance Casino and Ballroom.

It was there, at the casino's ballroom on 138th Street and Seventh Avenue, that the Rens played their "home" games— though most of the time they traveled. Their first-ever game was November 3, 1923, at the Renaissance Ballroom, a 28–22 win over a white team known as the Collegiate Five.

After the few games the Rens would play at the Ballroom, music took over the night, with greats such as Duke Ellington,

Count Basie, Ella Fitzgerald, Earl "Fatha" Hines, and Chick Webb playing the venue.

The Rens were a force through the 1920s and '30s and once won 88 consecutive games. And these were legitimate wins, not the wins that would be claimed by the Globetrotters after they became more about the show and less about actual basketball competition. The Rens played everyone and anyone and usually won. In 1932–33, they had a record of 120–8. Even Michael Jordan's 1995–96 Bulls weren't that good.

The Rens also made history. They beat the all-white Original Celtics in 1925, which sent shockwaves through the sports world. They became a popular draw among both black and white fans and in 1939 became the first all-black team to win a championship, after a 34–25 win over Oshkosh at the World Basketball Tournament in, fittingly, Chicago.

Coincidentally, the Rens beat the Globetrotters in the semifinals. It was the only meeting between the two teams.

Perhaps the most important contribution the Rens made to the game of basketball was their style of play that, over time, became a trademark of New York City basketball: the fast break and dazzling ball movement. And John "Boy Wonder" Isaacs is often credited for inventing the pick-and-roll play, which is such a big part of the game today and especially in the NBA.

The city has always loved the game, but the love affair was never as intimate as it was in the early 1970s, when the Knicks were an elite team in the NBA, with a cast of superstar players who played a smooth, intelligent, and selfless game. The era inspired Axthelm to write his book, which chronicled the team while also delving into the game's other stories that were hidden in the shadows of Madison Square Garden.

But while basketball certainly has its roots in New York with the Rens, the emergence of the college game as a showcase at the

Garden and, eventually, the arrival of the Knicks in 1946, there is a place in Manhattan where the game has a more intimate connection with the city.

And that, too, exists in Harlem.

Holcombe Rucker worked for New York City's Parks and Recreation Department in the 1940s and organized a basketball tournament among players in the city at a park at Seventh Avenue between 128th and 129th Streets. With a mission to use the tournament as a means to promote education, Rucker often used the phrase, "Each one, teach one," as the motto.

The tournament grew in popularity over the years, and by the 1960s it was not only attracting the best players from around the city but some of the best players in the game. The likes of Wilt Chamberlain and Lew Alcindor (later Kareem Abdul-Jabbar) took their game to Rucker's tournament, and it has become commonplace for young NBA stars to test their skills at the game's rawest level, on the street.

You can't name a New York City–born and bred basketball star who made his way to the NBA without first making a stop at Rucker. Everyone from Connie Hawkins to Mark Jackson to Stephon Marbury has been through its ranks.

The courts where the tournament is now played, on Frederick Douglass Boulevard and the Harlem River Drive, used to be known simply as the P.S. 156 playground. In 1974 it was named after Rucker, who succumbed to cancer at the young age of 38.

Since then, similar tournaments have developed around the city, with the popular West 4th Street Summer League downtown and the Sole in the Hole Classic in Bedford-Stuyvesant, Brooklyn. These parks produce some amazing basketball, but not everyone makes it to the NBA. The story of Earl "the Goat" Manigault, arguably the greatest player to never play in the NBA, is the most notable.

Most of these parks have seen upgrades to more NBA-style backboards and rims. But go to any New York City playground and you'll most often find the same simple setup of a pole, a metal backboard, and a steel rim with no net.

Deee-Fense!

Here, it's a war cry.

Maybe in more recent years, it was a demand, perhaps even a plea.

The origins of the world-famous "Defense" chant—DEEE-FENSE! (clap, clap) DEEE-FENSE! (clap, clap)—started in New York, but it didn't start at Madison Square Garden. It was actually at Yankee Stadium. But it wasn't baseball fans encouraging pitchers such as Whitey Ford and Don Larsen.

The New York Football Giants moved to Yankee Stadium in 1956, and Big Blue fans developed a strong affinity for the rugged, stonewalling defensive unit led by Sam Huff, Andy Robustelli, Jimmy Patton, and Rosey Grier.

In the famous 1958 season—the one capped by the NFL championship defeat to the Baltimore Colts, known as "the Greatest Game Ever Played"—Giants fans began to greet the dominating *D* as they ran onto the field by enthusiastically chanting "De-fense!" As the season went on, the chant grew until almost the entire stadium sang it in unison.

"It almost was a distraction," former Giants linebacker Harland Svare said in the book *New York Giants: The Complete Illustrated History*. "You couldn't hear anything."

During those years, there wasn't much to cheer about at the Old Garden, where the Knicks endured a decade of mostly losing seasons and no playoff appearances. It's hard to be enthusiastic about defense when your team is giving up a franchise-record 120.1 points per game in 1960–61.

The arrival of Dave DeBusschere in December 1968 established a new mentality based on the foundation of principles that Red Holzman, who took over as coach the previous season, had set. The Knicks reduced their points-per-game allowed by almost 10, to 105.1 in 1968–69, their lowest since the first season of the 24-second shot clock in 1954–55.

It was then the "De-fense" chant was brought from the Stadium into the new Garden. DeBuscchere's blue-collar work ethic and Willis Reed's physical prowess and shot blocking were one thing, but it was Walt Frazier's on-the-ball tenacity and quick hands that also had the crowd roaring for more. He made the NBA's All-Defense first team in 1969–70 with more votes than any player in the league.

"I think more and more people are getting conscious of steals and blocked shots and picking off passes," Frazier wrote in his book *Rockin' Steady*. "Like in the Garden, the game gets tight, the first thing they scream is, 'Dee-fense, Dee-fense.' They don't yell 'Of-fense.' That doesn't jingle nothin' inside."

It's true. The chant isn't a celebration as much as it is a bloodthirsty refrain. It usually starts after a made basket as the Knicks get into their defensive position. The louder the chant, the more it resonates in the heads of opponents. The clap is replaced with stomping feet, which makes it all the more savage and intimidating.

It was on this defensive mind-set that the Knicks won their two NBA titles in 1970 and '73, though they still gave up a lot of points (103.7 per game over the five-season span from 1969 to 1973).

The chant became a regular staple at the Garden, with fans getting creative to the point where one would hold up a large *D* and another would hold up a section of picket fence and run around the concourse that separates the upper and lower bowls of the arena. The dynamic backcourt of Ray Williams and Micheal Ray Richardson were tenacious defenders in the late 1970s and early 1980s that thrilled the fans, but their era was short-lived. Patrick Ewing came in 1985 as the Hoya Destroya, one of the game's most dominant defensive centers. His reputation for shot blocking drew comparisons to Russell, but it wasn't until Pat Riley arrived in 1991 that defense was back en vogue at the Garden.

And the "De-fense" chant returned as the battle cry of a new era.

"We set out to be the hardest-working, best-defending, most disliked team in the NBA," Riley said in a May 31, 1993, story in *New York* magazine.

In his first season, the Knicks defense sliced 5.6 points per game off their opponents' average and they held teams to a franchise-best 29.5 percent from three-point range. In 1992–93, they were the NBA's best defensive team and held opponents to a stingy 42.6 percent shooting.

The chant was no longer a battle cry, but—with players such as Ewing, Charles Oakley, and Anthony Mason—it became a rugged philosophy that included a no-layup rule, and opponents would often get regular introductions to fans in the first row.

As new franchises and new arenas sprouted up around the NBA in the 1990s, the "De-fense" chant was adopted by scoreboard operators everywhere to create atmosphere. In New York, there is no need for instruction or encouragement. This is where the chant was invented.

Pat the Rat

There was a time when Pat Riley was viewed as a savior.

In the spring of 1991, after the Knicks were swept out of the first round by the Chicago Bulls and the franchise was teetering toward falling back into the same pattern of failure that doomed the 1980s, the team had just said good-bye to their third coach—John MacLeod—in three seasons.

Dave Checketts arrived from Utah to take over the Knicks with the intention of finally getting the team back where it belonged, among the top of the league. Checketts had the brains, and in Ewing and Oakley he had the brawn. What he needed was a coach who could handle the New York spotlight.

Riley had left the Lakers after the 1989–90 season and worked the broadcasts as a studio analyst for the *NBA on NBC* during the 1990–91 season. As a four-time NBA championship–winning coach, Riley's profile and marketable cachet was exactly what Checketts felt the Knicks needed.

And after a bitter exit with the Lakers, Riley felt the Knicks were exactly what he needed, too.

"When I left the Lakers, then took the year off and worked with NBC, I saw myself possibly there [in New York], if in fact, there was a [coaching] change," Riley told D'Agostino in *Garden Glory*. "I was very highly motivated during the course of that year to try to see myself there. I can remember, when I would jog or work out, imagining myself giving halftime talks to Patrick, Mark Jackson, and Charles Oakley, or how I would do this or that, or where I'd live."

With Riley in charge, the Knicks became exactly what Checketts had envisioned: not only the toast of a basketball-crazed town, but one of the league's best franchises. The stars returned to celebrity row at the Garden (even well-known Lakers fan Jack Nicholson would show up from time to time), and the Knicks reached the 60-win mark (1992–93) for only the second time in franchise history and the first since Red Holzman's team did it in the 1969–70 championship season.

Though there was a tangible return to the glory days, Riley's Knicks were no glamour team. Sure, the coach continued to rock the Armani suits on the bench, but he left Showtime in Los Angeles. Those Lakers teams were built on the megawatt personality of Earvin "Magic" Johnson. These Knicks were built on the menacing scowl of Patrick Ewing.

"I didn't change the style; the players were who they were," Riley told me in 2008. "They were all defensive-oriented tough guys and had talent. So I just went with how they were. I didn't build anything, I didn't change anything.

"If Magic Johnson was with the Knicks, that would have been Showtime. It doesn't make a difference who else we had on the team. He was Showtime."

Riley to this day firmly believes those Knicks were just as much a championship-caliber team, but they would never win one. With the Lakers, he and Magic managed to overcome their greatest nemeses, Larry Bird and the Celtics, in 1985 and '87. But Riley and Ewing were never able to beat Michael Jordan and the indomitable Bulls.

In Riley's first season, the Knicks lost in a seven-game battle in the Eastern Conference semifinals in 1992. The following year, arguably the second-best season in franchise history, Riley was named NBA Coach of the Year. The Knicks won 57 games that season and rolled to the Eastern Conference Finals against Jordan and the Bulls. With the top seed in the East, this was the year they were built to beat them. They took the opening games at the

Garden to go up two games to none. They then proceeded to lose four straight to end the season in bitter frustration.

In '94 the Knicks finally got past the Bulls in the Eastern Conference semifinals—it still took seven games, even with Jordan out of the league playing minor-league baseball—and reached the NBA Finals after beating a new rival in Reggie Miller and the Indiana Pacers in the Eastern Conference Finals.

Riley had the Knicks one win away from a title after a 91–84 win over the Houston Rockets in Game 5 of the NBA Finals at Madison Square Garden. That was as close as they would get.

The following season, the Knicks won 55 games and were again favorites in the East, even with Jordan making a late return to Chicago that season. But with all their toughness, all their defense, the Knicks had no answers for Miller. And when Ewing missed on a finger roll down the lane in the final seconds of Game 7 on May 21, 1995, Riley had coached his last game in New York.

During the four years in New York a power struggle had developed between the very large egos in charge of the team. Riley wanted more of a say in personnel decisions, while players were growing more and more frustrated with his demanding style of coaching and discipline.

Checketts wanted him back and made a lucrative five-year offer for as much as $25 million. Riley asked for a percentage of ownership, which the Gulf & Western executives were not willing to grant.

It was then, on June 15, 1995, that Riley, with a year left on his contract, decided to leave the Knicks. He did so not in a face-to-face conversation with Checketts, or even a telephone call. Instead, the letter of resignation was sent via fax to the Garden offices at 2 Penn Plaza.

What made matters worse was news that Riley was already talking to the Miami Heat, whose young owner, Mickey Arison, had targeted Riley to turn the fledgling franchise around. Arison offered Riley a seven-year deal worth $35 million, with full control of basketball operations and another alluring detail: a minority ownership stake in the franchise.

The Knicks accused the Heat of tampering, and the NBA eventually ruled that Miami had to forfeit a 1996 first-round pick to New York as compensation. The pick turned into Walter McCarty, who lasted one season.

But what lasted a lifetime in New York is a hatred for Riley that was voiced loudly in his first appearance at the Garden as the Heat coach on December 19, 1995. The Knicks rolled to an 89–70 win as the sellout crowd roared "Pat the Rat!" chants down on Riley.

"What I felt versus what they felt was entirely different," Riley said after the game. "I spent four years here, and I think that they know what I put into this, and we were very successful. I always thought the fans of New York...are the very best."

The feeling would never again be mutual, and Knicks fans were only more incensed when Riley's Heat defeated the Knicks in a nasty seven-game battle in the 1997 Eastern Conference semifinals. That series saw the Knicks blow a 3–1 lead and included the Game 5 fight that led to several suspensions that left the Knicks shorthanded in Games 6 and 7.

There was some measure of revenge over the next three seasons, however, as the Knicks knocked out the Heat in each postseason. The biggest victory came in 1999 when the Knicks, as the eighth seed, upset the top-seeded Heat, who were believed to be on the way to their first NBA title.

Riley would eventually land that championship with Dwyane Wade and Shaquille O'Neal in 2006 (and then add a second in 2012). And it was during those NBA Finals, as the first coach to take three different franchises that far, when he reflected on the lost opportunity in New York. When he was inducted into the Basketball Hall of Fame in 2008, he was even more nostalgic.

"I'm sorry the end was so bad. I just want—I'm so sorry because it was my fault more than it was anybody else's. It ended up negatively, and I'm sorry about that. But New York was a great place for me."

When I asked if he had any regrets, Riley quickly replied, "Oh yeah, absolutely. If I had it to do all over again, I would have left, but I would have done it differently."

He then paused and flashed his million-dollar grin.

"Instead of faxing it, I probably would have..."

Thirteen years later, it was okay to laugh. And there was no need to finish the thought.

Heat-ed Rivalry

Pat Riley's sudden and power-hungry move from New York to Miami in 1995 changed everything about games between the Knicks and Heat. Visits to South Beach used to be enjoyable breaks in the midwinter schedule, against a team that had just one winning season in its first seven of existence before Riley arrived.

The Heat were actually built in the image of Riley's Knicks teams. Alonzo Mourning was acquired from the Charlotte Hornets to provide a similar presence as a defensive foundation in the paint, while Tim Hardaway, who was acquired late in the 1995–96 season, brought the exact combination of toughness and talent that Riley loved.

By the time the 1997 playoffs arrived, both teams were loaded up and ready to battle the Chicago Bulls for the Eastern Conference.

The Heat won the Atlantic Division with a 61–21 record, the best in franchise history, and the Knicks, with former Riley assistant Jeff Van Gundy now in place as head coach, went 57–25. Both were behind the Bulls at 69–13, and the most important element here is that by finishing first, the Bulls could avoid facing both the Heat and Knicks—their toughest challenges—until the conference finals.

It also meant the Knicks and Heat would slug it out in the conference semifinal round, and whoever survived would limp into the series against the Bulls.

Chicago knocked off a young and talented Hawks team in five games, and after an 89–76 win in Game 4 at the Garden, the Knicks looked to be on their way to another meeting with Chicago with a 3–1 lead in the best-of-seven series. The Heat battled back at home to win Game 5 96–81, but with Game 6 back at the Garden, the Knicks had every reason to be confident.

Then it happened.

Things started to get testy late in the game as Charles Oakley floored Hardaway with a hard screen that drew a foul. Mourning came over to help Hardaway off the floor and Mourning put his forearm into Oakley's chest. Oakley then got in Mourning's face and responded with a shove, and the teams got together. More shoving ensued, with Mourning putting his hand on Oakley's neck. Oakley responded with another shove and was ejected with two technicals.

During the scrum, Charlie Ward got into it with Heat power forward P.J. Brown. It was a minor dustup but worth noting, considering what would come next. With Hardaway at the line to shoot the free throw for the foul, Ward undercut Brown with a box-out that rode his hip right into Brown's knee. Brown grabbed Ward by the waist and flipped him over into a row of photographers.

If anyone ever questions the hostility between these two teams, consider this: Ward is a devout Christian who as a player would speak of Jesus Christ with the passion most NBA players have when they talk about cars and women. And Brown that season won the annual Walter J. Kennedy Citizenship Award for the player who displays outstanding service and dedication to community. These weren't two thugs looking for a fight, but what they started turned into one of the ugliest and costliest moments in Knicks history.

"The situation," Ward would say afterward, "just got out of control."

Bedlam ensued, as rookie John Wallace, in for Oakley, tried to pull Brown off of Ward. Several Knicks, including Patrick Ewing, Larry Johnson, John Starks, and Allan Houston, came over from the bench, which was only a few feet away across the baseline, to break up the fight.

The following day the NBA handed down six suspensions as a result of the fight, with the Knicks taking the worst of it. Four key Knicks were suspended by the NBA for leaving the bench, with Ewing and Houston ordered to serve their suspensions in Game 6 and Johnson and Starks for Game 7. The Heat lost Brown for two games.

Ewing had been such a key figure in the series—his dunk over Mourning sealed Game 1 and his block of a Hardaway three clinched Game 3—so his presence was undoubtedly critical. What angered the Knicks is that, while Houston, Starks, and Johnson clearly got into the scuffle along the far baseline, Ewing barely took but a few steps off the bench. But the NBA rule states a player is not permitted to leave the bench during an altercation, so Ewing was penalized.

"They just decided that they were going to make him an example," Van Gundy said. "And we could have lost all those other guys, but with Patrick at home in Game 6, we would have won by 10 points."

Instead, the Knicks lost Game 6 95–90, Mourning drilling a rare three-pointer late in the game to clinch the series-tying win.

The series ended with a 101–90 loss in Game 7 in Miami, with Hardaway pouring in 38 points and six three-pointers. Ewing had another dominant game, with 37 points and 17 rebounds, but the rookie Wallace, who started in place of Johnson, provided very little support (four points and four rebounds in 21 minutes).

"People are going to make excuses for us," Van Gundy said after the game. "I don't think our players are looking for excuses. Our coaches aren't either. We just got beat today."

When the teams met again in the first round a year later in 1998, the Knicks had a new excuse. Ewing suffered a broken wrist in December of that season and was done for the year. The Knicks made the playoffs with a 43–39 record and the seventh seed in the East. The Heat were once again the No. 2 seed and tops in the Atlantic Division at 55–27.

Without Ewing, Mourning and the Heat were expected to make quick work of the Knicks, who had to rely on career backup Chris Dudley as the starting center. Miami took a 2–1 lead in the best-of-five series after a 91–85 win at the Garden in Game 3. One defeat away from elimination, the Knicks planned to go down fighting.

The plan worked.

The Knicks battled to a 90–85 win that had the Garden crowd roaring as Hardaway bricked a three-pointer with four seconds left. Starks grabbed the rebound and dribbled out the clock, but behind him a melee ensued.

Before Hardaway's shot, Mourning had set a screen on Johnson, and the two remained together for the rest of the play. Johnson hit Mourning with a strong box-out, but his arms were up near Mourning's face. Mourning responded with a right hook that missed, and Johnson countered with a right that also missed. Mourning missed with another right, and Johnson caught Mourning's shoulder with a punch.

Oakley jumped in between the two and shoved Mourning away. That's when Mourning looked down and realized something was grabbing him by the leg.

It was Van Gundy, who in trying to break up the fight wound up on the floor under the two big men. "People ask me, 'What were you thinking?'" Van Gundy says when recalling that moment. "And I usually say, 'If I was thinking, I wouldn't have been hanging onto his leg.'"

Ewing, who was in a suit on the bench at the time, laughs about it now.

"Seeing Jeff grab onto Alonzo and then slide down his leg and hold on for dear life was funny," Ewing said with a chuckle during an NBA Entertainment profile of the rivalry.

It wasn't funny to Riley. "You just blew the season," Riley barked at Mourning as he left the court, according to the book *Just Ballin'*, by Mike Wise and Frank Isola.

Riley was right. With Mourning suspended (along with Johnson), the Knicks blew out the Heat 98–81 in Game 5 in Miami to win the series.

But perhaps the biggest blow in the rivalry between the teams came the following year when the Knicks and Heat met yet again in the first round. This time, rather than brawls and bad blood, the series was won by the Knicks changing their style to a more up-tempo game—with Ewing showing signs of age—and one heroic basket by Allan Houston in the final second of Game 5.

The teams met once more in the postseason in 2000, this time in the second round, and the Knicks pulled it out once again in a seven-game battle that ended with yet another series-clinching win in Miami. With the Knicks leading 83–82, Clarence Weatherspoon missed a short jumper and Latrell Sprewell grabbed the rebound with 2.1 seconds left and, though he never actually called a timeout, referee Bennett Salvatore blew the whistle and awarded one.

The Heat were furious. The Knicks were able to inbound the ball, and Chris Childs killed the remaining time by throwing the ball high into the air.

A few years later, in 2006, Riley and the Heat finally captured a championship, while the Knicks floundered through a playoff drought. The teams met again in the playoffs in 2012, but the injury-depleted Knicks, led by Carmelo Anthony and Amar'e Stoudemire, were overwhelmed in a five-game defeat to a Heat team now led by LeBron James and Dwyane Wade.

Riley torpedoed the Knicks' chances to land LeBron as a free agent in 2010 when he worked with Wade to lure the two-time MVP to Miami. After dispatching the Knicks, the Heat went on to win their second title in six years. The Knicks' wait for a third title extended into its 40th season.

H$_2$O and the Shot

Every franchise has those Where-were-you-when? moments. Allan Houston was exactly where the Knicks needed him to be.

"A day doesn't go by when I don't get stopped, and it's the one thing they all mention," Houston told Dave D'Alessandro of the *Newark Star-Ledger* in May 2009. "I've heard it in Tokyo, Hong Kong, Uganda, other places in Africa. And since New York is such an international place, you hear about it in every accent."

It was, of course, "the Shot." And for one of the game's purest shooters, the three-bounce clanker that fell in with 0.8 seconds left on the clock to win Game 5 of the first-round series against the top-seeded Heat in Miami was the most beautiful thing in the world.

"I thought I kind of short-armed it at first, but it hung up there," Houston said after the 78–77 win. "I got a friendly bounce from up above."

The Knicks didn't at all seem like a team of destiny that season, which had been shortened to 50 games because of the NBA lockout. This had turned into a transition year for a franchise that could no longer be carried by the creaky knees of Patrick Ewing. As president of the NBA players' union, Ewing spent most of the lockout in a suit, sitting through negotiations with the NBA in boardrooms.

When the lockout was settled and there was a season to play, the 36-year-old Ewing was in no shape to jump into a truncated schedule that would see several back-to-back-to-back games.

Houston had arrived as the headline free agent in 1996 to be the All-Star-caliber wingman Ewing had always craved. In his first three NBA seasons, Houston slowly developed into a scorer (19.7 points per game in 1995–96) and one of the league's best three-point threats (42.7 percent) for the Detroit Pistons. When he became a free agent that off-season, the Knicks targeted him ahead of star free agents such as Reggie Miller and even Michael Jordan, who would be much more of a long shot to acquire.

With the Knicks, Houston led a major off-season of retooling that included acquiring Larry Johnson from the Charlotte Hornets, signing point guard Chris Childs from the Nets, and adding veteran Buck Williams. With Ewing over 30, the window was closing on the pursuit of a championship.

Houston wanted New York, but the challenge of playing in an offense that featured Ewing almost exclusively limited him. Over the next three seasons, his scoring and shooting percentages dipped, and the Knicks never did become the championship-caliber team Dave Checketts and Ernie Grunfeld envisioned.

But Houston did play a major role in the transition of the team from the half-court, plodding system that was dominated by Ewing for 14 years to a faster, more perimeter-based attack.

20 x 5

Allan Houston signed a six-year, $100 million contract in 2001, which caused Jeff Van Gundy to crack, "I told Allan there's no truth to the rumor that his new number is going to be 20 times 5." The idea was that he would at least average 20 points over the next five years, but two years later, Houston would suffer a knee injury that would lead to a swift decline and an early retirement while the Knicks appeared to be burdened by a hefty contract. But in 2005 the NBA had a new collective-bargaining agreement and there was an "amnesty clause" that allowed teams the opportunity to release a player without having that contract count against the salary cap. It was called "the Allan Houston Rule," because of the size of Houston's contract, yet the Knicks decided not to use it for Houston. (They waived another large contract in Jerome Williams, instead.)

And he was instrumental in one of the most exciting spring playoff runs in franchise history. Ewing was hobbled in that first-round series with the Heat but gave all he could—as usual—against his protégé, Alonzo Mourning.

The Knicks hobbled into those playoffs. It wasn't until the second-to-last game of the season that they finally clinched a playoff berth—the eighth, and final, seed in the East. The lockout-shortened season was tough on Ewing, but it was also difficult on Jeff Van Gundy, who had little time to work in newcomers such as Latrell Sprewell and Marcus Camby.

The Heat finished with the No. 1 seed in the East, though they tied with the Indiana Pacers and Orlando Magic with a 33–17 record in the shortened season. They were primed for yet another shot at a title.

But the veteran-laden Knicks, despite a 27–23 finish, weren't a typical eighth seed. And that was made abundantly clear in Game 1, when the Knicks took a 20-point win in Miami. Houston had a terrific game with 22 points, but he struggled throughout most of the series.

The teams traded wins, and the series went back to New York tied at 2. Then Houston had 18 points in another blowout, a 97–73 victory, in Game 3 at the Garden. One win from elimination, the Heat came back with a 87–72 win in Game 4.

For the third-straight year, these two rivals would go the distance in a playoff series. And this time it would go all the way to the final second.

Houston struggled with his shooting in Game 5. He made just two of his first eight shots through three quarters and was 4-of-12 for a mere 10 points late in the fourth.

Terry Porter hit a pair of free throws with 58 seconds left to give Miami a 77–74 lead. Ewing pulled down his 11th rebound of the game—the man's will, considering that later it was learned he was playing with a partially torn Achilles tendon, was amazing—and was fouled. He hit both free throws to cut the deficit to one with 39 seconds left.

Sprewell then stripped Hardaway, a former Knicks killer who had struggled all series, and the Knicks called timeout with 24.9 seconds on the clock. On the ensuing inbounds, Sprewell caught the ball and began a move, but Porter knocked the ball out of bounds.

There were 4.5 seconds left. Triangle Down was the play.

With Charlie Ward inbounding, Ewing turned and Houston sprinted around him on a perfectly executed curl. He caught the pass just above the three-point arc with one of the Heat's best perimeter defenders, Dan Majerle, right on his tail.

Houston made a dribble move to the right elbow, with Majerle on his left and Hardaway stepping at him on his right. He elevated with a leaning shot as Majerle reached and tried to block the shot from behind. If not for the lean by Houston, Majerle might have gotten it.

As Houston released the shot, Ewing, who used to be the target in these situations in the past, raised his fist in anticipated triumph.

The shot was short.

But the rims at Miami Arena were very forgiving and the trajectory of Houston's shot—again, he had one of the best shooting forms in the league—bounced off the front rim and ricocheted high to the backboard. It kissed the glass and then gently fell through the nylon netting.

Houston didn't take the time to watch his shot. The second he let it go, he did the most fundamental thing that most coaches—fittingly, he is a coach's son—preach: he followed his shot.

Houston was almost eye-level with the rim when the ball fell through.

"I was gonna try and tip it in," he told D'Agostino in *Garden Glory.* "I just felt it come off a little short. It hit the front rim. Since I felt that, I just immediately jumped in the air and got ready to tip it.

"Fortunately," he added, "I didn't need to."

The shot propelled the Knicks into the second round, and the momentum of the Heat win carried them into a four-game sweep of the Atlanta Hawks. Then came more playoff magic in the Eastern Conference Finals against the Indiana Pacers.

And just like that, the Knicks were back in the NBA Finals.

"People always tell you where they were at that particular moment," Houston told D'Alessandro in that 2009 article in the *Star-Ledger.* "It's almost like being a part of their lives. How many times does that happen? So it's important in that way.

"And yeah, they still say that if that shot didn't fall, this or that would have happened with the team. But I never really believed in chance or luck—I believe things happen in a way [they're] supposed to happen. So, I don't know."

The Easter Epic

The Boston Celtics were once the team that set the standard for the championship-era Knicks. It was after a six-game loss in the 1969 Eastern Division Finals—Bill Russell's final season in Boston—that the Knicks developed the belief that they were good enough to contend for a title.

But on their way to the 1970 title, the Knicks never faced the Celtics, who, without Russell, failed to make the playoffs for the first time in 20 years. Boston didn't return as a contender until 1972, when the Knicks made quick work of them with a five-game win in the Eastern Conference Finals.

But in 1972–73, the Celtics were back as an NBA force. Led by the league's MVP, Dave Cowens, and a deep and talented roster, Boston won 68 games that season to reclaim their spot as the league's elite franchise. And that spring, they met the Knicks again in the Eastern Conference Finals.

Back then the series schedule was much different than what you see today. As the top seed, the Celtics had home-court advantage, but the sites would alternate game-by-game from Boston Garden to Madison Square Garden.

The Knicks were blown out 134–108 in Game 1 in Boston but held serve in New York three days later with a blowout of their own, 129–96 in a Game 2 that saw Red Holzman sick a three-quarter-court press against John Havlicek and the Celtics.

Back in Boston for Game 3, the Knicks took a 98–91 victory that gave them a 2–1 advantage in the series. And that win came with an added advantage: Havlicek suffered a shoulder strain in the third quarter when he tried to run through a pick by Dave DeBusschere.

Havlicek missed Game 4 at Madison Square Garden as a result of the injury, but the Knicks would also be without their own key player. Earl Monroe would be forced to sit out the game with a hip pointer.

"It certainly wasn't a coach's decision," Monroe recently joked of his DNP that day.

What a game to miss. On a sweltering Easter afternoon in New York, the Celtics jumped out to a 21-point lead in the first half and were ahead by as many as 17 points in the third quarter.

But there was no quit in these Knicks, who continued to attack. Behind Walt Frazier, who scored 15 of his 37 points in the fourth quarter, the Knicks outscored Boston 33–17. Frazier tied it at 89 on a fall-away jumper in the closing seconds to force overtime.

It took a pair of free throws by Phil Jackson to tie it at 101 and send the game into a second overtime. With both teams exhausted and both uniforms soaked in sweat, the game turned heavily in favor of the Knicks when Cowens fouled out. Willis Reed was already gone, so the front court was now even. But the Knicks still had Frazier, who scored 30 points in the second half and two overtime periods.

"I just remember it went back and forth," Frazier told D'Agostino in *Garden Glory*. "It was a quintessential game between the Knicks and Celtics in those days."

An 11–4 run to end the game gave the Knicks a 117–110 win and a commanding 3–1 lead in the series. As the New York crowd roared with delight, Celtics coach Tommy Heinsohn chased the referees, Jack Madden and Jake O'Donnell, all the way to the locker rooms.

Heinsohn's Celtics wouldn't go down easily, of course. Back in Boston, the Celtics escaped elimination when Paul Silas grabbed a miss by Jo Jo White with seven seconds left and drew a foul. Silas nailed both free throws to give Boston a 98–97 win.

Cowens and White combined for 51 points to overwhelm the Knicks 110–100 in Game 6 on a Friday night at Madison Square Garden.

That's when Ned Irish, the owner and founder of the franchise, stormed into practice the next day and berated the group.

"[Irish] basically told us we were all a bunch of bums," Bradley told D'Agostino in *Garden Glory*. "He said he didn't expect us to do anything in the seventh game and that we had a chance to win it in the Garden and we didn't.

"Of course," Bradley continued, "that was all psychological buildup."

The Celtics had never in team history lost a Game 7 at home. But there is always a first time for everything. Heinsohn's young group was made of championship material, but these Knicks had one more run in them.

Boston's time would come the next year, when they ended the Knicks championship era with a five-game win in the Eastern Conference Finals and went on to win the first of two championships in three seasons.

The Dunk

For nine years, Michael Jordan owned the Madison Square Garden stage with his high-flying, breathtaking aerialist show. It was often maddeningly conflicting for Garden fans, who were awestruck by Jordan's performances yet frustrated that he would do it at the expense of their beloved Knicks.

And Jordan had posterized the Knicks on many occasions, going back to the trademark rock-the-baby cuff dunk he threw down on that breakaway in his Garden debut during his rookie season in 1984–85. He'd also banged one on his good friend Patrick Ewing late in the first half of Game 3 in the 1991 playoffs at the Garden. It became another one of Jordan's famous dunks, dribbling out of a double-team in the corner with a quick spin, then stunning a straight-up Ewing with a quick elevation and slam.

One of the players Jordan left in the dust on that play was John Starks, who, after Gerald Wilkins was toasted, became Jordan's punching bag in many of the battles between the teams in the early 1990s.

But in 1992–93 it looked like the tide was ready to turn. The Knicks won 60 games to finish with the top seed in the East. That gave them home-court advantage when they faced the Bulls in the Eastern Conference Finals, which meant much-needed momentum to start the series.

Everything went according to plan. The Knicks won Game 1 98–90 behind a combined 50 points from Ewing and Starks, the latter determined to make Jordan work just as much on defense as Jordan made him work.

Starks had the toughest, most unenviable job of any Knicks player. Defending Michael Jordan is not only the game's toughest challenge because of his talent, but it can also be demoralizing because of his incessant trash-talking.

And in Game 2 Jordan was looking to beat the Knicks by himself. He took 32 shots, seven from three-point range and another 13 from the foul line. (Jordan recorded a total of one assist, in case you were wondering about his singular focus in this game.)

Starks was busy on the defensive end and as a result did not play as much of a role on offense. This game, instead, was all about Ewing (26 points, 10 rebounds) and Doc Rivers, who overwhelmed B.J. Armstrong with 21 points, three three-pointers, and eight of 10 from the foul line.

Starks had just 10 points on 10 field-goal attempts going into the final minute of the game (for the record, he did have nine assists). The Knicks had been up by 14 but were clinging to a three-point lead with less than a minute to go when Starks had the ball on the right side of the court with Armstrong defending him. Ewing came over for a pick-and-roll play on the high (right) side of Armstrong.

A slight hesitation dribble by Starks—and a gentle shove from Ewing—caused Armstrong to lose his footing and fall to the ground. Starks had a wide-open lane to the basket along the baseline and darted toward the right block.

The Bulls had been sending Starks to the baseline all game long, with help waiting to bottle him up in the corner. Starks noticed the scheme and believed he would see it again. And when he did, Starks was ready.

Before Bill Cartwright could even think about sliding down on the switch, Starks had already accelerated hard to the basket. Horace Grant slid over with both hands up just as Starks sprang off the hardwood just outside the lane.

The 6'10" Grant jumped straight in the air with his arms extended, but Starks seemed to keep elevating upward. Jordan came over a bit late and gave a half-hearted leap in the background, but when you're Michael Jordan, you have a sixth sense about these sorts of plays. You know a posterization when it's about to happen.

This one was coming—and it was moving in slow motion.

Starks' body turned sideways in the air to avoid Grant, and with a Jordanesque style, he put the ball in his left hand while leading with his right shoulder. Starks slammed it down at the apex of his jump as Grant and Jordan seemed to be already descending.

"I knew I had to go strong," Starks told D'Agostino in *Garden Glory*, "and I just went up and over the top."

The Garden exploded with a celebration that seemed to be a catharsis. The Knicks won the game 96–91, and it seemed Jordan and the Bulls were finally on the ropes. Pat Riley called Starks' dunk "the exclamation point."

And the Knicks were headed to Chicago just two wins away from the NBA Finals.

As history shows, the Bulls didn't lose another game in the remainder of that series and went on to win their third-straight championship.

But history also has a way of freezing a moment in time. Starks' dunk became one of the most famous—and popular—posters in Knicks history.

"Because of the situation and the team that we were playing, people still remember that," Starks told D'Agostino in *Garden Glory*. "That play put me on the map. It's funny, in basketball, one play can make your career. That particular play put me on the map and to this day people come up to me and tell me that it was the greatest play they'd ever seen."

Johnny Rocket

John Starks was working as a clerk at a Safeway in his hometown of Tulsa, Oklahoma—literally bagging groceries for a salary of $3.35 an hour. He had been kicked out of Northern Oklahoma College in 1985, and at the moment there was no reason to believe the NBA was in his future.

There was no reason to believe that, just five years later, Knicks general manager Al Bianchi would give him $40,000 just to come for a tryout.

Knicks fans can't help but love John Starks, who wore his emotions on his sleeve and gave 100 percent in every game he played.

Err Jordan

The Knicks never had an answer for Michael Jordan, but they did have one player who was so often a thorn in the side of His Airness. The first time John Starks walked out on the court to guard Jordan, he patted the superstar on the back. Jordan then greeted the CBA graduate with a condescending remark. "You'll be calling me 'Mr. Jordan' by the end of the game," he said. Starks thrived on challenges and, as time proved, tended to attack those who challenged him. So this little dis didn't make his knees shake as much as it got his adrenaline flowing. Starks' reply to Jordan? "We'll see," he said.

And that might have been all the money he would ever make off the Knicks, had it not been for that relentless and, at times, maddeningly bullheaded side of him that would endear him to the Garden faithful.

After the Reality Check at Register Three experience of bagging groceries, Starks got his basketball career on track by getting into junior college and then making his way to Oklahoma State. Even after a decent season at OSU (15.4 points per game in 30 games in 1987–88), the NBA didn't come calling right away. Instead, Starks found himself installing tin roofs as he looked for tryout opportunities with NBA teams.

The Golden State Warriors signed him as a reserve guard for the 1988–89 season and Starks appeared in 36 games for an average 8.8 minutes per game.

He spent the next season in Cedar Rapids, Iowa, in the Continental Basketball Association, where he drew interest from the Detroit Pistons. Starks' agent, Ron Grinker, told Starks that the Pistons, who were on the verge of a championship season, wanted to give Starks a 10-day contract.

"The next night we were in a close game when I got whistled for a foul," Starks recalls in his book, *My Life*. "I thought the referee had made a bad call, so I ran up to him and accidentally got too close and bumped him with my chest. The ref called a technical foul and the league suspended me for the rest of the season, even though the ref later said it was an accident. He tried to save me.

"It was a double-whammy," Starks continued. "The Pistons were supposedly scared away from signing me and Cedar Rapids missed out on making the playoffs. I worried that I'd blown my chance to make it back into the NBA."

After that season, Starks joined the Memphis Rockers of the World Basketball League, which had a summer-based schedule and accepted only players 6'5" and under. It was a dreamland for guards who hated having to pass the ball into the post to big men. This was a run-and-gun, chuck-and-duck game.

Starks also played in the Los Angeles Summer League, which is where NBA scouts used to flock to find undiscovered talent. Bianchi loved Starks' energy and toughness and felt it fit well into the type of player then-coach Stu Jackson wanted.

By the end of training camp in 1990, however, Jackson had planned to cut Starks, who had the similarly athletic Gerald Wilkins and the better-shooting Trent Tucker to beat out at the shooting guard position. But a player who would make overcoming odds a personal trademark isn't that easy to get rid of.

"It was the day before we were gonna cut him and he came down on a fast break in practice," Jackson recalled to D'Agostino in *Garden Glory*. "It was one-on-one, because we were pressing in practice. It's him and Patrick and the son of a gun challenged him. It was bizarre what he did! So he goes up and challenges Patrick and Patrick blocks the shot and goes completely through him because he's pissed that this guy challenged him.

"Down John goes in a heap, they cart him off, and that's the last I ever saw of John Starks."

Jackson, of course, lasted just 15 games into the 1990–91 season. Bianchi brought in John MacLeod to finish coaching the season. Starks, who suffered a knee injury as a result of the Ewing confrontation, was saved by league rules that prohibit teams from cutting injured players. Eventually he worked his way back and, with a young assistant named Jeff Van Gundy spending extra time with him on the practice court, Starks caught MacLeod's eye. Van Gundy liked to call him "Johnny Rocket."

He wound up playing 61 games that season, with 10 starts, and averaged 7.6 points in 19.2 minutes per game.

"Patrick really felt bad about [the injury]," Starks said, "but it turned out to be a blessing in disguise."

A year later, Pat Riley arrived and immediately developed an affinity for the rambunctious, reckless nature that Starks brought to the game.

By Riley's second season, Starks had supplanted Wilkins as the starting shooting guard and had emerged as a major player in the Knicks' rise to the NBA elite. The famous dunk over Horace Grant and Michael Jordan in Game 2 of the 1993 Eastern Conference Finals was the greatest highlight of his career. But the moment when he truly arrived came a season later, when he joined Ewing and Charles Oakley on the East All-Star team.

In less than 10 years, he had gone from bagging groceries to banging jumpers with the greatest basketball players in the world.

Starks still had his moments, of course. After almost shooting the Knicks to the NBA Championship in Game 6 of the '94 Finals, he had one of the epic slumps in the history of Game 7s, when he shot 2-for-18 in a painful defeat. He often lost his cool against the ultimate antagonist, Reggie Miller, which had the Garden crowd, and even his teammates, verbally spanking him on site.

But that's what Starks was as a Knick. He was your little brother. You scolded him, chastised him, maligned his decisions, and yet rooted like hell for him to get it right. He was a fighter, a battler, and he related most to so many of the people high up in the stands, some of whom actually did bag groceries or made minimum wage.

28 Da Bulls

The night before the 1988 NBA Draft, two franchises got together and made an amicable trade that would almost instantly set the foundation of a bitter rivalry.

The Chicago Bulls had a rugged rebounder in Charles Oakley but were even more enamored with their first-round pick from the year before, an athletic 6'10" forward named Horace Grant. What the Bulls lacked was a center.

The Knicks had a veteran center in Bill Cartwright, but he had been relegated to backup duties behind Patrick Ewing. Though Hubie Brown years earlier tried to play the two together, what Ewing really needed was a power forward to bolster the front court.

So the Knicks and Bulls swapped their excesses to fill their needs, and by the end of the coming season, the teams met in the Eastern Conference semifinals.

The Knicks won 52 games that season and, as the No. 2 seed in the East, made quick work of Charles Barkley and the seventh-seeded Philadelphia 76ers, with a three-game sweep that saw Rick Pitino's brash group grab a broom from next to one basket and literally sweep the court at the Spectrum after a series-clinching 116–115 overtime win in Game 3.

The Bulls, however, needed Jordan's heroics to pull off an upset over the third-seeded Cleveland Cavaliers. It came in the deciding Game 5, with a play forever remembered in both cities (but mostly in tragedy-riddled Cleveland) as "the Shot." Jordan elevated over Craig Ehlo for the famous buzzer-beater.

The '89 Eastern Conference semifinals would be the first of six playoff meetings between the teams over an eight-year span. The Bulls had a 3–1 lead in the series after winning a pair of back-to-back games at Chicago Stadium. The Knicks took Game 5 at the Garden and then Trent Tucker completed a four-point play in the closing seconds of Game 6 that put the Knicks on the verge of bringing the series back to New York for a Game 7.

But Jordan ended any plans for a return to the Garden that year, sinking a pair of free throws to clinch a 113–111 win.

"To this day I often think about what it would have been like to play the seventh game of that series, against Michael Jordan and the Chicago Bulls, in Madison Square Garden," Tucker told D'Agostino in *Garden Glory*. "Can you imagine how loud, how rocking, that place would have been?"

That opportunity would come in a few years but not before more heartbreak. The teams met again in 1991, but the Knicks, going through a coaching transition after Stu Jackson was fired, barely made it to the playoffs and were quickly dismissed in a three-game sweep.

In 1992, Pat Riley's first year at the helm, the Knicks put up much more of a fight, This time there would be a seventh game, after the Knicks pulled out a 14-point Game 6 victory at the Garden. That Game 7, however, wasn't one to remember for the Knicks, as Jordan and the Bulls rolled to a 29-point blowout win.

Chicago, You're Welcome

Did you know that the Knicks actually played a major role in helping the Chicago Bulls land Scottie Pippen? Before the 1986–87 season, Knicks general manager Scotty Stirling made several desperate moves that impacted the franchise for many years. On October 2, 1986, he used a first-round pick the team acquired from the Nuggets (for Darrell Walker) and sent it to the Bulls for center Jawaan Oldham. A few weeks later, he sent the team's own first-rounder to the Seattle SuperSonics for veteran Gerald Henderson and Seattle's No. 1. That pick Seattle got became the fifth overall pick, and they chose Pippen. The pick that went to Chicago fell at No. 8 and became Olden Polynice. A few weeks after the draft, the Bulls sent Polynice to Seattle for Pippen.

The rematch in 1993, this time in the Eastern Conference Finals, was the closest the Knicks ever were to finally overcoming Jordan's Bulls. To this point he had terrorized the Knicks all too often with his breathtaking, unguardable aerial attack and started to make a routine of breaking hearts in New York each spring.

This year was supposed to be different, and when the Knicks took a 2–0 lead in the series, punctuated by the emphatic dunk by John Starks over Horace Grant and Jordan, the belief was that the Bulls, after back-to-back championships, had finally met their match. The Knicks were gritty, tough, and relentless.

"This is real physical combat," Jordan said after the Game 2 loss. "We have to play above the referees."

Jordan also had to play amid reports that he was out gambling in Atlantic City into the late hours of the night between Games 1 and 2 in New York.

As much as that series invokes memories of Starks' dunk and the two euphoric wins at the Garden, the image embedded in that series is of the closing seconds of Game 5, when the Knicks, trailing 95–94, had a victory in hand.

Charles Smith, a 6'10" forward who was acquired from the Clippers in the latest attempt to land a quality small forward to join Ewing and Oakley in the frontcourt, had three attempts to score the go-ahead basket. Each time, however, Smith was blocked by Jordan, Grant, and Scottie Pippen.

The defeat snapped the Knicks' 27-game winning streak at the Garden. Coincidentally, it would be their last of the season there, as the Bulls won Game 6 to clinch the series.

A year later, Jordan was playing baseball and the Bulls had become Pippen's team. The Bulls were still a handful, but this time the Knicks had that Game 7 at the Garden that Tucker craved. Only this time, Tucker played for the Bulls.

It was a wild series that saw several bizarre moments, such as when Pippen refused to enter the game for the final play of Game 3 in Chicago. Bulls coach Phil Jackson designed a play for Toni Kukoc instead of Pippen and, according to reports from that game, Pippen was heard cursing and saying, "I'm tired of this." Kukoc nailed the game-winner to save the Bulls from a 3–0 deficit in the series.

The Bulls tied the series with a pair of wins in Chicago, which set up a pivotal Game 5 at the Garden. The Knicks trailed 86–85 on their final possession when the ball found second-year guard Hubert Davis. He put up a shot with 2.1 seconds that Pippen jumped out to defend and suddenly...a whistle.

"When I heard the whistle, it was like, 'What happened? Who fouled?'" Pippen told ESPN.com's J.A. Adande in a May 29, 2009, story. "I didn't think I had made a foul."

But referee Hue Hollins saw it differently. He felt Pippen made contact with Davis, who was promptly awarded two free throws. Davis, an 82.5 percent free-throw shooter that season, hit both and the Knicks won the game. Following a 14-point loss in Game 6 in Chicago, the Knicks finally put the Bulls away with an 87–77 win at the Garden.

"Somewhere, some team had to put them away," Pat Riley said afterward, "and for us, I think it was fitting."

"We didn't really like them," Patrick Ewing once told NBA.com. "They were in our way, and we wanted to get past them and win a championship. They had had enough success already, in our minds."

The rivals would meet just once more after that, in the 1996 Eastern Conference semifinals. Once again, the franchises were headed in different directions. Jordan was back from his baseball hiatus and led the Bulls to an NBA-record 72-win season.

The Knicks took just one game from Chicago in that series, a 102–99 overtime victory in Game 3 at the Garden that saw Starks counter Jordan's 46 points with his own 30-point afternoon. They lost Game 4 the following night by a mere three points.

That Game 3 defeat was the only blemish on Chicago's record against the Eastern Conference in that playoff year, as they swept the Miami Heat and Orlando Magic on their way to beating the Supersonics in six to reclaim the NBA title.

Though the teams would not again meet in the postseason, the rivalry remained heated through the rest of the 1990s. That following season, Jeff Van Gundy stoked the fires when he went on a Chicago radio station and suggested that Jordan uses his status as a living legend to get younger players to take it easy on him.

"He talks about young players, invites people to be in his movies—and it's all a con," Van Gundy said. "His way is to befriend them, soften them up, try to make them feel like he cares about them. Then he goes out there and tries to destroy them. The first step as a player is to realize that and don't go for it."

Jordan responded by spending the entire game cursing at Van Gundy while he dropped 51 points on the Knicks in an 88–87 win.

29 Big Chief Triangle

Phil Jackson's Knicks no longer exist. That era is gone, and with it went any nostalgia he may have for the franchise. He started his NBA career in New York and won his first championship there. He met thought-provoking conversationalists (like himself), such as Bill Bradley and Dave DeBusschere, and quirky personalities (also like himself) such as Jerry Lucas.

And it is where the hippie from North Dakota, with the wire-hanger shoulders and long, windmill-like arms, met the mentor that would direct him toward one of the greatest coaching careers in NBA history.

Red Holzman, a reluctant coach himself, saw it in Jackson: the keen understanding of the game, the confidence to lead men, and the wherewithal to explain things plainly.

Holzman was teaching Jackson how to be a coach when Jackson was just 24 years old and three years into his playing career. Jackson missed the 1969–70 championship season with a back injury, which afforded the time for him to view the game from the coach's eyes. He had a curiosity about the game and a thirst to know more.

"I asked him questions about coaching; he used to tell me, 'It's not rocket science, Phil. It's not rocket science,'" Jackson said of Holzman during the 2009 NBA Finals. "He was pretty basic about his basketball: see the ball on defense and hit the open man on offense. But he also had a great feel for people and how to get them motivated."

Jackson had his own unique way of dealing with players—one trademark is his annual tradition of handing out message-specific novels for his players to read—but some might say that Jackson's best coaching technique was that he only coached great players.

He also had the benefit of playing with one of the all-time greatest teams during the Knicks' championship era. Jackson, a 6'8", 220-pound forward, was a second-round pick by the Knicks in 1967 and quickly became a valuable reserve for his energy and defense.

He never put up gaudy numbers, but Jackson was a valued member of Holzman's bench brigade, which went by the nickname, "the Minutemen." He spent 10 seasons with the Knicks, played a key role in the 1973 championship, and then finished out his career with the Nets in 1979–80.

Jackson heeded Holzman's advice and pursued a coaching career upon retirement. He started out in the Continental Basketball Association, where he coached the Albany Patroons to a CBA title in 1984, and then went to Puerto Rico for the next three years before he landed a job in Chicago on Doug Collins' staff.

It is there he met Tex Winter, who promoted the Triangle Offense, which is a triple-post scheme he developed from former USC coach Sam Barry. The Triangle Offense became the foundation of Jackson's coaching philosophy, and when he took over for Collins in the 1989–90 season, the Bulls became one of the NBA's greatest dynasties.

It helped that he had Michael Jordan, too.

The Knicks had become one of the Bulls' fiercest rivals in the early 1990s, which turned Jackson from a beloved alumnus of the championship era to an enemy. He and Pat Riley exchanged barbs via the media on several occasions, but it wasn't until the scrappy little former Riley assistant spoke up that people really took notice.

Jeff Van Gundy, tired of the reverence given to Jackson, sarcastically referenced Jackson as "Big Chief Triangle," which was a confluence of disses that included his loyalty to Winter's offense and his well-known alternative lifestyle that includes Zen philosophy, yoga, and studying Native American culture.

Jackson countered by dismissively—and purposely—mispronouncing his counterpart's name as "Van Gumby."

But in the spring of 1999, it got personal. Jackson left the Bulls after the 1997–98 season and had considered an offer from the Nets. With the Knicks stumbling through the lockout-shortened 1998–99 season, Checketts reached out to Jackson to gauge his interest in taking over the job once held by his mentor.

Holzman passed away in November 1998 and Checketts called Jackson about bringing him into the organization because it was something Holzman had wanted.

And there were obvious concerns he might go to the Nets.

"I said, 'Look, we can't let him go across the river without talking to him,'" Checketts told D'Agostino in *Garden Glory*. "Even though he'd been the coach of the Bulls all those years, Phil was a Knick. He was a Knick. And he's a very good coach."

Checketts and Jackson continued the conversation as Van Gundy's Knicks pulled off an upset over the top-seeded Heat. The story then got out about the communication with Jackson, which sparked a media controversy that Checketts only made worse by denying he had spoken to Jackson about a job.

The Nets offer, though lucrative, was never a real option for Jackson, who had no interest in a rebuilding situation. And Jackson's Knicks possibility faded as Van Gundy's popularity soared during that improbable run to the NBA Finals.

The option to hire Jackson as head coach came up twice more, but neither time did an agreement come to fruition. In 2005, Jackson was on the radar but he opted to return to the Lakers after a brief hiatus. Then, in the spring of 2012, the Knicks considered the 11-time NBA championship coach, who had retired from the Lakers in 2011, but the Knicks opted to promote Mike Woodson to head coach instead.

Woodson, who took over for Mike D'Antoni late in the season, led the Knicks to 18 wins in their final 24 games, as well as a playoff berth. Woodson also had the strong endorsement of the team's star players, Carmelo Anthony, Amar'e Stoudemire, and Tyson Chandler.

Jackson apparently didn't have the same emotion for the Knicks stars. In an interview with HBO's *Real Sports*, he called the roster "clumsy" and suggested he had little interest in the job.

 The Trade (1968)

Red Holzman said of Dave DeBusschere, "[He] was our Holy Grail."

The Knicks had tried like hell to acquire the tough, smart, and defensive-minded power forward, but the Detroit Pistons would never even engage the conversation. The Knicks weren't the only team smitten with DeBusschere.

He was just 24 years old when the Pistons named him player-coach—The NBA was a trip in the '60s and '70s, wasn't it?—and when he would occasionally ask opposing general managers what Pistons players they might want in a trade, each offered the same response: You.

After three years as player-coach, the Pistons let DeBusschere focus solely on basketball and hired Donnie Butcher to run the bench in 1967–68. The Pistons were a sub-.500 team with an emerging star in Dave Bing. Though DeBusschere was holding his own in the frontcourt, Paul Seymour, who replaced Butcher during the 1968–69 season, felt Detroit was lacking one important element: a true center.

The Knicks had Willis Reed playing power forward at the time, with four-time All-Star Walt Bellamy at center. Reed preferred to play center, and the two didn't have the best chemistry together in the paint.

Pistons general manager Ed Coil contacted Knicks GM Eddie Donovan about Bellamy, and the two went back and forth for a while, with Coil making it clear there was one player the Knicks could not have for Bellamy: Dave Bing.

Did that mean DeBusschere was no longer untouchable?

Early in the 1968–69 season both teams were under .500 and struggling. The Pistons had lost eight straight from late November into early December and were 11–18. The Knicks got off to a miserable 6–13 start but righted the ship with a 12–4 push that got them a game over .500 after a mid-December win in Boston.

Bellamy had gotten into foul trouble that night against the Celtics, which allowed Reed to play most of the minutes at center. As Reed told D'Agostino in *Garden Glory*, Holzman coyly asked Reed if he enjoyed playing center.

"It was all right," Reed replied.

"Who knows," the coach replied, "you might be playing there more."

The team then traveled to Detroit to play DeBusschere and the Pistons, and Walt Frazier was watching television when the report of a trade came on the news: The Knicks—on December 19, 1968—agreed to send Bellamy and starting point guard Howard Komives to the Pistons straight up for DeBusschere.

The following night, DeBusschere led the Knicks with 21 points and 15 rebounds in a 135–87 blowout win at the old Cobo Arena in downtown Detroit. Motor City fans gave DeBusschere a standing ovation as he left the court.

"He didn't look like the guy who played eight games for me," Seymour said afterward.

The deal didn't work out for Seymour and the Pistons. He was fired later that season, and the following year, Detroit was under .500 yet again. They then sent Happy Hairston to the Lakers to fill a new need: a rebounding power forward (Hairston, a Brooklyn product who went to NYU, went on to face the Knicks three times in the NBA Finals, with a win in 1972). Bellamy, who, because of a schedule quirk, wound up playing 88 games in the 1968–69 season between the Knicks and Pistons, was traded to Atlanta the following season.

The trade, of course, fit perfectly in so many ways for the Knicks. First, with DeBusschere the natural power forward, it allowed Reed to play center full-time. DeBusschere's ability to hit shots from the perimeter also opened up the floor for Holzman's offense, which demanded constant ball movement and motion. His high basketball IQ only made the Knicks better as a passing team, and his athleticism made them better in transition.

And, of course, there was his defense and rebounding.

"From the moment he arrived, Dave changed the team," longtime Knicks broadcaster Marv Albert told the *New York Times* in 2003.

His impact was also felt in the backcourt, where the departure of Komives paved the way for Frazier, in his second season, to take over as the starting point guard.

The Knicks' fabulous five, the group that would go on to win the NBA title that following season, was set.

As Reed told the *New York Post* in February 2010, "That was kind of the last piece of the puzzle."

31 The Trade (1971)

Walt Frazier was excited about what the DeBusschere trade meant for him as the new starting point guard. But when rumors emerged that the Knicks were on the verge of acquiring Frazier's greatest rival, Earl "the Pearl" Monroe, he didn't know what to think.

"When Earl came," Frazier recalled in February 2010, "they said we were going to need two basketballs."

Red Holzman, however, knew better. Monroe was a basketball legend from the tough Philadelphia playground courts. He delighted crowds with his streetball-inspired improvisation, and many compared his performances to that of a jazz musician. But with all of the flash, wild off-balance shots, dazzling spin moves, and the adoration from inner-city fans who hailed him as "Black Jesus," there was a bona fide basketball player at the core.

Holzman believed if Monroe entered the team-concept environment that his proud hoop scholars maintained in New York, the Pearl would be happy as a clam.

"I had scouted Earl a lot," he told D'Agostino in *Garden Glory*. "People didn't realize that Earl wasn't just a showman, a guy who wanted to shoot. Earl was the type of basketball player who would do anything you'd ask him to do. If you wanted him to pass the ball, he'd pass the ball. His defense would fit in because we played a helping type of defense.

"Earl knew the game very well. He was very intelligent about the game. He was a great person. He just looked mean on the floor."

Holzman's Knicks weren't looking very good on the floor, either. Willis Reed's knees were so bad he eventually had to shut down for the season after just 11 games. The team had acquired Jerry Lucas in the spring, and that helped fill the void at center.

But in Baltimore, an opportunity was brewing. The Bullets had ended the Knicks' attempt to repeat as champions by winning Game 7 at the Garden in the Eastern Conference semifinals. Monroe outscored Frazier 26–13, and it took a late basket by Fred "Mad Dog" Carter to seal a 93–91 upset.

The Knicks had twice before eliminated the Bullets, so to knock off the defending champions on their home court was a significant victory for Baltimore. Consider that from 1968 to 1970, the Jets upset the Colts in the Super Bowl, the Mets beat the Orioles in the World Series, and the Knicks bounced the Bullets in the playoffs.

But in the late fall of 1971, New York was about to again come out on top over Baltimore.

Monroe was looking for a bigger payday with Baltimore and, as expected, things got uglier than the Bullets' uniforms that season. It turned into a war of words in the media, with Monroe questioning the Bullets' loyalty and team owner Abe Pollin and some other Bullets players questioning Monroe's interest in winning. And, as many players did during this era, Monroe used the ABA as leverage, as the Indiana Pacers expressed interest in the flashy superstar guard.

The Bullets finally agreed to trade Monroe, but he had a list of specific preferences. (Imagine NBA commissioner David Stern allowing this...oh wait, we're forgetting Carmelo Anthony!) Monroe listed Chicago, Los Angeles, or his hometown of Philadelphia as places he'd accept a trade to rather than bolt to the ABA and leave the Bullets empty-handed.

Holzman got right to work on a deal that no one saw coming, mainly because, at the time, the Knicks didn't have a need for another point guard when they had Frazier.

But Monroe got word from his agent that there was an agreement in place between the Bullets and the team he had tried so hard for years to beat, the Knicks. All he had to do was accept the move.

On November 10, 1971, Monroe was dealt to the Knicks for two important pieces of Holzman's bench, Mike Riordan and Dave Stallworth, plus cash.

And suddenly, the star-studded Knicks had one more star.

"That was probably the most tumultuous time in my career as a Knick, because now everyone's saying that Frazier is out, he's gonna get traded, they can't keep both of them," Frazier told D'Agostino in *Garden Glory*. "So it was a tough time for me."

Monroe arrived, wearing No. 33 at first before later switching to No. 15 (he wore No. 10 in Baltimore, but that was Frazier's number in New York). Unlike the DeBusschere deal, which had a more immediate impact, Monroe didn't quite fit in comfortably right away. At first he came in off the bench as Frazier's backup. Occasionally, the two would play together. His scoring dipped dramatically, from 21.4 points per game with the Bullets in 1970–71 to 11.4 points per game in 60 games with the Knicks in 1971–72. He took eight less shots per game and his assists totals were cut in half.

"I knew I wasn't going to play the way I wanted to play," Monroe said in February 2010.

And rather than clash, he and Frazier—who, despite the rivalry, had a healthy mutual respect—developed a chemistry together and became a fearsome backcourt tandem that reached the NBA Finals in 1972 and won the championship a year later, with Reed back at full health.

Today, the duo are in the Basketball Hall of Fame, among the 50 Greatest Players in NBA history and arguably the most talented backcourt tandem the game has ever seen.

"Earl changed his game," Frazier said. "He said, 'This is Clyde's team, I'm just coming to blend in.' He already had all the individual accolades. He just wanted a championship."

The Trade (2011)

It was just two nights after LeBron James announced to the world his Decision to take his talents to South Beach. New York was in a state of depression over one of the biggest losses in franchise history. For two years the franchise had dumped payroll and hoarded salary-cap space to get in position to sign James, the two-time MVP, and begin a long-awaited new era that would lead to a long-awaited NBA title.

James was in New York along with several other NBA stars as guests at the wedding of Denver Nuggets All-Star Carmelo Anthony and television personality Lala Vasquez. Players were teasing James about his choice to join forces with All-Stars Dwyane Wade and Chris Bosh on the Miami Heat. James let it be known the road to the title was now going through Miami.

James also told a few of the envious small-market stars at the wedding, including Anthony, that they needed to follow his lead if they want a chance to win a championship. Amar'e Stoudemire, another guest at the wedding, had signed with the Knicks earlier that week.

"If you want any chance against us in Miami," LeBron then told Carmelo, according to a story in *Sports Illustrated*, "you'd better team up with Stoud in New York."

Shortly after that, Hornets All-Star guard Chris Paul then made a toast to he and Anthony going to New York to join Stoudemire "and form our own Big Three." Everyone laughed.

Well, everyone except Nuggets owner Stan Kroenke.

By the end of the summer, Kroenke was forced to deal with the fact that this lighthearted joke, this toast that was meant to be all in fun, had now turned into a serious situation. Anthony was a year away from being able to opt out of his contract to become a free agent, and there was a strong sense that he had no interest in signing a three-year, $65 million contract extension that the Nuggets had put on the table that spring.

The Knicks, still smarting after missing out on LeBron, were lurking in the background. They had cap space to sign Carmelo if he did opt out.

The next nine months turned into an unprecedented pursuit that was a daily media obsession. The New Jersey Nets, who also had hopes to land LeBron but wound up completely shut out in free agency, did all they could to trump their cross-Hudson rivals to score Carmelo.

The Nuggets made it clear the Knicks didn't have much to offer that satisfied them and favored the Nets, who were aggressively putting together packages that included a host of draft picks and their own lottery selection from that season, power forward Derrick Favors.

It became a cat-and-mouse game, with the Nets believing they had a deal three different times during the 2010–11 season. In late January, after a second deal fell through, Nets owner Mikhail

Prokhorov held a bizarre press conference to announce the team was ending its pursuit of Denver's All-Star forward.

The Knicks jumped out to a 21–14 start behind an MVP-type first half from Stoudemire and cohesive play from a young core that included Danilo Gallinari, Wilson Chandler, and rookie Landry Fields. The cry for Carmelo had subsided for the most part, but when the team looked overwhelmed against star-loaded lineups including the Heat and Boston Celtics, the debate returned.

A six-game losing streak for the Knicks in mid-January coincided with Prokhorov's defiant stance, which turned the spotlight back on the Knicks. The trade deadline (February 24) was fast approaching, and rumors persisted that the Nets' troubles to complete a deal were based on Anthony's refusal to sign a contract extension as part of the deal. Remember Earl Monroe using the threat of the ABA and his list of preferred trade destinations? Consider Anthony's contract extension his own leverage in controlling his destiny.

There was really only one team the Brooklyn-born star wanted to play for: the Knicks.

"That's like the ultimate dream at the end of the day," Anthony said in an interview with ESPN in mid-January. "Who wouldn't want to go back home to play?"

By the All-Star break in mid-February, the Melo-Drama had reached its apex. All of the NBA's stars ascended to Los Angeles and, with the trade deadline just days away, all the talk surrounded Carmelo. The Nets, despite Prokhorov's announcement, jumped back into negotiations and once again believed they had a deal in place. If only Carmelo would agree to an extension.

When the All-Star Game began, many wondered what would happen if a trade went down during the game. Would Carmelo switch jerseys and go from the West team to the East?

During the game, the Knicks, with team owner James Dolan taking the lead, pushed to finalize the deal. There was little doubt that this would be the last game Anthony would play representing the Denver Nuggets.

Two days later, a complicated three-team deal involving an NBA-record 13 players was completed on February 22, 2011. The Knicks agreed to send Gallinari, Chandler, Raymond Felton, and Timofey Mozgov and a first-round pick to Denver along with Eddy Curry and Anthony Randolph to Minnesota, in exchange for Anthony, Chauncey Billups, Shelden Williams, Anthony Carter, and Renaldo Balkman from the Nuggets, plus Corey Brewer from Minnesota.

An exhausting process was finally complete. The Knicks got that second star they hoped to get in free agency the summer before and Anthony got the new beginning—and the big stage—he craved.

"It's a dream come true," Anthony said when the trade was officially announced. "I'm sitting here in one of the best places in the world, New York City."

X-Man

No one has ever made such a lasting impact as a Knick in such a short time as Xavier McDaniel.

In the early 1990s, when Pat Riley transformed the team into the next-generation version of the Detroit Pistons "Bad Boys," McDaniel seemed like the perfect fit.

Since Bernard King was let go in 1987, the Knicks had searched for years for a scoring small forward to complement Patrick Ewing in the middle. The position seemed to be the biggest hole in the lineup, and many guys came through over the years to try to fill the void.

In 1991–92 an opportunity came up that couldn't be overlooked. After toiling through a failed experiment with the poor-shooting Kenny Walker, the inconsistent Johnny Newman, and the underwhelming Kiki Vandeweghe—all of whom just didn't fit the rugged style Riley wanted to develop—the next candidate for the job appeared with a shiny bald head and a brash attitude.

The fourth overall pick by the Seattle SuperSonics in the 1985 draft, McDaniel finished second behind Ewing in the Rookie of the Year voting that season and became an All-Star by his third year. But despite his early success in Seattle, he was traded to Phoenix early in the 1990–91 season, and then the Suns decided to move him before the 1991–92 season.

McDaniel was acquired from the Suns on October 1, 1991, for Trent Tucker, second-year forward Jerrod Mustaf, and a couple of second-round picks. The deal came with a bit of a risk, because McDaniel had a $500,000 buyout clause in his contract that allowed him to become a free agent at season's end. He had until January 15 of that season to exercise the clause.

There was no mistaking that McDaniel fit right in with this rugged group that Riley had assembled, which not only included Ewing and Charles Oakley (whom McDaniel once fought during the 1989–90 season) but another bruising forward, Anthony Mason.

"It was a totally different attitude and mind-set," Vandeweghe told D'Agostino in *Garden Glory*. "Pat has a different way of doing things and commands a lot of respect. The players responded to that. It was typified by the first day in practice, with the big fight between Anthony Mason and Xavier McDaniel. You could see it coming from the first minute of practice. I was sitting there, part of the group that pulled the two apart, and I'm just going, 'Oh boy, this is going to be wild.' And it was."

Vandeweghe actually proved to be very effective as a scorer off the bench, which helped during the regular season, as McDaniel struggled to find any consistency. But once the playoffs arrived, McDaniel turned into X-Man.

And the Garden crowd *loved* the X-Man.

He was a physical dynamo against the fading Pistons in the first round, but McDaniel is most remembered for his defiant, aggressive battle with Scottie Pippen in a seven-game battle with the Chicago Bulls.

It was in Game 4 where McDaniel started to draw the ire of Phil Jackson, who was ejected from the game (a 93–86 win at the Garden that tied the series at two) and proceeded to complain to the press about all that McDaniel was getting away with as he defended Pippen.

"They're shoving our dribblers with two hands," Jackson said, "and that's against the rules."

When this was brought to McDaniel's attention, he replied, "Fuck Phil Jackson."

Nothing endears you more to a New York crowd than an expletive directed toward the enemy.

The love affair would be short-lived, however. After that thrilling series, McDaniel became a free agent and promptly signed a five-year, $13.2 million deal with the Boston Celtics.

"A lot of people in New York are mad at me," McDaniel admitted in his first visit to the Garden the following year. "But they are mad at me because I made a business decision for myself that was not in the best interest of the Knicks."

McDaniel said the Knicks told him they had no plans to offer more than three years. But Dave Checketts, in an interview with the *New York Times* after McDaniel signed with Boston, said otherwise.

"We would have paid him more money than the Celtics paid him," Checketts said. "We never got a chance."

There was talk that the Knicks never had a chance. Why? McDaniel was represented by super-agent David Falk, who also represented Michael Jordan. It has been suggested that Jordan told Falk to get McDaniel, who was a problem for Scottie Pippen, out of New York. Falk, however, also represented Patrick Ewing, so he had an interest in the Knicks' success, as well. But that hasn't silenced the skeptics.

34 Oak

There are many players who have left an indelible mark on the franchise. Many who were part of unforgettable championship runs, memorable moments, and perhaps provided a ray of light during an otherwise dark era. But you won't find another player who is more beloved than Charles Oakley.

"I'm just a piece of the pie, a slice of the pound cake," he told Mike Wise of the *New York Times* in November 1995. "Nobody knows me. I'm not the man. I still can't believe I'm even in the NBA.

"Me? Hah."

For 10 years, his presence as Patrick Ewing's right-hand man in the Knicks frontcourt was nothing to laugh about. In fact, Oakley often made opponents quiver. The burly 6'9" power forward brought a measure of toughness that became the foundation of the franchise's second-best era.

Loved—and often feared—by his teammates, Oakley was the bodyguard and the enforcer. He also believed in the "no layup rule" philosophy that started with the Detroit Pistons "Bad Boys" in the late 1980s. Oakley's Knicks carried that attitude of tough, physical basketball into the 1990s.

It was a style that motivated the NBA to crack down on the physical play and fighting that many critics believed was ruining the game. But Oakley gave no apologies—especially come playoff time.

"If something occurs during the game that calls for us to be physical, then whatever," Oakley said before the 1993 playoffs, when the league installed rules to suppress physical play, such as an automatic suspension if a player throws a punch. "The rules aren't going to affect me. If somebody goes out of their way after me, I'm coming after them, rules or no rules."

There were times Oakley took it too far, but his was an attitude that was only encouraged by Pat Riley when he arrived in 1991. Oakley was also a major part of Jeff Van Gundy's tough, physical defensive teams, which, unlike Holzman's beloved team in the early 1970s, were despised around the NBA.

"Teams don't like the way we play defense, up in your face for 48 minutes," Oakley once said. "But we're not going to step back."

He rarely stepped back or even sat down. Oakley's blue-collar effort became such a given, his double-doubles were often taken for granted. He once grabbed a franchise-record 14 offensive rebounds against the Celtics on January 3, 1989. Oakley had three 20-plus rebound games in 1993–94, when he was named to the NBA All-Star team.

Perhaps one of the most impressive playoff performances of his Knicks career also came against the Celtics that next season in the playoffs, when he had 26 points and 17 rebounds in the unforgettable Game 5 upset at Boston Garden.

His defense against opposing big men—in an era that included some of the best power forwards of all time, such as Charles Barkley and Karl Malone—and ability to take on centers when Ewing was in foul trouble were invaluable.

Oak may have intimidated his opponents, but he's among the most beloved Knicks alumni. (Getty Images)

In 10 seasons with the Knicks, Oakley played in 727 games, which includes an ironman streak of 107 starts (including 25 playoff games) during the 1993–94 season. He ranks third on the franchise's all-time list with 23,959 minutes, second in steals with 844, and is 15th in scoring at 7,528 points. His forte, of course, was rebounding, and he trails only Ewing and Willis Reed on the franchise's all-time list with 7,291 boards for the Knicks. His career total of 12,205 is 20th on the all-time NBA list.

And on the list of most quotable Knicks of all time, he's easily No. 1 and comes the closest to matching another beloved New York athlete, Yogi Berra, for his enjoyably confused axioms.

"If it ain't broke," he once said, "don't break it."

But New York's love affair with Oakley wouldn't last forever. In 1998 it was finally time to go. Motivated by the need to get younger and faster and distance themselves from the bruising era that produced deep playoff runs into spring but no championships, Oakley was traded to the Toronto Raptors for Marcus Camby.

Hurt by the move, Oakley refused to answer his phone, which held up the deal.

He has come back as a visiting player and after his retirement, as a spectator many times since and regularly receives cheers. It would be easier to find 1 percent of body fat on his chiseled frame than to find a Knicks fan who didn't appreciate what he brought to the Garden every night for 10 years.

"Oakley has been a consistently tremendous ballplayer for New York who has contributed mightily night after night," one of the franchise's most famous (and loyal) fans, Woody Allen, wrote for the *New York Observer* in 1998. "Of course, I'd hate to wake up in the middle of the night and find him hovering over my bed with that look on his face, but on the court he's worth every cent they pay him."

35 The Duo That Never Was

A new era began in 1985, with Patrick Ewing's arrival as the new savior of a franchise that only a year before had gone toe-to-toe with the eventual-champion Boston Celtics in the Eastern Conference semifinals. Ewing's arrival came with the unwitting courtesy of the team's current star, Bernard King, whose career-threatening knee injury late in the 1984–85 season led to the collapse that put the Knicks in position to land Ewing.

When King looks back on it, there were two moments in his career that brought him to tears—and they are both related. The first was just after that March night in Kansas City, when his knee shattered while he chased down Reggie Theus on a fast break. He was told the injury could effectively end a career just as he was leading the NBA in scoring.

The second came just over a month later, when the Knicks won the first NBA Draft Lottery and, as a result, the ability to land a franchise center like Ewing. If he could just get himself back, King believed he and Ewing had a chance to do something special.

The caveat, of course, was that King had to get himself back. And in those days, professional athletes weren't attempting come-backs from torn ACL injures; they were attempting new careers. But Knicks team physician, Dr. Norman Scott, performed the surgery, and King focused on what would be a long and arduous comeback.

Ewing's rookie season would be a nightmare, of course, and the Knicks stumbled to another losing record at 23–59. King was nowhere to be found, as he stayed away from the team while he went through the rehabilitation process, and that annoyed team executives.

In 1986–87 King started coming around again toward the end of what was yet another lost season. (Hubie Brown had already been fired and Bob Hill had taken over as interim coach.)

King was almost ready. He was running up and down the court, cutting and darting, taking jumpers, and feeling again like a basketball player. Ewing, meanwhile, was averaging 21.5 points, 8.8 rebounds, and 2.3 blocks per game, and his numbers were steadily improving as the season went on.

The Knicks played the Indiana Pacers at the Garden on March 19, 1987. Ewing had some issues with his left knee that had caused him to miss a recent game against the Boston Celtics, but he was back in the lineup on this night. It was late in the first quarter when he went to the post and slipped on a wet spot on the floor. The slip caused Pacers center Steve Stipanovich to fall over him. When they both got up, Ewing slipped again, but this time his legs split awkwardly, and back down he went. The diagnosis was a sprained knee. His season was over.

Just 11 games later, King was cleared to play.

He would get through the last six games of the season and prove he'd made it all the way back by averaging 22.7 points per game. His contract was up that off-season, and King was hoping the Knicks would bring him back at the same salary and let him and Ewing develop together.

But the franchise was going through major changes at the top. Al Bianchi took over as general manager and brought in former Brown assistant Rick Pitino, who had a successful run to the Final Four with Providence College. Pitino planned to install his fast-break, pressure defense system and King, on a knee no one knew for certain would hold up, was no longer in the plans.

Knicks fans, however, felt differently. They gave King a three-minute standing ovation when he made his long-awaited comeback that April, and in Pitino's first preseason game the following season, the Garden faithful began the night by chanting, "We Want Bernard!"

But Bianchi and Pitino wanted Sidney Green, a power forward from the Detroit Pistons who they believed would fit well next to Ewing. With it clear the Knicks had no interest in re-signing King, the Washington Bullets made a two-year offer for $2.3 million. The Knicks had 15 days to match and, of course, didn't.

Instead, they used the salary slot to acquire Green, and the Bernard King era in New York was unceremoniously extinguished. And with that began years of searching for a scoring small forward who could complement Ewing's low-post game.

"Ewing and I have talked about that privately," King once told me. "If we had the chance to play together, we would have won a title."

Ewing considered the thought, raised his eyebrows, and shrugged. "We'll never know," he said. Fifteen years he spent in New York and winning a championship was all that consumed him. The King debate only added yet another hypothetical to the catalogue of shortcomings—Game 6 against Chicago in '93, Game 7 in Houston in '94, leaving the bench in Miami in '97, his season-ending wrist injury in '98—that will never go away.

But King is adamant. Though both players were dominant post scorers, King believes his game after the surgery changed into a style that would have blended well with Ewing, who was one of the game's greatest jump-shooting centers.

"The type of player I morphed into after my injury was still a tremendous offensive player, but I think demonstrated in terms of my short-range game and my jump shot and my ball-handling skills on the open floor, I transitioned into a perimeter player that could post," King said. "That speaks to how strong the chemistry Patrick and I would have had. He would have had the block to himself."

Twenty-five years later, the Knicks made a deal to bring in Carmelo Anthony, who is easily the most talented scoring small forward the franchise has had since King's departure (Anthony, coincidentally, grew up in Brooklyn and idolized King's game). Anthony's arrival was intended to complement big man Amar'e Stoudemire. The Knicks finally had two bona fide superstars on their roster.

After the trade, Ewing looked back at all of the players he had during his tenure with the Knicks. John Starks, Allan Houston, Charles Oakley, Latrell Sprewell...each of them talented in their own right.

"They're not Carmelo," Ewing said with a wry grin. "They're not Carmelo."

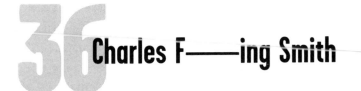

36 Charles F——ing Smith

There is a man who you'll occasionally see standing in the vestibule between the locker-room hallways, near that famous tunnel at Madison Square Garden. He is well dressed, well groomed, and stands like a towering column that reaches the high ceiling. His smile is pleasant and he articulates casual conversation with genuine warmth and interest.

If he were any other person in the world, he'd be someone who could walk confidently and proudly through the halls and the concourses of this old arena. "Once a Knick, always a Knick" is the motto used when a former player is introduced to the crowd here. But you'll never see this man introduced, even though he was a member of one of the franchise's most beloved teams, the 1994 group that reached the NBA Finals.

"Life grants us situations, both good and bad," Charles Smith told D'Agostino in *Garden Glory*. "But at the end of the day, it all depends on how you handle it as an individual."

ALAN HAHN

It's not right that the mere mention of Smith's name, let alone the glimpse of his image at the Garden, conjures such derision from fans. The Bridgeport, Connecticut, native has done so much admirable work in his retirement with his foundation that serves and supports children and families in his hometown. He's been a brilliant businessman and now works as executive director of the NBA Retired Players Association, which assists and advises players through the transition into retirement.

But if only he made that layup.

Or the next one after that.

Or the one after that.

Or that last one...

At this point you should be well versed in the 1993 Eastern Conference Finals between the Knicks and Chicago Bulls. You know about the Knicks earning home-court advantage to get the first two games at Madison Square Garden. You know about winning both of those games to take a 2–0 lead in the best-of-seven series.

You know about the Dunk.

The series went back to Chicago, where Michael Jordan and Scottie Pippen overcame the physical Knicks defense to win both games.

But before we go any further, a little backstory:

After Xavier McDaniel bolted to the Celtics, the Knicks were once again in the market for a small forward who would fit with Patrick Ewing and Charles Oakley in the frontcourt. Smith was going into his fifth season with the Los Angeles Clippers and had been a 20-point scorer.

So the deal was made on September 22, 1992, that acquired Smith and veteran guard Doc Rivers, plus Bo Kimble, in a three-team deal that sent Mark Jackson and a second-round pick to the Clippers, while a first-round pick went to Orlando, who sent Stanley Roberts to Los Angeles.

Smith was a natural power forward but, at 6'10", had shown the versatility to play all three frontcourt positions in his first four seasons. Pat Riley envisioned the long-armed, athletic Smith as a small forward who would give the Knicks a very tall front line.

Smith had to adjust his game in many ways, starting with being on the perimeter and not getting many plays called his way. He averaged 12.4 points in his first season, but in the playoffs he had some big games, starting with a 24-point performance in a series-opening win over the Indiana Pacers. Smith then helped the Knicks finish off the Charlotte Hornets in the second round with 19 points in Game 4 and 18 points and eight rebounds in the series-clinching Game 5. No longer were the Knicks missing X-Man. They saw Smith as the *X* factor.

The momentum carried over into the series with the Bulls, as Smith had 17 points in the Game 1 win and 12 points in Game 2. His minutes were limited because of foul trouble in Game 3, but Smith came back to score 15 points in Game 4. And in Game 5 back at the Garden, he had 12 points in a tight game that went down to the wire.

Then it happened.

With the Knicks trailing 95–94 with under a half-minute left, Ewing had the ball on the right high post and dribbled left against Stacey King. But on his way to the basket, Ewing slipped, and on his way down he managed to shovel the ball to Smith, who had slid into the paint to get into rebounding position.

Smith caught the ball literally under the backboard. He had to gather himself and power up but also back on the right side of the rim. But that allowed Horace Grant to block him from behind. But Smith recovered the ball and went up again—only this time

Michael Jordan slid to the baseline and slapped the ball out of Smith's hands on the way up.

Again, he was able to regain control of the ball, and he powered up yet again, this time on the left side of the rim. This time Scottie Pippen leaped and spiked the shot from behind. But once again, Smith had the ball in his hands with the seconds ticking off the clock, the Garden crowd growing more and more anxious and what seemed like the entire Bulls roster jumping over him.

Smith gave it one more leap, and Pippen timed it perfectly and swatted it yet again. But this time instead of down, he batted it to Grant, who had come over from the right side, and he deflected it away from Smith. Jordan then came up with the ball and threw it down the court to B.J. Armstrong.

Armstrong finished it off with a layup as the final buzzer sounded. Amazingly, Smith was the only Knick who pursued the play. He grabbed the ball after it went through the hoop and slammed it hard on the blue painted hardwood.

Smith would play three more seasons in New York, but fans could never forgive him for the four missed opportunities that led to one disappointing ending.

The dramatic highlight, which is readily available on YouTube, stands out as the source of the bitter defeat, with Smith as the goat. But a closer look at the box score shows Smith was not alone coming up small in a critical game. The Knicks missed 15 free throws in the game (20-for-35), including six by Ewing. And before Smith came up with three offensive rebounds on that final play, the Knicks had recorded only eight in the entire game. The Bulls had 17.

37 West's Celebrated Shot (That Didn't Beat the Knicks)

In the early 1960s, two fledgling basketball leagues drew an arc around each end of the court and designated any shots taken beyond it would count for three points. It was a novelty introduced to add some extra excitement to the game in an attempt to bring back the beauty of the jump shot at a time when towering big men like Wilt Chamberlain were dominating the game at the rim.

When the American Basketball Association (ABA) was formed in 1967, the league wanted to be more progressive than the rigid NBA, and along with the eye-catching red, white, and blue basketball, the ABA included a three-point line.

It wasn't until 1979, three years after the NBA-ABA merger, that the three-point line was added to the NBA game.

This procrastination would play a small but noteworthy role in the Knicks' first championship season.

In the 1970 NBA Finals, the Knicks and Lakers split the first two games at Madison Square Garden, and the series headed west to Los Angeles. The Lakers took a commanding 56–42 lead at the half of Game 3 and looked poised to take a 2–1 lead in the series, with still another game to play at the L.A. Forum.

But behind Dave DeBusschere and Dick Barnett, the Knicks whittled away at the deficit until the score was tied at 96 late in the fourth quarter. Wilt Chamberlain hit one of two from the line with 13 seconds left to tie the score at 100, and the Knicks called timeout.

Off the ensuing inbound play, Walt Frazier fed DeBusschere, who hesitated a moment and then took a contested, fading

16-footer against heavy pressure from Lakers forward Happy Hairston. The ball went through the net with three seconds left, and the Knicks had a 102–100 lead. Frazier pumped his fist and Bill Bradley casually backpedaled. With no timeouts, the Lakers had almost no chance to get off a good shot.

DeBusschere, always defensively focused, always thinking, saw Hairston take off immediately for the other end, and DeBusschere sprinted to catch him, with fears of a long pass for a layup.

A frustrated Chamberlain quickly grabbed the ball after it went through the hoop and tossed it to Jerry West. (Chamberlain barely stepped out of bounds, which should have been a violation—and probably would have been the subject of this chapter if things had ended differently.)

West took two dribbles to his right and then put up a right-handed push shot from just a step before the center-court circle, with one tick left on the clock. The ball sailed 60 feet on a perfect arc and nailed its target, just under the back rim.

The Forum crowd exploded.

DeBusschere, who chased Hairston down the court, was right at the rim when the ball dropped through.

"The ball went right in—*Boom!*—right through to tie the game and send us to overtime," DeBusschere recalled in an NBA Entertainment video on the game. "I just fell down on my back."

While the Lakers players ran out on the court to celebrate the amazing shot, West calmly walked toward the team bench. There was still an overtime to be played.

"Everyone was stunned," Lakers star Elgin Baylor said in that NBA Entertainment video about the game. "The Knicks were stunned. We were excited."

But the Lakers would have been elated—and would have come away with the win—if the NBA had a three-point shot back then. On this night, however, the shot was worth only two points and therefore merely tied the score.

It also didn't seem to disrupt what momentum the Knicks had going in the second half, as they continued to roll into the overtime period. An 18-foot jumper by Barnett gave the Knicks a five-point lead in the final minute, and that sealed the deal in a 111–108 win.

This would be a critical victory, because two nights later the teams would once again go to overtime, but this time the Lakers, behind 37 points from West and 30 by Baylor, pulled out a 121–115 win to even the series.

Back in New York for Game 5, the Knicks were dealt a devastating blow, when Willis Reed went down early in the game with a torn muscle in his hip. Through grit and determination—and a small-ball scheme that would make Mike D'Antoni smile—the Knicks pulled out the Game 5 win. But without Reed in Game 6 in L.A., Chamberlain and the Lakers served up a dominating 135–113 blowout win.

At this point, you're well aware of what happened in Game 7 (as all Knicks fans should be). Reed often points to the inspiring effort by DeBusschere and the Knicks to win Game 5 after he went down, but you can't overlook the importance of Game 3, either. Had there been a three-point line and West's shot proved to be a game-winner, the Knicks would have never gotten to that seventh game.

There would be no Willis Reed moment and no first championship.

L.J. and the Four-Point Play

When the three-point shot was introduced to the NBA in 1979–80, that subsequently brought to the game the potential for a four-point play.

There have been 47 four-point plays in Knicks history as of the 2012–13 season, only two of them in the playoffs. The first was Trent Tucker's shot late in Game 6 of the 1989 Eastern Conference semifinals.

It would be 10 years before it would happen again. But this one would be frozen in time forever.

Larry Johnson entered the NBA as an explosively powerful forward who could overwhelm you under the basket with a physically dominant game. In his first NBA season, he attempted just 22 three-pointers. But as his body started breaking down from the bruising style he played, Johnson started developing more and more a perimeter, finesse game. The three-point shot became a larger part of his game as he got older. But to consider him a serious long-range threat? No, he was average, if not mediocre, at best.

Still, all it takes, as Charles Smith learned, is one shot to become legendary.

The 1999 playoffs quickly turned into one of those inexplicable runs a team goes on in a given year, when every break, every bounce, and every bit of magic goes their way. The first-round battle with the rival Miami Heat, capped by Allan Houston's last-second winner in the deciding Game 5, sent the Knicks on their way.

Marcus Camby's high-flying dunk down the lane in Game 1 in Atlanta highlighted the sweep in the Eastern Conference semifinals.

And then there was Game 3 of the Eastern Conference Finals against another old rival, the Indiana Pacers.

This wasn't supposed to be the Knicks' year. This was Indiana's time. They were battle-tested, tough, and also a mix of experience and talented youth, led by Jalen Rose.

The Knicks took the first game of the series 93–90 at Indiana, and then Reggie Miller held off the Knicks 88–86 with a pair of free throws in the final seconds to even the series.

The Pacers looked poised to take Game 3 at the Garden, with an eight-point lead with under four minutes to go. But the Knicks scored seven straight to close to within one, until Mark Jackson, now with the Pacers, hit a pair of free throws with 11.9 seconds left to make it a 91–88 lead for Indiana.

Jeff Van Gundy called a timeout, and it seemed obvious what to do. Remember Game 5 in Miami?

Triangle Down, of course.

Only this time, Patrick Ewing wasn't there to set the pick. He played in the first two games of the series, and played a big part down the stretch in clinching the Game 1 victory, but after Game 2 it was revealed that he tore the Achilles that had been aching since the regular season.

Johnson was in Ewing's spot, but as Houston cut to curl, the inbounder, Charlie Ward (always good to have a Heisman Trophy winner as your primary passer), had his passing lane blocked by heavy pressure.

So Johnson flashed to the ball and Ward made the pass. With Antonio Davis draped over him, Johnson squared up, took a dribble to his left, pump-faked, and then...

"The Garden," Houston said, "literally lifted off the ground."

Referee Jess Kersey raised his arm to signal a three-point attempt and then tweeted his whistle. Nineteen thousand seven hundred and sixty-three witnesses, plus a few thousand more who claimed to be in the building, stared at the spinning ball, which soared through the net with 5.7 seconds left.

Larry Bird was just a step away from Johnson but wearing the clothes of a head coach now and no longer a player. All he could do was stare back at Kersey.

Years later, now as the president of the Pacers, Bird barely grins when the shot is brought up in conversation. "There was no foul," he says.

Kersey, a veteran official, begged to differ.

"His arm continued up in a motion to take a shot at the basket," he said after the game. "And that is a continuation play."

Johnson, of course, backed Kersey: "It was a good call."

But the shot only tied the score at 91. As the Garden rocked and Johnson flashed his trademark *L* symbol, which he formed with his arms, Chris Childs ran to Johnson to calm his emotions. "You gotta make the free throw!" he yelled to his teammate over the din.

Of course he did, to cap a 26-point performance and a pivotal win in the series. Afterward, he put the shot, and the win, in perspective.

"This could be a great win and a great show," Johnson said, "and we could still lose [the series] 4–2."

(That had to resonate with anyone who remembered Starks' famous Dunk from that '93 series against the Bulls, which wound up being the high point of a series the Knicks eventually lost in six.)

The Knicks would lose Game 4 by 12 points, but they then came up with a pair of gritty wins, 101–94 in Game 5 in Indiana and then a euphoric Game 6 celebration back at the Garden to clinch the series and an improbable ending to this run: a trip to the NBA Finals.

Robbed in '52

Perhaps Larry Johnson's miraculous four-point play was a gift from the basketball gods, who felt the Knicks were owed one from a long, long time ago.

Though it didn't actually lose the series, or happen late enough to directly impact the final score, there is a controversial call that goes back six decades into franchise history, during a time when the Knicks came achingly close to winning a championship.

From 1951 to 1953, the Knicks dominated the East in the early years of the NBA. The best shot at a title came in '51 against the Rochester Royals—who, at the time, were a fierce rival, with greats such as Arnie Risen, Bob Davies, and Bobby Wanzer. (Just nod your head in agreement; these guys were great players in their day.)

The Knicks had defeated the Celtics in the first round and then knocked off the Syracuse Nationals in a five-game battle to advance to their first NBA Finals appearance.

Here's the thing about those days, however. First, the Knicks were never expected to play that deep into the spring (the Finals were in mid-April). Second, the Knicks never had precedence at the old Madison Square Garden on 49th Street. The circus had been scheduled well in advance and tickets had been sold. And the people of New York loved the circus. After all, the very existence of the Garden in New York was entirely because of the circus and one P.T. Barnum. And the NBA then was nowhere near the attraction it is today.

So in New York's first Finals appearance, the games were played at the 69th Regiment Armory on 26th Street and Lexington Avenue. The Knicks had lost the first two games of the series in Rochester by blowout scores and then fell 78–71 in Game 3 at the Armory to fall behind 3–0 in the best-of-seven series.

A comeback win in Game 4 avoided the sweep, and the Knicks stayed alive two nights later with a three-point win in Rochester. They'd have one more date at the Armory and pull off yet another victory, 80–73, to force a seventh and final game back in Rochester.

The Knicks would lose a heartbreaker 79–75, but 60 years later they remain one of only three teams in league history to force a Game 7 after falling behind 0–3 in a best-of-seven series. (The other two: the 1994 Denver Nuggets and 2003 Portland Trail Blazers.)

A year later, the Knicks were back in the NBA Finals after again beating the Celtics in the first round and the Nationals in the Eastern Division Finals. The opponent in the Finals this time was the Minneapolis Lakers, who had the biggest star in the league, center George Mikan.

The marquee says it all.

The towering, bespectacled 6'10" Mikan was so popular around the country that when the Lakers came to play the Knicks in December 1949, Irish had the marquee read, Geo Mikan v/s Knicks rather than the Knicks vs. Lakers. The average New Yorker didn't know anything about the Lakers, but most people had heard of Mikan.

Knicks coach Joe Lapchick certainly knew who he was. In fact, Lapchick seemed almost obsessed with Mikan.

"He would go out of his mind every time he saw me play," Mikan said in a story for NBA.com. "He wanted to try to do something to stop me."

One effort he did make, which impacted the game of basketball to this day, was to get the league to widen the three-second lane from six to 12 feet, thus forcing big men such as Mikan farther away from the basket.

So there was already some animosity going into the '52 Finals. Adding more drama to the scene was that the Garden was again unavailable for the Knicks because of the circus, so the Knicks would have to use the Armory as their home court once again. And the Lakers' home arena, the Minneapolis Auditorium, was also booked, so the games were played in St. Paul.

The series opened with immediate controversy. Early in Game 1, Al McGuire drove in for a layup and was fouled on the play. Both officials, well-known referees Sid Borgia and Stan Stutz, whistled for the foul and called for two free throws.

Wait, everyone wondered. *Two?*

What Borgia and Stutz didn't see was that McGuire's layup went in after the foul was called. Amazingly, neither referee was aware the basket was good. Lapchick pleaded his case with both, but neither would overturn the call. Even Lakers coach John Kundla admitted to the officials that the shot went in, but still the referees did not budge.

Lapchick even went over to NBA commissioner Maurice Podoloff, who was sitting courtside, to make an appeal. But Podoloff did not use his authority to change the call.

So instead of finishing off an and-one, McGuire went to the line for two free throws. He made one of two. A potential three-point play was reduced to just one.

The Knicks went on to lose that game in overtime 83–79, and many of them believed the missing two points cost them a win.

"That might have changed the whole thing around," Al's brother, Dick McGuire, told D'Agostino in *Garden Glory*.

The Knicks came back to win Game 2 and then split Games 3 and 4 in New York at the Armory, including a 90–89 overtime win to tie the series at two games apiece. When the Lakers won Game 5, most New Yorkers had given up on the Knicks. Only 3,000 fans showed up for Game 6 at the Armory—Mikan affectionately dubbed it "the drill shed"—to see a 76–68 win that forced Game 7.

But this time the Lakers had their home court back, and the game was played at the Minneapolis Auditorium. This is significant because at this venue, with a court that was narrower than standard by a few feet, the Knicks had lost 11 straight games. On April 25, 1952, it became 12.

The teams would meet again the following year, and this time the Minneapolis Auditorium was again available. The Knicks put an end to their issues there with a 96–88 win to open the series, but the Lakers took the next four straight, including three in New York at—where else?—the beloved Armory, to win their second-straight title.

It would be 17 years until the Knicks would reach the NBA Finals again.

The Fighting 69th

The New York skyline is an ever-changing image, with historic architecture surrounded by modern buildings that have risen in between. There is the intimidating reach of the Empire State Building, with its long spearlike antenna poking at the heavens. Nearby is the majestic gold peak of the New York Life building, where the first two versions of Madison Square Garden once stood.

There is nothing left of the original Garden, much like there is nothing left of the third edition of the Garden on 49th Street. The current Garden on Seventh Avenue has stood since 1968—and as the years go by, Knicks history seems to be limited to the period that existed in that space above Pennsylvania Station between 33rd and 31st Streets. This is where the greatest successes of the franchise took place, so this is where the heart is.

But for Knicks fans who like to occasionally wrap themselves in nostalgia as if it's an old sweater, a trip to the 69th Regiment Armory is a must.

The building itself is a national historic landmark, so declared in 1965, and a New York City landmark since 1983. Built in 1906, the massive edifice is located on Lexington Avenue between 25th and 26th Streets. It was made to house the 69th Regiment, a brigade of Irish-Americans with a lineage that goes back to the mid-1800s, during a tumultuous time in New York City history that was fictionalized in Martin Scorsese's 2002 drama, *Gangs of New York*.

The Armory is still used to this very day to house the 69th Infantry Regiment, which earned the nickname, "the Fighting 69th" by General Robert E. Lee during the Civil War. In fact, one of their first nicknames was also the "Fighting Irish"—which, of course, has since been adopted by a well-known university in South Bend, Indiana.

The famous St. Patrick's Day Parade in New York that strolls down Fifth Avenue is traditionally led by the 69th Regiment.

The Armory became more than just a home and a place for the infantry to hold drills and ceremonies. There were art exhibits and track meets and roller derbies. And there was, of course, basketball.

Though the Knicks called Madison Square Garden home, they weren't always the priority tenant they are today. Early in the franchise's existence, when the circus came to town or the NHL's Rangers had a game, the Knicks had to find an alternative court.

"We just had to find a place in the city, somewhat in the vicinity of the Garden," Fred Podesta told the *New York Post*'s Leonard Lewin in 1994. "It came down to the armories. We found most of them unsuitable for what we needed. They didn't have the right configuration for basketball. The only one that fit the basic needs was the 69th Regiment Armory.

"It was the best of nothing, but it had a balcony and a high ceiling. We used to run boxing matches at Yankee Stadium in those days, and we kept four to five thousand portable seats there. We

The Old Armory

The Knicks played games at the 69th Regiment Armory over the franchise's first 14 seasons. The last time they played at the Armory was January 16, 1960, when a crowd of 3,000 came out to see the Knicks beat the Cincinnati Royals 132–106. It was around this time, coincidentally, that plans for a new Madison Square Garden were under way. The Knicks actually recorded their first official "home" win in franchise history at the Armory, with a 64–62 overtime win over the Pittsburgh Ironmen on November 16, 1946. The first actual home game, which took place at the Garden on 49th Street, was on November 11, 1946, a 78–68 overtime loss to the Chicago Stags.

not only had to move and store them at the Armory, we had to keep breaking down the setup according to Armory requirements, such as drills for the National Guard and other events."

The Knicks played a lot of games there, but the most famous were their three-straight appearances in the NBA Finals from 1951 to 1953. The Knicks went 4–5 in nine Finals games hosted at the Armory. In 15 playoff games there, the team was 8–7.

No, it wasn't the Garden. But it wasn't so bad, either.

"The Armory floor was much, much better," Dick McGuire told D'Agostino in *Garden Glory*. "The ball bounced much more truly. The Garden had a lot of dead spots where the ball could go down on you. It had a lot of dead spots where the Armory didn't. I enjoyed playing in the Armory, except that we didn't have as many fans there."

If you visit there today, you'll see the court is still in place, right in the middle of the event floor. So is the old-fashioned analog clock at one end of the building above a sign that reads, Next Home Game.

Perhaps somewhere in the drafts that blow through the old, cavernous building, McGuire and the boys are waiting for another shot at Mikan and those Lakers.

41 The Real Father Knickerbocker

Ned Irish never wanted to own a professional basketball team. To him, the college game was where it was at. And as a young sportswriter for the *New York World Telegram*, Irish found himself climbing through a window just to get into a college game he was supposed to cover. The idea that came to mind was rather obvious: this game needs a bigger venue.

"Anytime there was a big college game, you had to fight your way into the building," Irish was once quoted as saying. "I realized that basketball had outgrown these gyms."

At the age of 29, Irish (who went by "Ned," though his first name is actually Edward), earned himself the nickname "the Boy Promoter" when he organized the first college doubleheader at Madison Square Garden on December 29, 1934. Over 16,000 fans packed the Garden on 49th Street to watch New York University beat Notre Dame and Westminster College top St. John's.

In just one night, Irish had created a new and lucrative attraction that turned into an overnight success. College teams from all over the country began to schedule games at the Garden to be part of these doubleheaders, and fans filled the seats to see them play. Irish left the ranks of the ink-stained scribes—he had also once worked as public-relations director for the New York Football Giants—and became basketball director for Madison Square Garden.

From 1942 to 1949, an estimated total of more than 500,000 fans came to the Garden just to see college basketball. In 1938 he played a major role in the creation of the National Invitation Tournament, which for many years was recognized as the national championship. The games were played, of course, at the Garden; it's a tradition that continues today.

You want to know where the Garden got its moniker as the "mecca of basketball"? It was at this time, when college teams all wanted to make the pilgrimage to New York to play there.

Ten years after Irish's first doubleheader, a group of arena managers from several other major cities—Boston, Chicago, Detroit, Toronto, and Cleveland—got together to create a professional league with amateur players and well-known graduates from the college circuit. They wanted New York, and the Garden, to have a franchise.

"He didn't want professional basketball at that time," Irish's longtime assistant, Fred Podesta, told *Post* writer Leonard Lewin in 1994. "For one thing, it was going to be a loss situation for an indeterminate number of years. Most important, we had no Garden dates for it. We were booked 100 percent and were in the middle of what was to be the most productive season the building ever had."

But when a man named Max Kase, a sports editor at the *Journal American*, tried to get involved to form a New York–based team for the new league, Irish's competitive nature flared. According to *Sports Illustrated*, Irish let it be known he had the backing of a corporation—with $3.5 million in assets.

Irish agreed to be part of the Basketball Association of America, which later became the NBA. He was the first president of the Knicks, a position he held from 1946 until his retirement in 1974.

There are many mixed perceptions about Irish and his relationship with the Knicks. On one hand, there is the feeling that he never really cared about the franchise or its success, which is why for most of his tenure the team never won, despite playing in a basketball-crazed city and in a league of just 10 teams.

"The way college basketball draws," he once told *Sports Illustrated* in 1961, "the Knicks are nothing but a tax write-off anyway."

But when the Knicks reached their first NBA Finals in 1951, Irish was ready to celebrate a championship. For Game 7 in Rochester, Irish arranged for a plane filled with champagne bottles and beer in anticipation of a win that never happened.

Despite three straight trips to the Finals from 1951 to 1953, Irish had to wait until 1969–70 to savor a long-awaited championship. It happened in Game 7 at the new Madison Square Garden, which was by then a place where the Knicks were the main attraction.

In 1964 Irish was the first member of the Knicks organization to be enshrined in the Basketball Hall of Fame. Not bad for a sportswriter.

153

42 Tricky Dick

If Ned Irish was the founding father of the Knicks, Dick McGuire was the franchise's beloved older brother—and the mainstay who connected the history of the team from its very beginning right to the modern era.

McGuire came from basketball royalty, off the famous courts of Rockaway, Queens, with his brother, Al.

"I could talk," the boisterous Al McGuire once said. "My brother Dick could play."

And he let his game speak for itself. McGuire was the kind of player everyone wanted on their team. He was known as "Tricky Dick" (how's that for a New York City streetball nickname?): a terrific ball handler with amazing vision and the ability to make passes right on target. If you couldn't get an easy basket playing with Dick McGuire, then you might as well just quit the game.

"Back when Dick played, a great pass often got more applause than a great shot," legendary broadcaster Bob Wolff, who called many of McGuire's games, told the *Daily News* in 2003. "That's how times have changed. Dick could shoot, but he could really hit the open man. That's what made him one of the great passers and great players in the history of the game."

In 11 NBA seasons from 1949 to 1960, McGuire never averaged more than 9.2 points per game and rarely attempted more than eight shots per game. He was the setup man, the quarterback. As a rookie in 1949–50, he set a league record with 386 assists and topped that a year later with an even 400. Passing was his thing, but while that worked well on the NBA Finalist teams from 1951 to 1953, as the team fell on hard times later in the '50s, there was more pressure on McGuire, a seven-time All-Star, to produce.

"There were times when I would think, *God, tomorrow night I'm going to shoot more*," McGuire told *Newsday* in 1992. "But I don't think you can change what you are."

That would come up again in the 1960s, when McGuire returned as coach of the team. He finished his playing career in Detroit in 1960, and the Pistons hired him to be their coach for a handsome salary of $13,000. He left after four seasons, homesick for New York and his family there. But without basketball, McGuire was lost. He took a job as an insurance salesman just to pay the bills. But being in New York kept him in the loop on his former team, the Knicks, who, early in the 1965–66 season were looking for a coach. McGuire's former teammate, Harry Gallatin, was fired.

At the age of 40, McGuire was back with the Knicks. He would remain with the franchise for another 43 years until he passed away in 2010.

In his second season, McGuire led a young Knicks team—with players such as Willis Reed, Dick Barnett, Cazzie Russell, Walt Bellamy, Dick Van Arsdale, and Dave Stallworth—back to the playoffs for the first time in eight years. The following season, however, the team slumped to a 15–22 start, and McGuire knew he really wasn't cut out to be a coach. He wasn't demonstrative and didn't challenge players the way a coach sometimes needs to do. McGuire was soft-spoken and preferred to be one of the guys.

With the team preparing to move into the new Garden, Ned Irish ordered a change. No one was more relieved than McGuire, especially when he learned he wouldn't be out of a job.

Instead, McGuire was moved to chief scout and assistant coach, while the man who had held that position, Red Holzman, became the coach. The rest, of course, is history we've already covered.

But the move didn't only work out well for Holzman, who went on to become one of the NBA's all-time greatest coaches, it was a better fit for McGuire, too. He was always happier with making the assist, and as a scout, he spent the next four decades finding talent and advising on personnel decisions.

Over the years, he became the patriarch of the franchise. In 1992 his No. 15 was raised to the rafters in a deserving honor. A year later, McGuire was enshrined in the Basketball Hall of Fame (joining his brother, Al, who was enshrined as a coach in 1992).

Though most fans these days have little to no recollection of McGuire as a player, you need to understand just how admired he was during his time.

"For the position I played, watching Dick McGuire then was watching what is known now as a role model," the great Bob Cousy told the *New York Times* in 1992.

McGuire was the epitome of New York basketball, as the point guard who controlled the game like a quarterback in football. These days, the city game has the same foundation, only passing has become the second option, which has led to the disappearance of the team concept McGuire embodied.

"I don't think we were as good as these guys are today," McGuire once told the *Daily News* when talking about the modern players. "These guys are so much better than we were, it's not even close. But I think if they had learned how to play like we played, they would enjoy the game a lot more."

43 The Action to Get Jackson

If we're going to mention Dick McGuire, you have to consider what might have been the best assist of his post-playing career. It was after the disastrous 1986–87 season, when Patrick Ewing went down with a knee injury and Bernard King returned from his own to prove, at the very least, that he could play again, when the executives at Gulf & Western decided it was time to clean house.

Gone was interim coach Bob Hill and interim general manager Scotty Stirling, who were relieved of their duties two days after the final regular-season game. But management didn't use the same haste to hire replacements, so it was left up to McGuire to run the draft.

The Knicks were back in the lottery that year, but this wouldn't be one fans hoped the NBA would rig. Their pick was already gone to the Seattle SuperSonics as part of the November 12, 1986 trade that Stirling made to bring in veteran guard Gerald Henderson.

But that wouldn't have been so bad if Stirling had not also agreed to another ill-fated deal that season. The Knicks had Denver's first-round pick in 1987 as part of the Darrell Walker trade on October 2, 1986—one of the few gambles Stirling got right. The Nuggets wound up with the No. 8 pick in the draft.

That pick, however, would be owned by the Chicago Bulls, who gladly took it off Stirling's hands in exchange for Jawaan Oldham, a center who never panned out and from the day he arrived couldn't wait to leave.

And you wonder why this franchise is always such a mess. While it takes years to build a championship-caliber team, it often only takes one or two dumb moves to destroy one.

So despite a 24–58 record, the Knicks were fortunate to at least have one first-round pick in the 1987 draft: it was No. 18 overall, and it came from Seattle (by way of Milwaukee) as part of the Henderson trade. With a record as poor as theirs, the Knicks had many needs. But with veterans Henderson and Rory Sparrow, point guard wasn't seen as one of them.

Plus, without a head coach, there was no style of play to consider when making a selection. So McGuire did it the only way he knew how: he made the simple play.

Mark Jackson was a player from the same Queens playgrounds on which McGuire came up as well as the same St. John's University program. He also was a rarity of the modern game: a passer, facilitator, and floor leader.

But while he had a successful four-year career at St. John's, there were questions about Jackson's ability to play at the NBA level. He wasn't much of a shooter from the perimeter (again, a game only McGuire could appreciate) and scouts were skeptical of his foot speed as a defender. Some scouts didn't even project him as worthy of a first-round pick.

The Portland Trail Blazers had the 17th pick, but the rowdy crowd at the Garden's theater was already anticipating the Knicks selection. This year, the fans couldn't care less about what the scouts were saying. Their choice was made.

"We want Mark! We want Mark! We want Mark!"

The St. Albans, Queens, native sat alone in a row of seats where the draftees waited to hear their names called. His heart was racing and his emotions were overflowing. Up until the Knicks selected, he was hoping the scouts were right and that the other teams would pass on him.

"Next to graduation from St. John's, those five minutes between the time the Portland Trail Blazers picked 17th until the Knicks picked me were the hardest five minutes of my life," Jackson said in Bill Reynolds' book, *Born to Coach*, which was an account of Pitino's first season in New York. "I felt like Dorothy from *The Wizard of Oz*. I was sitting there clicking my heels, saying, 'There's no place like home.' The fans are screaming and chanting, and I'm getting ready to cry. All of a sudden, Kenny Smith walked up and [sat] next to me. That's the only thing that saved me."

Smith, who came up with Jackson through the famed New York City High School Catholic League, was taken sixth overall by the Sacramento Kings. He was the first to offer a hearty handshake when commissioner David Stern announced the Knicks' choice, to the raucous delight of the crowd.

Two weeks later, the Knicks hired Al Bianchi—another guy with Queens roots—as the general manager. Shortly afterward, Bianchi would name Providence College coach Rick Pitino, whose career began as a Catholic League player on Long Island, as the Knicks head coach.

By the middle of Jackson's rookie season, he had climbed over both Henderson and Sparrow to become the team's starting point guard.

"At the time, it was a big shock," Jackson told Reynolds. "A lot of teams would have thought twice about having a rookie point guard. A veteran coach might have stayed with the veterans. But a rookie coach was more than willing to give me a shot."

Pitino gave him a chance, but McGuire provided the opportunity. The two would remain forever linked in franchise history.

Jackson was named the NBA's Rookie of the Year for that season, edging out his good friend Kenny Smith. He is the last Knicks draft pick to win the award.

Jackson would play seven seasons with the Knicks (1987–92 and 2000–02) and is ranked second in franchise history with 4,005 assists, just behind one of his idols, Walt Frazier (4,791) and, fittingly, just ahead of McGuire (2,950).

44 The Bomb Squad

The Rick Pitino era was brief, but it was entertaining. Pitino spent those two seasons trying—and, at times, succeeding—to convince naysayers that his intense pressure defense and wild up-tempo offense could win at the NBA level.

It wasn't so much the system as it was its demands. Constant effort, which was maniacally enforced by the relentless coach whose previous experience with professional players was as Hubie Brown's assistant for two seasons from 1983 to 1985.

But as exhausting as Pitino's style was on defense, the reward was how much fun you could have on offense. He encouraged his players to push the pace, fill the lanes, and, most of all, take full advantage of the three-point line.

During the 1986–87 season, the Knicks attempted 375 shots from beyond the three-point arc. In the eight seasons since the NBA adopted the three-point shot in its game, that was the highest total—by well over 100—the Knicks had taken in a single season.

In Pitino's first season in New York in 1987–88, his team beat that total by almost 200 attempts. And by year two, they doubled that with an astounding 2,241 shots from downtown, as Marv Albert would say. Their total, the first time an NBA team had ever eclipsed the 1,000-attempts mark, led the NBA by 323 attempts.

More important than the frequency of attempts, of course, is the frequency of shots made. In the first year, Pitino's team hit 179 for a 31.6 percent clip. That following season the Knicks hit 386, which was more than six NBA teams (including Larry Bird's Celtics) even *attempted*, for an above-average rate of 33.7 percent.

No one benefited more from the style of play than one of the NBA's most lethal marksman in the early years of the three-point line: Trent Tucker. He took 296 threes that season, which was fourth-most in the NBA.

"Rick allowed me to do the thing I did best," Tucker told D'Agostino in *Garden Glory*, "and that's shoot from downtown."

Johnny Newman wasn't too far behind, with 287 attempts, followed by 240 by Mark Jackson and 172 from Gerald Wilkins. Even Charles Oakley got into the act, with 48 attempts (though he hit only 12).

The aforementioned group of long-range shooters came to be known as "the Bomb Squad" during that 1988–89 season. The group even got together—Rod Strickland was included, though he wasn't nearly as prolific at 19-for-59 from three-point land—for a promotional poster that had them standing in front of an old fighter jet. The poster has since become a rare collector's item among Knicks fans.

It wasn't until the mid-to-late 1990s that the Knicks would take more than 1,000 three-pointers. The arrival of Mike D'Antoni in 2008 brought a return to the Bomb Squad mentality, as the 2008–09 team attempted a franchise-record 2,284 three-pointers.

In D'Antoni's three full seasons in New York, the Knicks consistently broke 2,000 in three-point attempts.

But it was Pitino who was one of the early believers in the three-point shot. Years later, when he coached the Boston Celtics, forward Antoine Walker was once asked why his team shot so many threes.

"Because," Walker replied, "there aren't any fours."

45 Fall Back, Baby!

At basketball's very core—along with the most basic fundamentals of dribbling, passing, and shooting—is an element that is as much a part of the game as the ball itself: trash-talking.

The sport has produced some of the world's greatest trash-talkers, with some of the most entertaining—and demoralizing—material. Charles Barkley was relentless. Michael Jordan was vicious. Reggie Miller was nasty. And Larry Bird was deadly.

But no one had a more maddening habit when it came to trash-talk than Dick Barnett. The 6'4" guard from Gary, Indiana, had a unique shooting form that was often impossible to duplicate but amazingly accurate.

"Within 18 to 22 feet of the basket," he once said in a *Sports Illustrated* article in 1966, "once it goes up, those other cats can forget it."

Barnett was an entertaining conversationalist. He'd often use terms of endearment like "darlin'" or "honey"—even when talking to men, such as his teammates—as opposed to "man" or "dude." One time during his career with the Lakers, when Los Angeles trailed the Cincinnati Royals by two with four seconds to go, Barnett caught a pass for the final shot. He pulled up for a 35-footer in front of the Lakers bench, turned to teammate Rod Hundley while the ball was still in the air, and said, "We're in overtime, darlin'!"

The Lakers went on to win in overtime.

Barnett was from humble beginnings, but there was nothing humble about him. It's not that he was arrogant, but he was smart—street smart, too, and he knew it. Barnett, also a natty dresser, had swagger before there even was such a thing.

He could play, no doubt, but Dick Barnett was the king of trash-talk.
(Getty Images)

The origins of his famous slogan—"Fall back, baby!"—are said to have begun at Tennessee State, where he played his college ball from 1955 to 1959.

"He would go to the gym and practice by himself, and he'd talk to an imaginary opponent out on the court," John McLendon recalled to William C. Rhoden in the *New York Times* in 1992. "He'd be making all these moves and talking, and that's what he'd say when he'd shoot the ball: 'Fall back.'"

But there have been conflicting stories. According to *Sports Illustrated*, in Barnett's years as a Laker (1962–65), he would actually yell, "Let's go back!"—encouraging his teammates to get back on defense because his shot was going in. It became popular among his teammates, and eventually many of them took to calling it out, too.

Elgin Baylor then let Chick Hearn, the legendary Lakers play-by-play announcer, in on the funny motto. Hearn then turned it into a signature call of, "Fall back, baby!" whenever Barnett nailed a jumper.

And even those jumpers had a style all their own. Barnett had a curious form, with his body leaning away from the basket and his legs kicking under him. It worked well enough for him to become the fourth overall pick by the Syracuse Nationals in the 1959 NBA Draft.

Barnett was miserable in Syracuse and took a risky jump to the short-lived American Basketball League, where he played for a Cleveland franchise owned by a man named George M. Steinbrenner. And in typical Steinbrenner form, that team won the league's championship.

Barnett got back into the NBA in the following season when the Lakers bought his contract. He spent three seasons in L.A., where his popularity grew but so did his impatience. Despite two trips to the NBA Finals in three seasons—both losses to the dynastic Celtics—Barnett wanted a new experience. The Lakers were in the hands of Jerry West and Elgin Baylor.

In New York, Barnett was one of the first pieces of what would eventually become a championship team. He was the starting shooting guard and quickly became a fan favorite. That first New York season, he averaged a career-high 23.1 points per game and took a career-high 17.9 shots per game.

That's a lot of fall back, babys.

Barnett retired after the 1973–74 season with two championship rings, though, at the age of 36, his role was to be greatly reduced with the arrival of Earl Monroe. He didn't graduate when he left Tennessee State, but throughout his career he continued earning credits until he earned his bachelor's degree in California. He then achieved a master's degree at NYU during his tenure with the Knicks.

And in 1991 he earned a doctorate from the Fordham School of Education. If you meet him today and call him Dick, he might be inclined to correct you. It's *Doctor*, darlin'.

46 The Ship Be Sinkin'

When a relentlessly energetic guard from the University of Montana caught Willis Reed's eye, he made the immediate connection. Reed had seen this combination of speed, defensive tenacity, and uncanny court awareness before in a point guard. In fact, he had won two championships with him.

On Reed's recommendation, the Knicks selected Micheal Ray Richardson and immediately a high ceiling was set. Richardson was dubbed the next Walt Frazier, whom the team had traded the season before. In his second season, Richardson became the first NBA player to lead the league in assists (10.1) and steals (3.2).

By his third season, the Knicks won 50 games and Richardson had become a leaguewide star. He dazzled the Garden crowd with his explosive drives and electrifying steals. He hounded an opposing point guard at one end of the floor and attacked him at the other. It didn't matter who you were, either.

"Every time I saw him, he went right at me," Magic Johnson said in the outstanding NBA Entertainment documentary *Whatever Happened to Sugar Ray?* "And Micheal would always talk trash, the whole game."

Longtime NBA writer for the *New York Post*, Peter Vescey, added, "Isiah Thomas tells me, to this day, the one guy who he was scared of was Richardson. He owned him."

But the young star from Lubbock, Texas, was engulfed in his newfound stardom in New York City at a time when a destructive disco scene emerged, laced with the temptation of cocaine and alcohol. It was a developing issue that went mostly swept under the rug during his days with the Knicks, mainly because it did not impact his performance on the court. (A few years later, while playing for the Nets, Richardson's drug and alcohol abuse troubles would surface and, eventually, destroy what should have been a Hall of Fame career).

Richardson relied on the support of his closest friends after the 1981 playoffs that saw the young team overwhelmed by an experienced Chicago Bulls team with a first-round sweep. During the off-season, Knicks general manager Eddie Donovan attempted to add some veteran talent with the intention of making a more playoff-ready team.

But Donovan's decisions showed he was out of touch with his team and, most importantly, his star player. First, Ray Williams,

Richardson's terrific backcourt mate and close friend, was headed to free agency and therefore traded for veteran Maurice Lucas. Another one of Richardson's friends, Mike Glenn, was also sent away, rather than re-signed, for a second-round pick. Though Richardson still put up big numbers, the team finished 33–49 and failed to make the playoffs.

That group hovered just under .500 through the middle of the season, and a playoff berth was within reach if only they could have put together a winning streak. Donovan signed another veteran, Paul Westphal, late in the year, but it only got worse. The Knicks lost 16 of their last 21 games. It is during this tailspin that Richardson had a famous conversation with a reporter that remains one of the most quoted sports lines of all time.

"What do you think is happening to the team?" he was asked.

"The ship be sinking," Richardson replied.

"How far can it sink?"

"Sky's the limit," he said.

When aging legend Red Holzman retired, the Knicks brought in an abrasive new coach in Hubie Brown. As Richardson tells the story in a video segment on CourtsideJones.com, before the 1982–83 season, Brown went around the room and berated each player for his shortcomings. When he reached Richardson, he plainly said that every team has an asshole, and Richardson was it.

As Brown continued on to the next guy, Richardson cut him off. "Wait a minute, Hubie," he then said. "On this team there are two assholes. You and me."

Richardson was traded the next day to Golden State for Bernard King.

47 Yes...and It Counts!

It may be the most popular phrase in basketball. It can be whispered, uttered, or screamed, and each time it means the same thing: a made basket.

Sometimes the greatest trademarks come from the simplest things. For a young broadcaster from Brooklyn, a lifelong Knicks fans and former ball boy, it just came naturally.

Marv Albert had been calling Knicks games since he was a child. Of course, no one other than his family heard any of these self-produced broadcasts, which he would do in front of the family television.

"I was influenced by a number of broadcasters," Albert said during an interview with Charlie Rose on September 4, 1996. "I was able to observe the style; my father had bought me a tape recorder for one of my early birthdays, and I would turn the sound down on the television and I got a crowd record, actually, from [former Knicks broadcaster] Les Keiter, and I would put the record on and do the game from the TV set."

Albert is a broadcasting legend now, but in the late 1950s, he was on the outside and hustling any way he could to get in. Working as a ball boy got him access to the inside, where he would talk to players, hear stories, and put faces with the names of people he needed to know. It got him access to his idol, sports broadcasting pioneer Marty Glickman, who called Knicks and Rangers games. Glickman took a liking to Albert, and the two developed a friendship.

And in the winter of 1963, when Glickman was in Paris and a major snowstorm kept him from getting back to New York, he summoned his protégé to get ready for his big break.

The Knicks played the Celtics on January 27, 1963. And the night before, Albert, at 20 years old, got the last train to Boston. Less than four years later, Albert realized his childhood dream: he was the full-time play-by-play announcer for the Knicks.

Albert came on the scene at exactly the right time. The Knicks were a team on the rise and gaining popularity in New York City as they moved into the new Madison Square Garden. And it was in that first playoff game there, on March 23, 1968, against the Philadelphia 76ers, where a trademark call was made.

As the final seconds ran out on the first quarter, Dick Barnett, Mr. "Fall back, baby!" himself, kicked up his legs and hit a jumper from the corner.

But Albert didn't follow the typical call that had been coined by Chick Hearn in Los Angeles. Instead, he instinctively blurted something he had heard many times from the exclusive vantage point of his days as a ball boy.

"Sid Borgia was a very colorful referee," Albert explained to D'Agostino in *Garden Glory*. "When a player scored and was fouled, he'd say, 'Yesss, and it counts!' He had all these flamboyant ways about him. So it came from that. I picked it up during my ball-boy days, sitting near the court and hearing it.

"Dick Barnett hit a 'Fall back, baby' fling at the buzzer to end the first quarter, and it just came out.

"Then I started to incorporate it [into the broadcasts], and the fans would repeat it back to me. For whatever reason, it just caught on."

Albert called Knicks games for 36 years, including the two championship seasons. As the NBA grew in popularity in the mid-1980s, so did Albert's profile. Through the '80s and '90s, he became known as the voice of the NBA and worked national broadcasts that included so many of Michael Jordan's greatest moments. Along the way, "Yes, and it counts!" became embedded in the basketball lexicon.

"When you try to look for a catch phrase, whatever the sport, it's usually forced," Albert told D'Agostino. "It just happened to work in basketball at a time when the Knicks were becoming very popular and very good."

His connection with the Knicks, however, frayed in the early 2000s, and then Madison Square Garden made the stunning decision to sever ties with the legendary voice, which had become synonymous with Knicks basketball, after the 2003–04 season.

Albert still does national broadcasts on TNT and is now a football commentator with CBS. Albert's son, Kenny, who followed his famous father's footsteps in the business, now works Knicks games as the No. 2 play-by-play announcer behind Mike Breen. On April 17, 2011, when the Knicks played the Celtics in Game 1 of their first-round series in Boston, Marv called the game for TNT while Kenny called it for the MSG Network. It was the first time he and his father worked a Knicks playoff game together.

When he glanced across the broadcast table to see his son, you have to wonder what might have gone through Marv's mind. Actually, it's not that hard to predict.

Yes!

48 Dancing Harry

When you attend a Knicks game these days, the game-operations staff will go out of their way to provide you as much auxiliary entertainment as possible during breaks in the action, just in case the home team isn't living up to its end of the bargain. They'll show videos on the massive GardenVision screens, bring out the

Knicks City Dancers, bust out the T-shirt cannons. They'll pump music through the sound system that will make your skull vibrate with the bass.

And occasionally they'll turn the camera on a fan somewhere in the upper bowl who will entertain the crowd with some dazzling footwork. Or they'll just show you one of the following: an old man who shockingly knows how to breakdance or a fat guy who can shake what his mama gave him (and who probably shouldn't have allowed him seconds).

Pretty much all of these people are planted by the well-meaning game-operations crew, who have learned over time that panning the crowd for spontaneous reactions can lead to unfortunate acts of stupidity by random knuckleheads who've had a little too much to drink.

But in the early 1970s, these kinds of things weren't part of the show. Back then they had this simple yet brilliant concept that the game was the show. People often used timeouts as an opportunity to talk about the game or, in the expensive seats, talk business. These days, the noise is so overwhelming, you need to wait for the ball to go back in play just to have a chance to hear someone speak.

It was in Baltimore where the entertainment of the game, passion for the team, and the creative spontaneity of one confident spectator turned into a enjoyable sideshow. A sausage salesman—which sounds like a lewd put-on but is actually true—named Marvin Cooper got to know one of the Bullets' biggest stars, Earl Monroe. When the two would shoot pool, Cooper would dance and sing to musicians such as Marvin Gaye and Sly and the Family Stone. Monroe suggested he take his act to a stage.

Cooper thought Monroe's stage was as good as any. He began getting up during timeouts and dancing in the aisle at the Baltimore Civic Center. The crowds loved his moves, and in time he would step onto the sidelines of the court to show off his fancy footwork. He became known as "Dancing Harry," with wild outfits of large bell-bottoms and big hats. He'd also extend his arms toward opposing teams to perform hexes, which made the crowds roar even louder.

When Monroe was traded to the Knicks, the glamour had been taken out of the Bullets. They were still a good team, but without the Pearl, the games just didn't have the same atmosphere.

In the spring of 1972, Cooper contacted the Knicks to see if they would allow him to move his show to the Garden. He was told no. Dancing Harry had been the enemy, going back to the previous season's bitter playoff defeat to end their drive for a second-straight title. Dancing Harry wasn't welcome at the Garden—especially not for a playoff game against the Boston Celtics.

Cooper made the trip to New York anyway and managed to get into the building at halftime and found a seat two rows behind the Knicks bench.

"Boston was killing the Knicks, by 20 points, I think," Cooper recalled to the *Daily News*. "Willis turned around, he saw me sitting, he said, 'What are you doing sitting down, Harry?'

"I told him the front office didn't want me to dance," Cooper continued.

"The hell with the front office, Harry," Reed replied. "Do something!"

So Dancing Harry made his Garden debut, and the crowd went wild.

"The whole place erupted," Cooper continued. "I could not hear, there was so much noise."

The Celtics lead disappeared in the second half, and the Knicks came away with the win.

Dancing Harry became a permanent fixture at the Garden during the 1972–73 season. The organist would provide the music and he would go into his dances and, of course, toss hexes toward

Before there were the Knicks City Dancers, there was Dancing Harry.
(Getty Images)

the road teams. He became an instant celebrity, with endorsement deals with clothing and shoe companies and requests to make appearances at nightclubs and even hotels in the Catskills.

Despite his appeal to fans, Dancing Harry wasn't as appreciated by some of the players. Frazier, for one, would gripe, "We win the games, and Harry gets all the press."

Ned Irish finally put a stop to it the following season when he instructed the ushers to inform Cooper he would not be allowed to dance. When he got up to do his thing anyway, he was promptly ejected.

Cooper then took his act to Long Island, where Dancing Harry emerged at New York Nets games at Nassau Coliseum. Julius Erving and the Nets won the ABA title that season. He then became an official mascot when the Indiana Pacers hired him to entertain the crowd at Market Square Arena.

The Knicks invited him back to the Garden in 2003 for the reunion of the '73 championship season.

"Every time I go back to New York, I get chills," he told D'Agostino in *Garden Glory*. "I went to a Knicks game [in the late 1990s]. I had my cape on, and John McEnroe asked me if I was going to perform. I remember so many fans. One time when I was in the Garden, Fred Astaire tapped me and told me, 'Go out there! Go out there!' I mean, Fred Astaire! Can you imagine?"

Just about every team in the NBA has a mascot these days. But the Knicks are one of the few franchises without a mascot. Dancing Harry, though he was borrowed from Baltimore, was the closest thing there was.

49 The Voice of the Garden

He greeted you as if you were an invited guest, and he opened the night with a pitch that sounded like the curtain was rising.

"Good evening, everybody," he would begin. "Welcome to the magic world of Madison Square Garden, the world's most famous arena."

When John Francis Xavier Condon took the mic, that was the signal to stop what you were doing, get to your seat, and get ready for the show. Condon's voice was heard by three generations of Knicks fans, starting at the old Garden in the team's very first season in 1946.

There's a funny story about how his career began. Condon was at a game between the Knicks and Celtics when he was asked to give the public-address announcer role a shot. Then he just kept coming back, night after night.

Over 40 years later, Condon joked to *New York Times* writer Sam Goldaper, "You know, they never came back and told me I had the job. Maybe I ought to call them and find out."

Condon was a classic announcer, with a personable yet authoritative tone. He would raise his voice with excitement—"That was BER-nard King!"—but never ever venture into the realm of giddy, which is where today's over-the-top announcers start the night and only elevate into cliché shtick. Condon combined knowledge of the game with the ability to explain it quickly and simply. And he did it with a twinge of a New York accent.

"No basket, noooooo basket," he would sing after Rockets center Ralph Sampson would tip in a ball that was still on the rim. "That was goaltending."

But when a young Michael Jordan was on a hot streak, Condon's voice would grow impatient, as if glaring at the Knicks bench.

"That was Michael Jordan."

It was a style that the team's current announcer, Mike Walczewski, often imitated as he began his own career.

"I used to imitate John because I wanted to be like him," Walczewski said in a feature on him for the Knicks Web site in 2004. "I have the highest respect for this job. I have fun, but I take it very seriously. The way I perform my job today is a tribute to him."

Walczewski took over the job in 1989 when Condon, at the age of 75, succumbed to cancer. Over the next decade, "Wally" would create his own signature calls—his most popular has to be "PAT-trick Ewing"—while still maintaining the classic control that Condon set as the standard before him.

And in an era of screaming, singing, and even incoherent rambling that leaves you wondering who got the basket and if it was a three-pointer or a two, Walczewski not only tells you who scored, but he'll also give you the score. Sure, that much is lit up on the scoreboard, but some scripts are meant to be followed.

"It's a Garden tradition," Walczewski said. "I think it puts a unique stamp on the job."

It's just one more thing that separates going to the Garden to see an NBA game from anywhere else.

Visit the Old Garden

As the nearly $1 billion transformation of the current Madison Square Garden is under way, there is already a sense of nostalgia about the building as it once was. But by remaining in the same structure, at the very least this new version of the Garden will retain its history.

But there will always be something romantic about the old Garden on 49th Street, with its fancy marquee and looming balcony. And, of course, the atmosphere. It is here where Madison Square Garden became "the Garden."

"The old Garden was a social history of America," Bill Bradley wrote in his book, *Life on the Run*.

Bradley played many games there as a collegiate star at Princeton, but by the time he returned from his years at Oxford to begin his Knicks career, the new Garden was almost finished. In 1968 the home on 49th Street, with its bustling sidewalks where, as a rookie, Bradley almost stepped right into oncoming traffic (had it not been for an alert stranger, Dollar Bill would have been reduced to loose change), was considered outdated and obsolete.

The plan for a new Garden effectively destroyed two New York City landmarks. First, Pennsylvania Station, which was crushed and buried into an underground facility, with the new arena built above. And second, the third version of the Garden, which was demolished by a wrecking ball immediately after the new building opened. There was no thought of preservation here. To quote Joni Mitchell, they paved paradise and put up a parking lot.

Truth be told, the old Garden was hardly a visual paradise. Aside from the magnificent marquee, which lit up 49th Street with its glittering white bulbs, the building itself was a nondescript rectangle that, without the marquee, might be mistaken for a warehouse or uninspiring office building. It was also located in an area of Manhattan called Clinton, or, as real New Yorkers know it, "Hell's Kitchen."

Inside was a different story, however.

"It was the place to be for basketball," said John Andariese, the longtime Knicks broadcaster.

"There was no atmosphere like Madison Square Garden," former Celtics great Satch Sanders told me in April 2011. "Out of all the arenas, there was just never the same kind of feel."

Sanders grew up in New York City and starred at NYU in the late 1950s. He played many games at the old Garden in college and as a visiting player with the Celtics.

"Because the sport was such a big part of the city, the fans were very knowledgeable," Sanders said. "And that's good and bad. You like the fans to make a lot of noise about the game, but you didn't need them to be that knowledgeable about *everything*.

"The other thing you had in those days were a lot of people betting on the games," he continued. "So the abuse was tinged with some anger over what might have occurred on the court."

And at halftime, bookies would gather in the famous lobby to offer up new odds for the second half. The Garden lobby was the traditional meeting place at every event.

And when the new Garden was built, a tradition came to a stunning halt.

"It was shocking when that building went down and there was nowhere to go at halftime," Andariese said. "It was so weird."

The floor was loaded with dead spots, but the rims were, too. Players often referred to the Garden rims as "sewers" because, as Bradley explained, "almost everything went down them."

And for the better part of its existence, the home team seemed to go down with regularity each season. Once the Knicks became more of a main attraction in the late 1950s and early 1960s, the teams weren't very good.

"But people loved the players," Andariese said.

By the late 1960s and early '70s, once the Garden was gone and the crowds had moved to Midtown South, the area by the old arena became a meeting place of a seedier attraction. The stretch of Eighth Avenue from 42nd Street up to 50th Street became notoriously known as the "Minnesota Strip," which some say is a reference to the crowds of Midwestern tourists that flocked to Broadway shows. But local legend suggests the moniker was used by the New York City police to describe the area's darker side, which saw a large number of the teenage girls from the Midwest who had turned to prostitution.

Twenty years later, the old Garden property was sold and the massive World Wide Plaza complex was built, with a 49-story tower and an illuminated peak that blends well in the classic skyline. When the parking lot was excavated to begin the construction in 1989, workers discovered a time capsule of sorts: the basement of the old Garden, dressing rooms, and other rooms, still intact.

Today there is nothing left of the old Garden. No signs, no landmarks. But if you walk up Eighth Avenue from the current Garden, you can stop midway between 49th and 50th Streets and know the famous marquee once hung right above you and that there was a time in the city's rich history, and the game's proud lineage, that this spot was one of the most famous in the world.

51 Good...Like Nedick's!

Before the days of the club-seating menu and waiter service that come as part of the lower-bowl seating at the new Garden, there was only one easy choice to make when it came to grabbing a bite to eat at a Knicks game in the old Garden.

Nedick's was as much a Garden tradition as the Knicks themselves. It was a fast-food chain started in 1913 by partners Robert T. Neely and Orville A. Dickinson (Nedick's being a combination of their last names, of course). It began as a stand on 23rd Street and Broadway. The restaurant, which boasted affordable prices, gained popularity, according to the *Daily News*, with stories about how a young actor named Gregory Peck lived on a "nine-cent Nedick's breakfast" while working his way up in the profession.

Nathan's in Coney Island is a New York City institution, but Nedick's was by far the more popular brand. Like Nathan's, Nedick's also benefited from its prime location—next to the Garden marquee on 49th Street. The restaurant was an instant hit with fans, reporters, and even players.

In 2003 the *New York Times* called Nedick's "the Starbucks of New York"— somewhat fitting since at the World Wide Plaza, where the old Garden and that famous Nedick's used to stand, there are now not one but two Starbucks.

Nedick's offered a typical fast-food menu but were best known for their signature hot dogs with various toppings. And the smell of the butter-toasted buns filled the lobby as an aromatic siren song, luring you in for a hot dog and another famous addition, orange soda.

"When I was working with the Guardian Angels in the subways, Nedick's was our oasis," Curtis Sliwa told the *Daily News* in 2003. "We'd say we were going to 'the Orange Room.' It was upscale dining for the blue-collar guy."

Nedick's was so much part of the fabric of the Garden and Knicks basketball that legendary announcer Marty Glickman came up with the catch phrase, "Good...like Nedick's!" whenever one of the Knicks stars of the time—be it Carl Braun, Harry Gallatin, or Richie Guerin—made a big shot.

When the old Garden came down, so did Nedick's. It ceased operations in 1981. A brief revival in the early 2000s reintroduced Nedick's to New York City and Penn Station eaters, but the magic was lost.

Get Your Jersey at Cosby's

Though Nedick's didn't make the move from the 49th Street Garden, there was another famous storefront that did: Cosby and Co.

For 50 years, and especially in the era before officially licensed apparel and the Internet, Cosby's was always *the* place to get your jersey or anything Knicks. And, if you're a traditionalist, it still is.

Cosby and Co. was founded by Gerry Cosby, a New England–born goaltender who played for the Massachusetts Rangers, who won the 1933 World Ice Hockey championship in Czechoslovakia. Cosby allowed just one goal in five games and upset the defending champion team from Canada in the gold medal game.

He went on to play for the New York Rovers of the Eastern League and also worked as a practice goalie for the Rangers. It was there where he started to develop ideas to improve hockey equipment, which eventually led to him opening his own sporting-goods store in 1938.

His storefront at the old Garden was at the corner of 49th Street and Eighth Avenue. Cosby's store was like a candy shop for athletes and fans who got to see and feel—and even wear—the same gear that was being worn on the ice and basketball court. Mr. Cosby appreciated anyone who shared his passion for sporting goods.

When the old Garden came down in 1968, Cosby and Co. moved across the way to Pennsylvania Plaza before opening up a location in the lobby of the new Garden in the late 1970s. It was a cramped store but had a wondrous display of jerseys from not just the Knicks and Rangers but seemingly every major professional team. They had game-worn jerseys, game-used equipment, and just about anything autographed you can imagine.

Much like Nedick's from the old Garden, Cosby's often became the meeting place at the new Garden before games, where you could kill time gawking at jerseys and collectibles. Circling the small rectangular store, surrounded by glass display cases as if it were a jewelry shop, was like browsing a museum.

And if you had the money, you could walk out of there with a customized jersey, fresh for the game, knowing that you had the exact same thing being worn on the court. Cosby's has been responsible for stitching the names and numbers on the actual game jerseys for the Knicks for over a half-century.

For instance, when the Carmelo Anthony trade went down on February 22, 2011, Cosby's was on call to get the uniforms for the six new Knicks players done in time for their anticipated debut the following night.

Anthony wore No. 15 in Denver, but he couldn't take that number with the Knicks because it had been twice retired in honor of Hall of Famers Dick McGuire and Earl Monroe. Anthony chose No. 7, which he chose by taking his high school number (22, which was also retired, for Dave DeBusschere) and subtracting his Nuggets number.

Sure enough, the blue No. 7 that Anthony pulled on that night (the Knicks wore their throwback uniforms for that game) in his debut against the Milwaukee Bucks came straight from Cosby's.

The store has since moved from the Garden lobby to a bigger location just a short walk across Seventh Avenue on 31st Street. But the tradition still carries on strong. If you attend a Knicks game and you're looking to buy a jersey—or just browse an amazing collection of uniforms and gear—head to Cosby's.

53 The Blue and Orange

One of the special things that comes with being an original franchise is the tradition of the uniform and maintaining its classic look. Over the six decades of NBA basketball, teams have come and gone, uniforms have changed, colors have been added… But aside from a brief—and regrettable—stint in the early 1980s, the Knicks have maintained the same basic style.

When the team was formed in 1946, the nickname was chosen as a connection to the proud history of the city and the identity of its people. The colors—orange, white, and blue—also represent the city; they are the official colors in the New York City flag.

So why does New York City's flag have the colors orange and blue? It is emblematic of the early history of the city, which was founded by Dutch settlers in the 17th century. The official flag of the Netherlands from 1625—when the Dutch founded New Amsterdam, which would later become New York—is orange, white, and blue.

The first Knicks uniform was like most in those days: simple. Like the Boston Celtics—who with the Knicks comprise the only two of the league's original franchises still located in their founding cities—the team used "New York" as its identity for both home and away, a tradition that remained for most of the franchise's existence and is still used today. The lettering was blue, trimmed in orange, and the shorts had a belt.

Why a belt? To keep the shorts from falling down, of course. (Sorry, couldn't resist.)

In 1961–62, the uniform changed subtly, with a Roman font used in the lettering of "New York," which still arched across the chest in blue trimmed by orange over the bold numbers in the same color format. The belted shorts remained through the 1967–68 season.

Along with the switch to a drawstring inside the shorts—and remember, this was the late 1960s, we're talking shorts as a fitting *adjective*, not just a noun—the uniform had a noteworthy change that also remains the look to this day: the lettering was reversed to orange with a blue outline.

And if you know what the Baltimore Bullets were wearing in those days, you'd agree that what the Knicks did was subtle. Thankfully subtle.

Curiously, it took another year for the Knicks to change their road uniforms to match the home threads (Cosby and Co. must have been behind schedule).

For some god-awful reason in 1979, someone came up with the brilliant idea (sarcasm) to turn completely away from tradition. Why on earth would someone want to do that? I'll share here an unfounded rumor of an unnamed marketing guy who worked for the Knicks at the time and was a proud graduate of the University of Pennsylvania, which happened to reach the Final Four in a dramatic run in 1979. Penn's colors are a deep blue and red.

Teams were constantly changing styles, especially after the ABA merger. Since the 1990s, when licensed apparel became a welcome part of revenue, having alternative uniforms has been good for business. But in 1979 it was just about changing an image. The

Making Some Green

The Knicks in green? Red Holzman is rolling over in his grave. There was a time when anything green was an unwelcome sight at Madison Square Garden. But in the era of NBA marketing and revenue from jersey sales—and the popularity of unique jerseys—anything is possible. The Knicks debuted in green (with orange and black stripes) on St. Patrick's Day 2006 and enjoyed a 105–103 win over the Detroit Pistons. It became an annual tradition on or around St. Patrick's Day, but then in 2008–09, the green jersey was added to Christmas Day 2009, as the Knicks were in green to play the Bulls (in red) to create the holiday color scheme. The plan was repeated on Christmas Day 2010 with the Knicks and the Heat.

Garden's other tenant, the New York Rangers, swapped out their classic look ("Rangers" written diagonally down the front) for a uniform with the team's shield logo on the front and a design that resembled, well, pajamas. (Actually, to me they *were* pajamas because at the age of six, I owned a pair thanks to my hockey-loving parents. Two years later, I became an Islanders fan. Twenty years after that, the Islanders introduced the silly fisherman logo, and I almost completely gave up on hockey as a result.)

The Knicks of the late 1970s were a shell of the great team they had been in the early part of the decade. With the Rangers skating across the Garden ice in pajamas, the idea must have sounded good to make total fools of the Knicks, too. (Coincidentally, the Rangers went back to their classic uniforms for the 1978–79 season and promptly reached the Stanley Cup Finals. The prosecution rests, Your Honor.)

So along with a slight change in colors (orange was changed to maroon and the blue became a deeper blue…mysteriously similar to Penn's colors at the time), there was a departure from the classic look of "New York" across the chest. The Knicks went completely out of the box on the new design, with the number on the chest and "Knicks" across the stomach. It was similarly reversed on the back, with the number above the player's last name.

Thankfully, this design lasted only four seasons before returning to the classic style from the championship era. And since 1983 the uniform has gone through some subtle changes—black was added to the color scheme in the 1990s, for example—but the main scheme has remained the same: "New York" across the chest in orange lettering with blue trim.

The Knicks did briefly bring back the ugly jersey era when they wore the 1979–83 edition a few times in an ironic celebration of a heritage marketing scheme. These days, when there's heritage to celebrate, the Knicks wear the uniform from the championship era.

Despite my biased disgust, some fans actually liked the Penn Quakers–colored, ABA-inspired uniform the Knicks wore from 1979 to 1983. The good news is, you can probably find one to purchase online, because in the mid-2000s the NBA started reintroducing past uniforms as part of the Hardwood Classics collection. The bad news is, you'll look awful.

54 Go New York, Go New York, Go!

The best thing about living in New York is that an opportunity awaits you every day. Jesse Itzler had enjoyed some mild success as a young musician who made, as he put it, "frat rap" in the early 1990s, at a time when Vanilla Ice was doing all he could to destroy any chance of a white guy ever getting respect in the hip-hop world. Thankfully, the Beastie Boys already broke the barrier in the 1980s and another Brooklyn crew, 3rd Bass, was doing quality work in the underground.

And then there was Itzler, a Long Island native whose first effort, *Thirty Footer in Your Face*, produced a Billboard Top 100 song ("Shake It Like a White Girl") and another single ("College Girls Are Easy"), under the stage name Jesse Jaymes in 1991. Two years later he was asked to write a radio jingle for a children's clothing company owned by a woman named Nancy Grunfeld. You may have heard of her husband, Ernie. You know, the former Knick who, at the time, was general manager of the team.

Itzler saw an opportunity and used the connection to pitch the Knicks, his favorite team, a theme song. And so the anthem came to be, with its turbocharged refrain, "Go New York, Go New York, Go!" that brings the Garden to its feet to this day.

The song debuted during the 1993–94 season, just in time for the franchise's long-awaited return to the NBA Finals.

Just about every team in New York has a theme song. The Yankees have the famous "Here Come the Yankees" fight song, the Mets have the adorable "Meet the Mets"...even the Rangers have the triumphant "Rangers Victory Song," which sounds straight out of a college stadium.

The Knicks have had other songs written for them in the past, such as "We Are New York and We Love Basketball," which debuted with Earl Monroe's arrival, and Paulette LaMelle's "Get Ready, Here Come the Knicks." And in 2005, Doug E. Fresh's "Take Me Home," with the lyric, "True New Yorkers wear orange-and-blue," was adopted for a short time as the team's official theme song.

But only Itzler's "Go New York, Go New York, Go!" song had staying power, despite its cheesy lyrics and repetitive call-and-reply refrain. Over the years there were changes made to the song. Itzler's record label, Alphabet City All-Stars, reintroduced the song in 2000. Then in 2009, hip-hop legend Q-Tip released his own version, with the "Go New York, Go New York, Go!" refrain included. And in 2011 Swizz Beatz put yet another spin on it in time for the playoffs.

Itzler arrived at exactly the right time, in an era where music pumped from high-tech sound systems displaced the classic organists who used to play during timeouts. The 1990s was the era of arena rock, and Itzler's song became a trendsetter.

He went on to record 50 songs for pro teams and came up with the Emmy Award–winning "I Love This Game" theme for the NBA.

"There's nothing like going to the Garden and hearing your song on the loudspeaker with 20,000 people waving their towels," Itzler told CNNMoney.com in 2004. "It's as close to being Jay-Z as I'll ever be."

55 Gawk at Celebrity Row

When the Garden became *The* Garden, when the Knicks became one of the city's great attractions, and games became not just something to see but to be seen, celebrity row came to be. And since the early 1970s, when the earning power of young actors such as Woody Allen afforded them the opportunity to sit as close to the action as possible, celebrities became an added attraction to Knicks home games.

Allen was one of the pioneers among the most faithful celebrity Knicks fans. He started out at the old Garden, though up in the stands, and eventually became a courtside fixture at the new Garden. Actually, Woody is rarely on the court. He prefers a seat behind the broadcast table (perhaps so he can get a peek at the monitor for replays).

Back then Dustin Hoffman, famous from his role as Ben Braddock in *The Graduate* (1967), started making regular appearances at the Garden along with his pal Robert Redford (who often rocked his cowboy hat, a nod to his breakthrough role as the Sundance Kid).

Sure, the Lakers, too, always drew an A-list crowd at the Forum, especially during the Showtime era. (And when Pat Riley came to New York in 1991, Lakers superfan Jack Nicholson was even spotted at the Garden.)

And in the 1990s, the Knicks' version of Nicholson—and perhaps the next generation's Woody Allen—had worked his way down the sections to become another courtside fixture. But unlike anyone else who ever took a seat along celebrity row, filmmaker Spike Lee actually had an impact in a game. Or so goes the legend of Game 5 of the 1994 Eastern Conference Finals, when Reggie Miller, inspired by trash talk from Lee, scored 25 points in the fourth quarter to lead a stunning comeback win for the Indiana Pacers that put the Knicks one defeat away from elimination.

"They really wanted my neck," Lee joked to the *New York Times* several years later.

Lee engages in regular conversations with many of the league's stars, and there are times fans sitting higher in the Garden will growl at Lee to keep quiet. And there are times when opposing stars have a lot to say to him (Kevin Garnett spent most of the game shouting expletives at Lee in a 2011 game).

But more often than not, the mood is much more jovial among the regulars, who include Matthew Modine, *The Sopranos'* Steve Schirripa, comedian Chris Rock, and Tracy Morgan.

And then there was a time when Nate Robinson backpedaled his way to actor Will Ferrell to slap five after a made basket. Robinson, a huge fan of Ferrell's movies, often borrowed the phrase, "Shake and bake!" from *Talladega Nights* when he'd get on one of his trademark hot streaks.

Mostly everyone who sits along celebrity row. (The tickets these days are generally comped by the team, by the way. It's good business for both.) is showed on GardenVision and gets at least polite applause if not, like Howard Stern or Rock or Morgan, a rousing ovation. But not everyone is appreciated by the Garden faithful. For instance, Donald Trump, despite his tremendous support for the team—he was to play a major role in recruiting LeBron James in 2010—gets booed. And the night during the 2010–11 season when teenybopper heartthrob Justin Bieber slipped into a courtside seat drew such a nasty reaction that Bieber didn't return for the second half.

Only in New York, right?

But nothing will top the time late in the 2002–03 season when Latrell Sprewell stood on the sideline right in front of celebrity row ready to inbound the ball and he felt a tug at his arm. He turned quickly to see an inebriated Calvin Klein—yes, the famous designer—attempting to start a conversation. The 60-year-old Klein, a huge fan of the NBA game, was literally on the court.

Security escorted the fashion legend back to his seat, where he crash-landed on a few people. Two weeks later, Klein checked into a substance abuse–rehabilitation center. Shortly after that, the "Calvin Klein Law" was signed by Mayor Michael Bloomberg. The law prohibits anyone from entering the playing area of a major sporting event in New York City and carries a fine of up to $5,000. And if contact is made with an athlete, it could result in a year in jail and up to a $25,000 fine.

There are no laws, of course, about the athletes making contact with the spectators, which can happen from time to time.

Paul Pierce did just that when the Celtics completed a four-game sweep of the Knicks in the first round of the 2011 playoffs. "Don't worry," he told Lee. "You guys are on the right track."

New York City taxi mogul Andrew Murstein then said, "Take care of the Heat for us."

Pierce looked back and winked.

56 Dollar Bill vs. Cazzie

In many respects, during the early 1970s, *the Knicks* were the celebrities to see at the Garden. Clyde, Pearl, and Fall Back, Baby were icons. Reed and DeBusschere were admired for toughness that most men only dreamed they had.

There was no debating the appreciation up and down those Knicks rosters—until you came to one name: Bill Bradley.

Make no mistake—Bradley was a star. He might have been the biggest star on the team, with a name that was known throughout the sport before he even came to the NBA in 1967. Bradley was a legend at Princeton who would draw standing-room-only crowds at the biggest venues in the country. He was the player a young Ned Irish would have pointed to as proof of the vision he had for the college game some three decades before.

"You can't imagine how big a star Bradley was," former *Daily News* beat writer Phil Pepe told D'Agostino in *Garden Glory*. "He was the Michael Jordan of his day, as a college player. He was a one-man team...I'll never forget Lenny Shecter writing a column saying that someday this guy was going to be President of the United States."

(As it turned out, he came close. Bradley, a longtime New Jersey senator, ran for president in 2000 but withdrew during the Democratic primaries and put his support behind Al Gore.)

But this wasn't your ordinary college jock taking his game to the pro level. He was drafted by the Knicks in 1965 and put his basketball career on hold for two years at Oxford University on a Rhodes Scholarship. The Knicks would have to wait.

Though Bradley was from Crystal City, Missouri, Irish argued—and won—that playing at Princeton made him eligible to the Knicks as a territorial pick that year. The following year the Knicks used the first overall pick to take another college superstar, forward Cazzie Russell. And so began a rivalry that had Knicks fans divided for years.

When Bradley arrived in 1967, he signed a $100,000 contract. In his story for the *New York Post* the next morning, beat writer Leonard Lewin coined the nickname "Dollar Bill."

Russell already had two years under his belt and had become a starter at the small-forward position. Bradley, at 6'5", played forward in college but was labeled as a shooting guard. But in the NBA, Bradley wasn't quick enough to play shooting guard. And it showed.

From there developed separate legions of fans: those for Cazzie and those for Bradley. You couldn't root for both.

"To the fans our competition highlighted our differences," Bradley wrote in his book, *Life on the Run*. "He was flamboyant; I was not. He was black; I was white. He verbalized constantly; I was careful with words, preferring to listen. He was an explosive player who generated much excitement through his one-on-one skills; I was a methodical player who often needed a screen to get my shot and concentrated on floor play.

"Finally, we had a history of competition that dated back to 1964 when my Princeton team played Cazzie's Michigan team twice. The game in Madison Square Garden on December 28 permanently etched our adversary roles in the minds of the basketball public. Princeton had a 14-point lead when I fouled out with four minutes remaining. Cazzie and Michigan caught and beat

Princeton in that stretch, avoiding a loss which would have jolted them from their No. 1 national ranking. Although I outscored Cazzie, his team won."

The tables would turn on January 21, 1969, when Russell broke his ankle and was out for the rest of the season. Bradley took his spot and, like Lou Gehrig with Wally Pipp, never gave it back. Though for a short while, after Russell returned the next season, not everyone agreed.

"We divided the basketball fans in New York into warring camps," Bradley wrote in his book. "The press and public emphasized our dissimilarities. Cab drivers would tell me Cazzie should start. Cab drivers would tell me I should start. People at courtside would do the same. If Cazzie or I missed several shots during warm-ups, someone would invariably yell that the other one of us should be starting. Both of us had a hard time accepting anything less."

Though the two maintained a mutual respect, the tension created a healthy level of competition. They were teammates when the Knicks won their first championship in 1969–70, with Russell a key member of Red Holzman's Minutemen. But with Reed ailing before the 1971–72 season, the Knicks needed a center, and Holzman had to find his best but most expendable asset to help fill the huge void left by Reed's injury, which limited him to just 11 games that season.

Holzman traded Russell to the San Francisco Warriors for Jerry Lucas, one of the great unsung trades in franchise history. For one, it brought in Lucas, an outstanding center with a quirky personality and high intelligence who fit right in with this group. But it also meant Holzman had settled the long debate among the fans.

"Red had picked *me*," Bradley wrote. "The effect was exhilarating."

The effect was Bradley's best pro season, with 15.1 points and four assists per game on 46.5 percent shooting. The following season, Bradley improved even more with 16.1 points and 4.5 assists, and he played all 82 games, plus all 17 playoff games, which, of course, led to the second NBA championship.

The win was celebrated after a 102–93 victory in Game 5 at the Forum in Los Angeles. As the final buzzer sounded, Bradley leaped into Reed's arms.

Longtime Garden photographer George Kalinsky got the famous shot of the exuberant Bradley hugging Reed—but he knew where to look.

"Before Game 5," Kalinsky told D'Agostino in *Garden Glory*, "Bradley comes over to me and says, 'We're gonna win...Not only are we gonna win tonight, but when we win, watch where the captain is, because I'm jumping in his arms.' And that's what happened."

 **Nate the Great**

During the bleakest of times through the worst era in franchise history, there was, at least, one source of entertainment that made some of the most depressing nights at the Garden at least a little better.

If Nate Robinson could be compared to anyone we've so far mentioned in this book, the best we could do is describe him as Dancing Harry in uniform.

The 5'9" dynamo was an unfettered bundle of adrenaline, who loved the fun of basketball, the thrill of crowd reactions, and the bright lights of the Garden stage. He was a pure entertainer, a showman. Despite his diminutive stature, Robinson proved himself to be one of the game's all-time greatest dunkers. He has two slam-dunk titles (joining Kenny "Sky" Walker as one of two Knicks to win the NBA's showcase event on All-Star Saturday), including the unforgettable time he donned the Knicks' green uniform and jumped over defending champion Dwight "Superman" Howard, making newscasts around the country.

He called himself "KryptoNate." Nike put up a billboard of this new alter-ego outside the Garden on 34th Street and Seventh Avenue. The littlest man in the NBA was now bigger than life in New York City.

"He's like a freak of nature," LeBron James once said.

In reality, he belonged on the Harlem Globetrotters (and, quite frankly, I believe he could revive that show if only they had the money to lure him away from the NBA) and not on a losing team that only looked worse when the giddy little guard bounced around the court as if the scoreboard had been shut off and no one was keeping score.

And as maddening as he could be to his coaches, the Garden fans loved him.

They called him Nate the Great. No, actually, he called himself that.

"They don't call me Nate the Great for nothing," he once said when Larry Brown was tough on him as a rookie. "I've got to live up to the name."

He often did with his spontaneity, which in the blink of an eye could turn a forgettable loss into a night you'd be talking about for a week.

Did you see him score 41 points off the bench against the Hawks?

Did you see Nate make Jose Calderon literally fall on his butt with that crossover?

Did you see him block the shot of 7'6" center Yao Ming?

Did you see Nate catch that one-handed rebound dunk against the Celtics?

Nate Robinson blazes past Spurs forward Tim Duncan for the easy score.
(Getty Images)

Of course along with these jaw-dropping moments came the gritted-teeth reactions from coaches such as Brown, Isiah Thomas, and Mike D'Antoni, who were often infuriated with his penchant for breaking plays and freelancing. And, of course, preening for the crowd.

He was eventually traded to the Celtics toward the end of the 2009–10 season and left behind a legacy as one of the franchise's all-time most entertaining personalities that unfortunately came during the franchise's worst era. The losing made it harder to enjoy him, but then again, some people feel the way he played didn't lend itself to a winning team.

"I'm just me. I don't really think about it too much, but I don't worry about what people think," Robinson once told me about his naysayers. "I really don't mind the criticism. I am who I am. God made me for a reason, just like everybody else around the world."

No, God didn't make anyone else in the world like this one.

58 Reggie F——ing Miller

Michael Jordan, the ultimate Knick killer, incited fear mixed with an undeniable dose of admiration that caused an overwhelming conflict of emotions throughout the Garden faithful.

But Reggie Miller? He was a true villain, unquestionably the most reviled opponent in franchise history.

"He's always going to be part of Knickerbocker infamy," Spike Lee told *Newsday* in 2005.

Lee, of course, has played a role in creating it.

The Knicks had finally slain their nemesis, the Chicago Bulls (sans Jordan), in the 1994 Eastern Conference semifinals, and all that stood between them and their first trip to the NBA Finals was the Indiana Pacers. After winning the first two games at the Garden in relatively comfortable fashion, the series was suddenly tied after a pair of blowout losses at Market Square Arena in Indianapolis.

Lee then made a bet with Miller before Game 5. If the Knicks won, Miller had to visit Mike Tyson in prison. If the Pacers won, Lee would have to cast Miller's wife in his next movie.

It appeared like Miller was headed to iron bars and Iron Mike as the Knicks carried a comfortable 70–58 lead into the fourth quarter. Lee got a bit excited and began to taunt Miller. And suddenly, a switch was flipped.

The Knicks franchise has seen its share of devastating performances by opponents before. George Mikan drove Joe Lapchick mad in the '52 and '53 NBA Finals. Earl Monroe basically stole the chance for a back-to-back championship in '71. Larry Bird put an end to the Bernard King show in the '84 conference semifinals. And, as always, there was Michael in '89, '91, '92, '93, and '96.

But what happened in the fourth quarter of Game 5 on June 1, 1994, would send shudders through the franchise—shudders that turned to shivers every time Miller stepped foot in the building from that moment on.

It started with a three-pointer just seconds into the quarter. And then it just kept coming. Bombs dropped from every angle, and with each came a message for Lee, who would yell back. As the Knicks lead suddenly turned into a deficit, Miller turned to Lee and put his hands around his neck and let him know: *Your team is choking.*

"I wanted to drive a stake through their heart," Miller said.

Behind 25 fourth-quarter points by Miller, the Pacers pulled off a 93–86 win to take a stunning 3–2 lead in the best-of-seven series. Indiana was headed home needing just one win to reach their first NBA Finals.

When asked what had gotten into Miller, Pacers power forward Antonio Davis said, "I think it was Spike Lee. Tell him thanks for us."

Pat Riley was furious at Lee and the next day called him out for getting involved with the opponent. Lee was on the back page of every New York tabloid. He was also courtside at a hostile Market Square Arena for Game 6, front-and-center, wearing his team's colors. The Knicks came through with one of their biggest playoff wins of that era, 98–91, to send the series back to New York for Game 7.

"I felt like I had more at stake than the players," Lee joked to the *New York Times* in 1999.

The Knicks won the series and avoided a devastating collapse, but a year later, Miller and the Pacers were back. The Knicks were up by six points with 18.7 seconds left and appeared to be on their way to a series-opening win. But Miller drilled a three-pointer with 16 seconds left to slice the lead in half. On the ensuing inbounds, Anthony Mason—not the best decision-maker on the team—attempted to pass the ball to Greg Anthony, who stumbled. Miller helped him with a push to the lower back that went unnoticed—or was ignored—by the referees, and as Anthony fell to the court, Mason had already let go of the pass. The ball went right to Miller, who took two dribbles to the three-point line, turned, and fired. Just like that, the score was tied at 105.

John Starks was fouled by Sam Mitchell with 13.2 seconds left and went to the line but missed both. On the second miss, Patrick Ewing set himself for the rebound, but Miller got to it first and was fouled by Mason. Miller nailed both free throws with 2.1 seconds left for the win. The shocking, maddening win. Eight points in 8.9 seconds.

And as he bolted off the Garden court, fans near the tunnel could hear him taunt what he only said symbolically a year before: "Choke artists!"

The Knicks would lose that series, though they would battle back once again after going down 3–1 to force a seventh game at the Garden. Ewing missed a finger roll at the buzzer. Miller decided to save any more talk of choking. Instead, he was all choked up.

There was some measure of revenge in 1999 when the teams met again in the Eastern Conference Finals. Larry Johnson had the four-point play in Game 3 and Miller was the one who choked this time, with a 3-for-18 shooting performance in a 90–82 series-clinching win for the Knicks.

The final word, however, came a year later when the two rivals met once more for a trip to the NBA Finals. In Game 6 at the Garden, with the Knicks trailing 3–2, Miller scored 17 of his 34 points in the fourth quarter to close the Garden down for the summer in a 93–80 win.

The villain had done it again. New Yorkers trudged home miserable, cursing his name. And you know what? He was cursing right back.

"To Reggie, New York fans are condescending, overindulged, spoiled basketball supremacists," Miller's famous sister, Cheryl, told *Newsday*'s Barbara Barker in 2005. "He's loved playing at the Garden. Every time he came to New York, he was going to show them exactly how basketball needed to be played."

59 Take In a Game from the 400s

In March 2011 the Knicks announced that ticket prices would be raised by 49 percent for the 2011–12 season. The highest increases were coming in the lower bowl, where the average fan in the past may have been able to sit on rare occasions.

In the old days, maybe you could sneak around the building during a game to slip into a choice seat that had been left vacant for the night, the same way Marv Albert and his brothers used to do it at the old Garden. Get to know a few ushers and you're in. But those days don't exist anymore.

Today it's expensive just getting in the building, no matter where you sit. Before the 1991 renovation, which added skyboxes high above the event floor, the upper bowl was known as "the Blue Seats." Just a guess: this was because the seats were, well, blue.

The Blues were a rowdy lot, the boisterous, unwashed masses who were disconnected from the cake-eaters in the lower bowl. Down there was Wall Street; up there were the street sweepers.

And as long as you rooted for the Knicks, you were one of them.

I wrote a column for *Newsday*, partly in reaction to the ticket-price hike and also about my early introductions to the Garden from those beautiful blues:

> The Garden buzz was something I had only read about. The roar was something I only heard through the television. Those bright stage lights were a bit discolored on my parents' Zenith.
>
> My first time in the building was sometime in the mid-1980s to see the circus. I remember I spent most of the time staring at the copper ceiling. The second time was to see St. John's, with Boo Harvey and Michael Porter, play against Rik Smits and Marist in a semifinal game of the ECAC Holiday Festival in 1987.
>
> It wasn't until April 1991 that as a gift, I got tickets to see the Knicks for the first time. Pretty good matchup, too: They played Michael Jordan and the Bulls. If I'm not mistaken, Gerald Wilkins was hurt that night, so starting in his place was a CBA refugee named John Starks. But it was a second-year player named Brian Quinnett, a second-round pick, who stole the show off the bench by outscoring

Jordan 16–5 in the second quarter as the Knicks took a stunning 62–44 lead.

But a reality check was in store as Jordan scorched Quinnett and the Knicks in the second half. The Bulls outscored the Knicks 30–12 in the third and rolled to a 101–91 win.

It was hard to go away entirely disappointed. I mean, I finally got in the building. Well, sort of. I literally had my back to the wall behind me in the 400s, the former Blue Seats, where the salt-of-the-earth fans still exist in a stratosphere so high and far from the court that at one point, I could swear I took a high-five from Lady Liberty when Quinnett drilled one of his two three-pointers in the game.

What I realized that night was that we may have been far from the stage, but the chants and the energy and the passion all seemed to develop from the 400s. It then would cascade down the upper bowl like a waterfall and splash over the silver spooners in the lower bowl and onto the court.

Just being in the building mattered for certain moments. I wasn't there to feel Patrick Ewing's outstretched arms hugging the crowd after Game 7 of the Eastern Conference finals in 1994, but I was for Larry Johnson's four-point play in 1999. I can't imagine that any other event produced as spontaneously loud a moment as that.

My colleagues on the beat often roll their eyes at the fact that after almost five full seasons and nearly 200 home games, I still maintain a sense of wonder about being courtside at the Garden… In fact, I couldn't contain my smile as I felt that famous buzz before Game 3 of the first-round series against the Celtics in 2011. It was my first playoff game at the Garden as a reporter. I was literally on the court (press row is right on the baseline), and for a kid who only experienced such things though his television, it was literally a thrill to be there.

I did also have the fortune of being on the court—actually on the hardwood and, to add to the thrill, on camera for MSG Network—when Carmelo Anthony and the new-look Knicks took the floor February 23, 2011, for the first time after the blockbuster trade. Al Trautwig was in my ear and asked me to describe the scene. I didn't initially look toward Carmelo, who wore a big smile the entire night.

Instead, my instinct was to look upward, into the darkness of the 400s, the old Blue Seats, toward the place I sat 21 years before, with my back to the wall, just happy to be in the building.

A nearly billion-dollar transformation project has to get paid for somehow, so despite frustrations, you can't begrudge the business decision to raise prices to inject more revenue. Of course this is the right time; with Carmelo and Amar'e Stoudemire and the return of this franchise to high-end status, it's basic supply-and-demand economics.

But something has to be left sacred, and if there is somewhere to be spared from the price hike, let it be for those hardy souls in the 400s. Let it be for the place where the energy builds and boils over until the entire arena is caught up in the buzz. Let it be for those with their back to the concrete wall, straining to decipher Landry Fields from Shawne Williams, just happy to be in the building.

60 Jeff Van-GUN-Dy!

There is a story Rick Pitino once told about a time during his brief tenure as Knicks coach when he was on location to shoot a commercial for a BMW dealer who gave him use of a car for his first season in New York. A half-hour shoot turned into an ordeal that took an entire afternoon, mainly because every time the camera would roll, a fan would drive by, see Pitino, and yell, "Go back to college!"

But Pitino's Providence pipeline served the Knicks well in the 1990s. Jeff Van Gundy was a graduate assistant under Pitino on that Friars team that reached the Final Four in 1987. Van Gundy remained at Providence when Pitino went to the Knicks, but the connection paved the way for Van Gundy's arrival two years later, when Pitino left for Kentucky and his assistant, Stu Jackson, was promoted to head coach. Jackson was also a member of Pitino's Providence staff and when he was looking for a third assistant, Jackson brought in Van Gundy.

"I was amazed at how good these guys were," Van Gundy told D'Agostino in *Garden Glory*. "Stu never introduced me, so they may have thought I was a ball boy or something."

That didn't last for long, as the young assistant immediately gained the respect of the most important players on the team, starting with Patrick Ewing. Van Gundy was a hustler, a worker. Pat Riley was so impressed by him that he kept him on the staff after he arrived in 1991. "You can be a head coach in this league," the nattily attired Riley once told him, "but you've got to start dressing better."

But unlike Riley, he wasn't the Armani type. And unlike Pitino, he wasn't the kind of guy who drove a BMW. Along with his short stature, drawn eyes, and balding head, Van Gundy completed the Everyman look a short while later by driving a Honda Accord.

No, he wasn't Hollywood. But that was okay because this was New York, where Van Gundy resembled so many of the bleary-eyed, rumpled suits who wandered into the Garden after yet another brutal day on Wall Street in the early 1990s. (Coincidentally, as Van Gundy's look improved over the years, so did the stock market.)

He was the son of a coach and might as well have been a long-lost nephew of Red Holzman, who would have appreciated Van Gundy's focus on defense and the selflessness he demanded. Offense? Well, that's another story. Van Gundy's teams were often the best in the league at stopping you, but they made scoring look a lot harder than it should. In other words, his teams fit the coach: not very easy on the eyes.

But, like him, they most often found a way to come out on top.

Van Gundy got the job as a result of a mutual realization between the Knicks and Don Nelson that Nellieball was just not fit for Ewing or New York. (Nelson actually tried to get the Knicks to trade Ewing in 1995.) Van Gundy finished the 1995–96 season as interim coach. His first win was a surprising 32-point blowout over Michael Jordan and the Bulls in Chicago. It was one of only 10 losses the record-breaking Bulls would suffer that season.

After finishing the season with a 13–10 record, the Knicks swept the Cavaliers but then were eliminated by the Bulls in the Eastern Conference semifinals. It was looking to be a big off-season, as the Knicks had salary-cap space and were prepared to spend big. There were some flirtations with Indiana Pacers coach Larry Brown, but Van Gundy had earned the job.

Over the next two seasons, the Knicks remained among the league's elite but couldn't overcome two major setbacks—the costly suspensions in Game 5 against the Miami Heat in the '97 playoffs and Ewing's season-ending wrist injury in 1997–98. Then the 1998–99 lockout season looked to be a disaster. The team, with new additions such as Latrell Sprewell and Marcus Camby, struggled through the shortened schedule, while Ewing battled nagging injuries throughout the season. It took a 6–2 finish just to clinch the final playoff berth in the East.

Meanwhile, Garden president Dave Checketts, perhaps anticipating a quick exit in the playoffs, considered Phil Jackson to replace Van Gundy. It was a reasonable thought, all things considered. Jackson had left the Bulls in '98 and had six rings to show for it, plus the connection to the franchise as a former player. And, as Checketts would later explain, Holzman had always asked him to bring Jackson back to the franchise one day.

All of this would have been fine if only it had stayed confidential. In New York, however, nothing stays confidential. Especially not when the Nets were also looking to land Jackson and were waiting for an answer.

Despite his connection to the Knicks' championship era, Jackson had since become more associated as an enemy in this generation. Van Gundy, however, was already somewhat of an endearing character—especially after he took on two of the game's high-profile coaches, Riley and Jackson, in a war of words. Plus, the guy didn't shy away from a scrum. Forget the Mourning incident; he got two black eyes trying to break up a fight between Derek Harper and Jo Jo English.

After the Knicks stunned the Heat in the first round in '99 and were putting the finishing touches on a sweep of the Atlanta Hawks in the second round, news broke of Checketts' contact with Jackson. Checketts issued a denial through a Garden spokesman, and Van Gundy was bombarded with questions before Game 3 of the series with Atlanta.

The media frenzy was to be expected. But what came as a surprise was what happened after PA announcer Mike Walczewski opened the pregame introductions with his usual opening line, "The Knicks are coached by Jeff Van Gundy."

The Garden crowd roared with an ovation.

And afterward, as recounted in the book *Just Ballin'*, Ewing was annoyed with the news.

"I'm not playing for Phil Jackson," he told reporters. "There's no way. They can trade me if they get Phil."

The drama continued to unfold, as Checketts eventually admitted there was contact with Jackson, but it was preliminary. As the series with Atlanta was an absolute bore at that point—the Knicks held a 3–0 lead going into Game 4—the tabloids and sports talk radio were dominated with the anger over Checketts going behind his coach's back and then lying about it.

The Knicks obliterated the Hawks with a 79–66 win in Game 4 at the Garden, which prompted chants of, "Sweep! Sweep! Sweep!" from the giddy crowd. With the knowledge that the Indiana Pacers and that sinister Reggie Miller would be up next, the chants then turned to, "We want Reggie!"

But as the final seconds ticked down, the party took a turn from a celebration to a rally. The cause being the unassuming coach with the sad eyes who paced the sideline in front of the Knicks bench.

Jeff-Van-GUN-dy!

(clap, clap, clap-clap, clap)

Jeff-Van-GUN-dy!

(clap, clap, clap-clap, clap)

In the jovial locker room afterward, the players picked up the chant, teasing their coach.

"I said that what usually comes after that is 'sucks,'" Van Gundy told D'Agostino in *Garden Glory*. "So it was good that they eliminated the 'sucks' part."

And after the team completed its surprising run to the NBA Finals, Checketts eliminated Jackson, or anyone else, as a candidate. Van Gundy signed a contract extension.

He continued to have success with the Knicks, with a 50-win season in 1999–2000 and one last run to the Eastern Conference Finals. That year also marked the end of the Ewing era, however. Van Gundy tried to talk Ewing into staying with the franchise— after all, Van Gundy probably wouldn't be there if it weren't for the Big Fella—but it was too late. That next season the Knicks won 48 games but looked very old in a five-game loss to the Raptors in the first round of the playoffs. It was the first time the Knicks had failed to advance in the playoffs since 1991.

Checketts resigned that spring and, with a lot of changes in the works and questions about the direction of the franchise, Van Gundy stepped down as head coach 19 games into the 2001–02 season. The team wouldn't spend much time over .500 for the remainder of the decade.

"I still have great regret about it," Van Gundy revealed to D'Agostino in *Garden Glory*. "Because I know I'll never have another job like the New York Knicks. You know there's only one like that."

French Toast

One of the first indications that the Knicks were heading in the wrong direction toward the end of Jeff Van Gundy's tenure came on June 30, 1999, a day that will live in infamy in not only franchise history but NBA Draft history.

It doesn't rank among the all-time greatest draft-day blunders, such as Portland's decision to pass on Michael Jordan to select injury-riddled center Sam Bowie or the Trail Blazers' second devastating mistake, passing on Kevin Durant for injury-riddled center Greg Oden. But the decision to take a 7'0" Frenchman named Frederic Weis with the 15th overall pick was a mistake that resonated for years.

Team president and general manager Ernie Grunfeld was fired during the 1998–99 season, which left a vacancy at the top of the franchise and, like in 1987, the Knicks went into the '99 draft without a general manager. But this time they didn't rely on Dick McGuire, who at the time was 73 and settled into an advisory role.

Grunfeld's assistant, Ed Tapscott, was promoted to interim general manager, and the draft was going to be his show.

With Patrick Ewing in the twilight of his career, the feeling was that the Knicks needed to find his eventual replacement at center. That draft that year, however, didn't have any true centers among the class of college entrants. But in Europe, there was a 7'2" prospect named Frederic Weis who had some serviceable skills and the potential to develop into a quality NBA player. Or at least that's what Tapscott was led to believe.

To be fair, Weis wasn't supposed to become the next Ewing, he was only supposed to be an understudy who, with time and guidance, could step into Ewing's place once the Big Fella retired. There were two problems with this theory: (1) Ewing had little interest in being a mentor. And (2) Jeff Van Gundy had no interest in coaching a limited talent with even more limited ability to communicate in English.

Clearly there wasn't much communicating going on at all in the days leading up to the draft. The coaching staff was a little busy at the time. The team lost Game 5 of the NBA Finals on June 25. Five days later, they were on the clock at the MCI Center in Washington. Weis was available.

But so was Ron Artest.

Had this draft been in the usual place, the Garden theater, the reaction would have been similar to the last time a St. John's star sat in the green room with the Knicks on the clock. Remember Mark Jackson? Artest sat there with his heart pounding until he heard the words, "Frederic Weis."

Then his heart broke.

Tapscott bypassed Artest, a burly, physical small forward who came up in the Queensbridge projects idolizing those rugged Knicks teams of the 1990s. It was a mistake that impacted both the Knicks and Artest, who went to the Bulls with the very next selection. Artest only spent two and a half seasons in Chicago before he was dealt to the Indiana Pacers. It was there he developed into an All-Star and the NBA's Defensive Player of the Year (2003–04).

The following season, however, he played a primary role in the ugly brawl in Detroit, where he went into the stands to fight a fan who had dumped soda on him. The incident led to a 73-game suspension.

Meanwhile, Weis never played a single game for the Knicks. He showed up for a workout the summer after he was drafted and looked lost. Van Gundy reportedly had little time for him. Weis never came over for training camp that season and instead remained in Europe. The following year, he played for France in the 2000 Olympic Games in Sydney.

The good news for Weis was that he came away with a silver medal in that tournament. The bad news was that he became an international embarrassment when Vince Carter, playing for Team USA, literally jumped over Weis' head for a posterization that to this day remains one of the most amazing plays in the history of the Olympics.

The French media dubbed it "Le Dunk de la Mort": the Dunk of Death.

Years later, Donnie Walsh put a bit of a fitting end to the Weis error when he traded the center's rights to the Houston Rockets. The player he got in return? Patrick Ewing's son, Pat Jr.

Damaged Goods

In a way this was all Howard Eisley's fault. If he had made that layup with 1:55 left in a preseason game against the Phoenix Suns,

Antonio McDyess wouldn't have needed to follow it up for a dunk attempt.

And if that put-back wasn't necessary, McDyess' left kneecap wouldn't have exploded. He wouldn't have missed the entire 2002–03 season and the Knicks wouldn't have missed the playoffs with a 37–45 record.

And Scott Layden wouldn't have lost his job.

And Isiah Thomas wouldn't have taken over the franchise.

And Stephon Marbury would have never been a Knick.

But Eisley's layup *did* miss and McDyess, who had 23 points and 15 rebounds and whose presence gave the Knicks hope of a revival after failing to make the playoffs the previous season (the first time in 15 years), felt compelled to do what he was brought there to do: finish plays.

"Our whole training camp was focused on him, his game," coach Don Chaney said at the time. "We did a lot of post-ups and pick-and-rolls."

The McDyess injury was no fender bender; it totaled the car. What no one knew was that he would recover a lot quicker than the Knicks would.

After the 30-win failure in 2001–02, Layden decided to use the Knicks' lottery pick that season to make a bold move. He traded the No. 7 overall pick (Nene Hilario), along with Marcus Camby and Mark Jackson to the Denver Nuggets for McDyess (and Frank Williams plus a future 2nd round pick).

A bold move, yes. McDyess had been one of the NBA's most ferocious power forwards and a devastating dunking machine for the Denver Nuggets. By the 2000–01 season, he was an All-Star. But early in the following season, while attempting a dunk in practice, he suffered one of the most painful knee injuries there is: a ruptured patella tendon. He returned to appear in just 10 games that season before reinjuring the knee again and shutting it down for the rest of the year.

But he was expected to make a full recovery, one that would have him ready in plenty of time for the 2002–03 season. He was still very much in his prime at 28 years old. And with Ewing long gone, the Knicks needed an inside presence to complement Allan Houston's perimeter game.

This looked like a good gamble for Layden, and three games into the preseason, McDyess was back to terrorizing helpless rims. Then Howard Eisley missed that layup and moments later, McDyess limped off the Garden court and slammed the scorers' table. Four days later he had surgery. He missed the entire season.

He returned a year later to make his regular-season debut on December 1, 2003. He had two points and three rebounds in 13 minutes. The Knicks lost by one. They did a lot of losing at that point in the season.

McDyess would appear in 18 games as a Knick but found his era in New York had already ended. Thomas replaced Layden on December 22 and saw McDyess, and just about everyone else, as someone else's guy. This was, in some ways, Bernard King all over again.

On January 5, 2004, Thomas made his first major move by trading McDyess—who just put up 14 points and 11 rebounds in 26 minutes against the Nets—to the Phoenix Suns in an eight-player deal that fulfilled Marbury's dream of becoming a Knick.

When the deal was completed, Thomas called McDyess and said, "Five years from now, you're going to thank me."

"I just didn't get that comment," McDyess said. "I guess he says he did me a favor."

In hindsight, Thomas was right. McDyess finished the season in Phoenix and remained healthy. He signed as a free agent with the Detroit Pistons, where he spent the next five seasons on a team that went to the Eastern Conference Finals every spring but one. He remained relatively healthy, with no major issues with his knees, for the remainder of his career.

The Knicks made the playoffs only once during that span. And Thomas lost his job after the 2007–08 season.

63 Starbury

It's not entirely fair to label Stephon Marbury as the image of the Knicks' darkest era in the first decade of the 21st century. Marbury spent only three full seasons in New York, while playing parts of others. But he wasn't the one making foolish trades and offering senseless contracts while negotiating against no one. He wasn't the one who failed to show up in shape year after year. He wasn't the one who drafted Donnell Harvey (with DeShawn Stevenson and Michael Redd on the board) and Michael Sweetney (David West, Nick Collison, Luke Ridnour, Travis Outlaw, Kendrick Perkins, and…).

But in New York, the star gets all the attention. When you're winning, it's great. But when you lose, it can crush you.

So considering how bad the Knicks were through the mid-2000s, it's understandable that Marbury was usually at the center of just about all of the controversy. Some of it was the result of the intense media scrutiny that comes with the job, but some of it he brought upon himself with bizarre behavior: the Starbury logo tattooed to his shaved skull, the way he would preach about finding God only to admit to committing adultery with a team intern, strange late-night videos of him dancing shirtless and eating Vaseline.

And then there was this: "I'm the best point guard in the NBA."

It's how he described himself to a reporter from the *Newark Star-Ledger* in January 2005. He said it when the Knicks were

16–13 and on deck for a New Year's Day game was Jason Kidd and the Nets, who had swept the Knicks in the first round of the playoffs that previous season.

"Don't get me wrong—I love Jason Kidd. He's a great point guard," Marbury explained. "[But] how am I comparing myself to him when I think I'm the best point guard to play basketball? That doesn't make any sense. I mean, how can I sit here and compare myself to somebody if I already think I'm the best?

"I'm telling you what it is: I know I'm the best point guard in the NBA. I don't need anybody else to tell me that. When I go on the basketball court, if I think about what you're all saying, I'll lose my mind."

Some might have argued he already had.

Upon reflection, Marbury's point was credible: if he goes into a game thinking his opponent is better than he is, the opponent has the mental advantage. So he has to tell himself he's the best. Plus, Marbury wasn't far removed from his last All-Star appearance (2002–03) and was among the league leaders in scoring and assists.

Still, he clearly wasn't the "best" in the league, not with MVP Steve Nash and Allen Iverson, Chauncey Billups, Gilbert Arenas, and, yes, Kidd, at the top of their games. But that wasn't quite his point.

No matter. All you had to do was pull the one quote out of the context, and it came off as a statement of extreme arrogance.

Marbury outplayed Kidd in the next game—31 points and eight assists to Kidd's 13 and three—but the Nets beat the Knicks 93–87. The comment began getting used against him as the Knicks went on to lose 11 of their next 12 games and cost Lenny Wilkens his job. Marbury's once-celebrated homecoming—the Garden roared when he was introduced for his debut—soured quickly as the Knicks failed to make the playoffs.

Much of the blame was placed on Marbury, but arguably he had very little talent around him. Still, several of his teammates were annoyed at his selfish play. Kurt Thomas, one of the last remaining connections to the proud era of the 1990s, had several heated exchanges with Marbury.

Thomas brought in Larry Brown in 2005–06 and made more bold, though unnecessarily risky, moves in trading two unprotected lottery picks for young center Eddy Curry, who had talent but serious motivation issues, and throwing $30 million at a career backup center Jerome James.

By then Marbury and Isiah Thomas were very close—the two even lived in neighboring homes in Westchester—and their relationship led to a player having unprecedented power at the Garden. So when Brown, who is notoriously tough on point guards, tried to control Marbury's shot-dominant game to fit it into a team concept, there was little chance the coach was going to win that battle.

Brown then pushed Thomas to trade for Steve Francis, with the intention to get Francis to unseat Marbury as the starting point guard. But Francis instead became friends with Marbury, and the two turned on Brown.

Without real leadership—the star player was usually the leader—the players also turned on themselves. A heated team meeting turned ugly as Quentin Richardson threatened to fight Marbury. The atmosphere was now toxic.

After Brown was fired, Thomas moved into the coaching role and his relationship with Marbury became strained. It started when Marbury admitted in a videotaped deposition (for a sexual harassment case against Thomas) that he had sex with a team intern. Marbury's behavior in the deposition only brought on more public criticism of Thomas and the Garden.

Marbury and Thomas then reportedly got into a fight on the team's charter to Phoenix early in the 2007–08 season. After the plane landed, Marbury hopped on a flight back to New York. He missed the game in Phoenix but met the team in Los Angeles. The players, tired of Marbury's insubordination, voted against letting Marbury play after he abandoned them in Phoenix. But Thomas played him 33 minutes. The Knicks lost.

Then, following a loss to the Suns on December 2, 2007, Marbury's father, Don, died of a heart attack he suffered during the game. The loss of his father devastated Stephon, who tried to play but eventually took an excused leave of absence to grieve. He wound up playing just 24 games that season.

When Donnie Walsh took over the franchise, he decided against arranging a buyout of the final year of Marbury's contract to cut him loose. The move backfired, as new coach Mike D'Antoni wanted nothing to do with coaching Marbury. After giving him token minutes off the bench in the preseason, he decided not to play him at all in the regular season. Marbury tried to keep his cool but was burning inside.

Then, after a roster-shaking day of trades, D'Antoni told Marbury the short-handed Knicks needed him to play in Milwaukee on November 21. D'Antoni offered the chance at playing 30 minutes a night, because, as a result of the trade, the Knicks now had a deficiency in the backcourt. But Marbury declined.

A week later in Detroit, D'Antoni went to him again about playing and, again, Marbury declined. The team immediately suspended him. Later in the season he was bought out and he signed with the Boston Celtics, which wound up being his last stop in the NBA. He has since continued his career in China.

By the end, Marbury had become calloused toward most of the media. He often had heated exchanges with beat writers, aside from one, Marc Berman of the *New York Post,* who covered him with a sympathetic perspective.

And the shame of it all is that the losing and the controversial moments overshadowed the other side of Stephon, the one that, in 2005, broke down into tears when he announced a $1 million donation to aid the victims of Hurricane Katrina, which devastated the city of New Orleans.

Then, in 2006, he started up a brand, Starbury, which made high-quality sneakers and athletic apparel at affordable prices. The intention was to make the same quality merchandise sold by major brands such as Nike and Adidas but remove the markups.

The move, of course, created some controversy in the basketball world, as star players were asked about their own multimillion dollar endorsement deals for items most poor families—from places many of these players are from—couldn't afford.

LeBron James, however, said he had no plans to follow Marbury's lead in creating a discount line.

"Me being with Nike, we hold our standards high," James said. "It does come with a price that's pretty high, but at the same time, you're getting great quality for it."

Marbury scoffed at James' remark.

"Better to own," he said, "than be owned."

64 End of an Error

When Isiah Thomas first arrived as president of the Knicks in late December 2003, he charmed the audience with his vision of bringing the once-proud franchise back to the upper-echelon of the NBA and the Garden back to again being the hottest spot during the cold New York winters.

"I want to see smoke rising off the building," he said.

Four years later, the only smoke was that which was coming out of the ears of irate fans. Instead of a return to greatness, the Knicks reached new lows both on the court and off of it.

Thomas came to New York on a recommendation by Magic Johnson, who was the original target when it was decided that it was time for the understated, over-his-head Scott Layden to go. Johnson didn't want the job, but one of his closest friends, the man whom he kissed before tip-off during the NBA Finals, was available. Thomas had success coaching the Indiana Pacers the previous three seasons but had been let go when Larry Bird took over basketball operations and decided to replace Thomas with his friend Rick Carlisle.

As for experience, Thomas did have four years in Toronto, where he was part owner and executive vice president of the expansion Raptors. The team was terrible, but he did draft three of the game's top young players in Damon Stoudamire, Marcus Camby, and Tracy McGrady.

The honeymoon in New York was good to Thomas, who immediately got to work to retool the Knicks with a couple of major moves that were loudly applauded. You see, New Yorkers love immediate moves and action. It's only afterward, once it fails, when people are critical for impetuousness.

He acquired Brooklyn-born point guard Stephon Marbury, a two-time All-Star, and then replaced Don Chaney with veteran coach Lenny Wilkens. The team went 10–6 to finish the season and clinch the last playoff spot in the East with a 39–43 record. Before the final regular-season game of the season, Thomas took a microphone and walked to center court and said to the Garden crowd, "Welcome to the playoffs."

He'd never get to utter those words again.

It wasn't for lack of trying. In the summer of 2004, armed only with a midlevel exception that could only pay about $5 million per season, Thomas tried to get free agent Kobe Bryant to come to the Knicks. Bryant had won three titles with the Lakers, but there was a lot of tension with Shaquille O'Neal and the departure of coach Phil Jackson, and Thomas was hoping Bryant might want a change of scenery.

"New York is a special place," he told J.A. Adande of the *Los Angeles Times*. "And it's a place that hasn't won in a long time. I know the challenge for me was to go to New York and try to unlock the safe and win the championship. If you can do it there, that's better than doing it anywhere."

Bryant decided instead to stay in Los Angeles for $136 million.

From that point, Thomas seemed lost. In August 2004, he traded four expiring contracts for Jamal Crawford and Jerome Williams, which brought in a combined $81 million in remaining

For a while it seemed like "Fire Isiah" eclipsed even the "De-Fense" cheers.

salary. In July 2005, he gave Jerome James, a decent defensive center with serious conditioning issues, a five-year, $30 million contract. Then three months later, he effectively made James the most expensive backup center in the NBA by working out a sign-and-trade for Eddy Curry, an up-and-coming big man. The interest in Curry made perfect sense, but sending the right to swap first-round picks in 2006 and '07 (with no lottery protection) to Chicago as part of the deal—especially when the Knicks were essentially negotiating against themselves—did not. Both picks naturally landed in the lottery.

And the Knicks ended up writing some very large checks, not only for their astronomical payroll ($125 million in 2005–06), but also for being way over the NBA's luxury-tax threshold. For the 2006–07 season, the Knicks paid a record $45.1 million in luxury tax. The small-market teams, which get a share of the tax money, loved the Isiah Thomas era.

The Knicks not only went through a carousel of players, but Thomas was constantly changing coaches, too. When Marbury was tired of dealing with Wilkens, he had Thomas dump him late in the 2004–05 season. The following year, another veteran coach with a successful résumé, Larry Brown, stepped into the job and immediately clashed with Marbury, too.

Brown's tumultuous season signaled the beginning of the end of Thomas, who, to his credit, did try to work with the coach. At Brown's request, Thomas made two midseason deals, one for an out-of-shape Jalen Rose and another that sent young forward Trevor Ariza—one of the things Thomas got right was finding this UCLA product in the second round in 2004—for Steve Francis. When the season was over, Brown included both on a list of players he felt had to go.

Instead, it was Brown who went, and the team wound up having to lay out even more money: $19 million in a settlement over the remainder of his contract. Rather than hire another coach, team owner James Dolan ordered Thomas, who was heading into the final season of his contract, to move to the bench.

"I'm saying this right with Isiah here," Dolan said during an interview on MSG Network in June 2006. "This is his team. He made this bed. There is nobody better than him to make this thing go forward. But he has to do that, and he has one season to do that."

Dolan said he'd need to see "evident progress" in order to bring Thomas back. On March 10, 2007, Francis hit a game-winning shot to beat the Wizards in Washington and jumped up on the scorer's table to celebrate. The win moved the Knicks (29–34) into eighth place in the East, the demarcation of the final playoff berth, with 19 games left in the season.

Two days later, Dolan cited proof of "evident progress" and gave Thomas a two-year contract extension. Dolan didn't want to make the move at the time and preferred to wait until after the season. But behind the scenes, Thomas pushed for the extension and insisted the players needed to know he was in charge.

The Knicks then finished the season by losing 15 of their final 19 games and once again failed to make the playoffs. On draft night, Thomas made one last dramatic—and expensive—move by trading for power forward Zach Randolph.

In the fall, Thomas was the subject of a sexual harassment case brought against him by a former Garden executive. The trial, which eventually ended in a settlement, became a major controversy that further tarnished the franchise and the Garden.

After enduring a brutal 23-win season in 2007–08, Thomas was demoted from his role as team president and replaced by Donnie Walsh, who then replaced him as coach with Mike D'Antoni.

Though officially no longer employed by the franchise, Thomas still continues to haunt fans with a behind-the-scenes presence through his friendship with Dolan, which is often cited by the media. Thomas even once said his dream was to come back and run the team again—which infuriated Walsh and sent fans into a panic—but he has since backed off such statements and now says he no longer wishes to return.

Donnie Basketball

Just a few days into his new job as president of the Knicks, Donnie Walsh's cell phone rang. It was yet another reporter. He had to get right to work in hiring a new head coach, and the New York media was in its usual frenzy, desperate for a scoop.

The rumor was that Walsh was to meet Mark Jackson to discuss the job. He was to fly that night to Los Angeles, where Jackson was working as an analyst for ABC/ESPN. So the questions came rapid-fire.

Are you meeting with Mark Jackson?

"I have no meetings scheduled with anyone today."

What about tomorrow?

"What about tomorrow? I'm telling you about today."

Are you in Los Angeles?

"No, I'm not in Los Angeles."

Well, can I ask where you are, then?

"I'm in the bathroom!"

Walsh is a native New Yorker with the thick accent to prove it, but for the better part of the last two decades, he lived and worked in Indianapolis, as general manager and later president of the Indiana Pacers. They had one newspaper, one radio station, and just a few local television stations. The coverage was often so easy-going that Walsh would look forward to engaging conversations with writers from around the league, just to hear what's going on in other markets.

At the age of 67, with plenty of money in the bank, Walsh didn't have to take this job. In fact, just after he was surrounded by a horde of reporters who pelted him with detailed questions about how he would rebuild the long-lost Knicks, Walsh wondered why he did it. But then he walked out onto Seventh Avenue, right by the marquee that glowed his name. The street was alive as it usually is, with hundreds of people bustling by, and many of them who recognized his face shouted best wishes to the new leader of their wayward franchise. And that's when he knew: this was exactly what he wanted.

Though he could do without all the reporters.

"I'm not the great new hope, all right?" Walsh said when he was introduced to the media as the team president on April 2, 2008. "I'm just a guy gonna try to come in and create a team, and it's not going to happen overnight. So I don't want any illusions. But I think it has to get better right away. I think the people in this city are paying money to go to games, and they have to see a competitive team. They've got to see a team that makes sense, so they can say, 'Okay, this is gonna get better.'"

Walsh outlined his plan, which was to get the payroll-burdened franchise under the salary cap in two years, which just so happened to coincide with one of the biggest free-agency classes in NBA history: LeBron James, Dwyane Wade, Amar'e Stoudemire, Joe Johnson, Chris Bosh, etc. You could rebuild a franchise quickly with a summer like that.

Walsh got right to work. He didn't wind up hiring Jackson, who was a leading candidate until the Phoenix Suns suddenly decided to part ways with their coach. Mike D'Antoni, who averaged 58 wins in his last four years there and had one of the most popular offensive systems in the game, was available. Walsh grabbed D'Antoni and believed he now not only had the lure of New York and the Garden on his side, but also one of the league's most popular coaches, too.

Still, to get the team under the cap by 2010 wouldn't be easy. There was only one team in the league that was known for taking on big contracts, and Walsh was now running it.

But as the Knicks got off to a 6–3 start, the value in some of their players started to rise. Walsh struck quickly. On November 21, 2008, he traded two starters, Zach Randolph and Jamal Crawford, for players with contracts that expired by 2010. The move saved the Knicks $27.3 million in salary off the books for 2010–11. It also put them in play to make a full maximum contract offer to James. For the next two seasons, it became a conversation Walsh went out of his way to avoid.

The following season, as critics claimed the Knicks would need a second star to lure James, Walsh pulled off yet another major move that carved even more money off the 2010–11 payroll. He sent Jared Jeffries, another one of Isiah Thomas' terrible contracts, and underwhelming rookie Jordan Hill to the Houston Rockets for Tracy McGrady's expiring contract. The move cut almost $10 million more, and the Knicks were projected to have enough room under the NBA salary cap to land two maximum-contract players.

In the end, LeBron chose to go to Miami, but the moves still allowed Walsh to rebuild the team through free agency. He signed Stoudemire and added point guard Raymond Felton as the main pieces.

But the failure to get LeBron was troubling for Walsh, especially after the team endured two more losing seasons as a result of him paring the roster and making personnel decisions based on contract length. In the end, some viewed it as being all for naught without LeBron James in orange-and-blue.

Walsh also took some criticism for his draft decisions. In 2008 the team selected 6'10" Italian Danilo Gallinari, who was limited to just 28 games as a rookie because of a back injury. He passed on others such as Eric Gordon, a second-team All-Rookie selection. And in '09, he passed on several point guards, such as Brandon Jennings, Ty Lawson, Darren Collison, and Jrue Holiday to take Hill, who turned into a bust.

And there were also issues with his health, including a neck injury that resulted in him needing a wheelchair during the summer of 2010. There were reports that James was taken aback by the image of the 69-year-old Walsh in a wheelchair during his meeting with the Knicks.

And after James chose the Heat, team owner James Dolan tried to bring former team president Isiah Thomas back into the franchise as a consultant. The sense was that Dolan felt that Thomas had a better connection with the game's star players and that would help the Knicks as they targeted other free agents.

Through all of this came reports that Walsh may decide to retire because of his health and other issues. That, of course, prompted Walsh to snap back at the media.

"I'm sure there are guys around me that are predicting my death, right?" he once said to me.

It's funny in a way, because he was the one who brought new life back to the franchise.

And in the so-called failure to land LeBron, Walsh never panicked and made any desperate moves. He maintained the cap space left over and spent the next nine months working on one of the biggest trades in franchise history, for Carmelo Anthony. The Knicks had their second star.

Walsh, at 70, decided after the 2010–11 season that he did not want to continue his tenure as team president and general manager (though he remained with the franchise as a paid consultant for the 2011–12 season). The Knicks accomplished their first winning season in a decade and clinched their first playoff berth in seven years in 2010–11. Despite Walsh's decision, he insisted in no way was the job complete.

"I really did look into my soul, and I can't do this job at less than 100 percent," Walsh said when the announcement was made. "And I really don't know [if] I can commit to doing this job for two [more] years at less than 100 percent."

Walsh has since returned to the Pacers as director of basketball operations. And, though his tenure with the Knicks was short, Walsh's contributions have revitalized the franchise.

"In a relatively short time with the Knicks, Donnie made a tremendous impact [that] will be felt for many years to come," said owner James Dolan.

The LeBronathon

In 2010 the Knicks had a chance to get the best player in the game. And the effort was an exhausting two-year process.

The NBA's tampering rules prohibited Walsh from ever referring to this player by name, but everyone knew. How could you not? At 25 years old, 6'8", and 250 pounds, with the agility of a wide receiver and the power of a linebacker and the skill set that threatened a triple-double every night, LeBron James was exactly the kind of player you could build a championship team around.

In fact, that's just what the Cleveland Cavaliers were trying to accomplish. The Cavs tanked the 2002–03 season for a shot at the No. 1 overall pick, and for one of the rare times in the NBA draft lottery's history, the team with the league's worst record actually won the top pick. (There were no "frozen envelope" controversies mentioned that season, but didn't anyone find it odd that the Cleveland franchise happened to be in perfect position to draft the dynamic high school sensation from nearby Akron?)

Over the two years between Walsh's hiring and July 1, 2010, when the free-agency period officially began, a fierce rivalry quickly grew between Cleveland and New York. You would think the teams had a history of playoff battles between them, but the Knicks hadn't been in a playoff game since 2004.

It became such an obsession with the media, the current Knicks players—most of whom knew they were merely there as placeholders until their contracts ran out in 2010—had their own running joke about the situation. The punch line to any issue was "once LeBron comes."

For instance, if there was a problem with the dining choices on the team charter, a player would joke, "We'll have a better selection once LeBron comes."

Though the players mocked the idea of James leaving his hometown Cavaliers, an NBA Finalist in 2007, for a losing franchise, New Yorkers saw LeBron as the savior.

When the Cavaliers came to the Garden, the building rocked like a spiritual revival. One fan literally ran out onto the court during a stoppage of play, which caught the ushers and security by complete surprise. When the young fan, clad in a Cavs jersey, was face to face with his hero, he was so stunned he was speechless. James, who had 50 points in the game, just laughed, gave him a quick pound, and tapped his heart as if to say thanks as the fan was pulled off the court by security.

Early in the 2008–09 season, just days after Walsh pulled off a pair of trades to carve out the space needed to offer LeBron a max contract in 2010, the Cavaliers came to the Garden for a game. The reception was over the top. Afterward, LeBron said all the things New Yorkers hoped to hear:

"It's humbling that a city like New York respects the way I play basketball," he said.

"I think July 1, 2010, is a very big day," he said.

And finally...

"If you guys want to sleep right now and don't wake up until July 1, 2010, then go ahead, because it's going to be a big day."

At that point, he owned New York. Most of the major newspapers posted countdowns to July 1, 2010. At *Newsday*, we called it the LeBronathon.

By the 2009–10 season, the anticipation was so high that the Garden would be filled with fans with customized Knicks jerseys with James' name and No. 23 on the back. On the day of his one and only visit to New York that season, the Yankees—LeBron's favorite baseball team—celebrated their 2009 World Series championship with the traditional ticker-tape parade down the Canyon of Heroes.

LeBron was invited by several Yankees players, including his close friend, pitcher CC Sabathia, to be a special guest on one of the floats—so he could experience what it was like to win in New York. James politely declined.

"My parade," he said, "starts at eight at night."

The next day, James spoke openly about free agency with the New York media for the last time.

The Knicks were headed for yet another nosedive in the second half of the season and failed to make the playoffs for the sixth-straight time, the franchise's second-longest drought. But by April no one was focusing on the playoffs. The anticipation to get to July was full throttle.

When James' Cavs team was on the verge of a surprising elimination by the Boston Celtics in the second round of the playoffs, the Beantown crowd at TD Garden mocked him with chants of, "New York Knicks! New York Knicks!" That was the level of absurdity this thing had reached: a Boston crowd chanting for a New York team.

Celebrities even started getting into the act. In early June, before making a presentation at Spike TV's Guy's Choice Awards, actor James Gandolfini (star of LeBron's favorite show, *The Sopranos*) made an impromptu pitch to LeBron, who was in attendance.

"First things first. LeBron, I would like you to come to New York, if you could," Gandolfini said. "If you miss Cleveland, you just have to drive across the bridge to New Jersey. It's pretty much the same thing."

The Knicks got everyone in on the act, from Donald Trump to Alec Baldwin to Chris Rock and, of course, Spike Lee.

Even New York City mayor Michael Bloomberg made a video with the slogan, "C'mon LeBron!" (Though Bloomberg, aware that the Nets were soon headed to Brooklyn, only spoke about New York City and carefully avoided talking about a specific franchise.)

The Knicks had planned a lavish recruiting effort for July 1, which would have involved every hot spot in the city. But LeBron's group—they deserve a book unto themselves—decided he would instead have teams come to him. And first at bat on the very first day of free agency were your New York Knicks.

The meeting, held at his marketing company's offices in downtown Cleveland, opened with a video. It was the final scene of *The Sopranos*—only the ending was different.

Tony Soprano had a beard (and, apparently, wasn't dead after all) and was living with Carmela in a witness-protection program. He was telling his wife he had an important friend who was coming to town and the friend needed a place to stay. That friend's name was LeBron James.

Carmela looked on her computer for a place in midtown Manhattan and said she found the perfect spot. The screen flashed to a photo of Madison Square Garden.

LeBron loved the celebrity pitch and also a breakdown by an outside firm on how, by moving to New York, James can earn $1 billion through his career. Earlier in his career, James had said that one of his goals was to be the first billion-dollar athlete.

James came away from each of his meetings—the Nets, Bulls, Heat, Clippers, and Cavaliers—expressing the same gratitude, and the teams expressed the same optimism. The Knicks didn't know what to think. There were agendas served and allegations tossed around and, of all the teams in the mix, the Knicks seemed to be the preferred punching bag.

Concerned that their plan to build a championship-caliber team might not have been made clear, the Knicks sent two representatives, MSG Sports president Scott O'Neil and team executive Glen Grunwald, back to Cleveland to meet with James' agent and business partner to further explain their strategies: one important point of emphasis was that they were on the verge of locking up All-Star forward Amar'e Stoudemire, whom James had unsuccessfully lobbied the Cavs to acquire at the trade deadline.

Still, the feedback was hardly encouraging. Rumors started to emerge that LeBron might consider joining his pal Dwyane Wade and Chris Bosh with the Heat. Pat Riley, always looking to stick it to the Knicks, made an aggressive play to clear just about every player off his roster, including young prospect Michael Beasley, to open up enough room to sign *three* maximum-contract players.

Meanwhile, the Cavaliers held firm the belief that LeBron would never leave home.

His choice was announced on ESPN, on a 30-minute show titled, *The Decision*. When word got out that the show, aired on ESPN, would be shot live at a Boys & Girls Club in Greenwich, Connecticut, just a short drive from New York City, the assumption was that James was ready to choose the Knicks.

I reported in *Newsday* that day that LeBron was going to the Heat. And that night, he confirmed the story by saying that infamous phrase that stunned the sports world and shook at least three franchises to their respective foundations: "I'm going to take my talents to South Beach."

Considering the amount of effort, time, and money the Knicks had invested in this ordeal, it might have been the most devastating loss in franchise history.

The First Star

When considering the star that got away, it's apt to mention the first star the franchise had. Dick McGuire may have been the catalyst, but he still needed a finisher at the end of his passes. And most of the time back in the early years of the Knicks' existence, it was Carl Braun.

At a wiry 6'5" and 180 pounds, Braun was one of the game's first great shooters and scorers. He joined the Knicks in their second season, 1947–48, after playing his collegiate ball at Colgate. Braun could fill it up from anywhere and had range that, in today's game, would rival three-point specialists like Ray Allen. In the days before the 24-second shot clock, Braun thrilled crowds with high-scoring performances and shooting exhibitions.

"Carl was a real scorer...He was a natural outside shooter," Harry Gallatin, one of his teammates, told D'Agostino in *Garden Glory*. "He had a two-handed overhead shot that no one could block. Carl had tremendous range."

In his first season, Braun put up 18 shots a game and averaged 14.3 points in 47 games to lead the Knicks in scoring as a rookie. (Though, really, the franchise and league were so new, if you weren't a rookie you were only a second-year player.) His scoring rate would increase slightly, and Braun started taking less shots and distributing more. And behind him, McGuire, and Gallatin, the Knicks became one of the best teams in the league.

"We back-doored guys an awful lot, me and Carl," McGuire told D'Agostino in *Garden Glory*. "He was such a good shooter that he'd fake to come to me on a back door, and it was always easy to just throw the pass right through there."

He played 12 seasons with the Knicks and averaged 14.1 points per game with 10,449 points—a mark that still ranks today as the fifth-highest total in franchise history. He was a five-time NBA All-Star from 1953 to 1957. Braun did play in one of those three Finals with the Knicks, but it wasn't until his final season, 1961–62, that he won the NBA championship. And then it was with the Celtics, as a reserve player at the age of 34.

The middle of his career was interrupted from 1950 to 1952 when he fulfilled his military commitment. He immediately re-signed with the Knicks.

"He loved the game," his wife, Joan, said in an interview with TCPalm.com after his passing in 2010. "And he would have paid the Knicks to play for them."

But Braun also would have appreciated a little recognition over the years. He is one of several original Knicks who went overlooked—and sometimes even forgotten—over the years. McGuire had his number retired in 1991 but only after Dave Checketts came in and felt it necessary to honor the longtime Knick, who also served as coach and scout.

Braun didn't stay with the team after his career and instead went on to become a very successful stockbroker on Wall Street. He was around to see the Knicks finally win championships in the early 1970s but eventually retired to Florida and lost touch with the franchise.

It wasn't until Donnie Walsh, a Bronx native who grew up idolizing those old Knicks teams, reached out in 2009 to give

Braun some closure. Walsh wanted to honor Braun as the franchise's "Player of the Decade" for the 1940s.

"When I first called Carl, I could tell he was really upset," Walsh said in a story posted on the team Web site in November 2010. "He was really going on about the Knicks and he included me, and I said, 'Hey Carl, I wasn't here when all that stuff went down. I'm just trying to honor you now because you were a great player, and we're trying to let people know that.' Then he seemed to get a little easier."

Unfortunately Braun, at 81 years old, couldn't make the trip from Florida to New York to join the ceremony at the Garden. His daughter accepted the honor on his behalf.

A year later, Braun passed away, coincidentally just a week after McGuire succumbed to an aortic aneurysm.

"When I was a kid, he was bigger than life in my eyes," Walsh said. "I wanted get him back because, no matter what had happened before, I wanted to show him that the franchise had feelings for him, and we wanted him to have feelings back. I don't think he agreed with everything I said, but at the end I think he came to peace with it."

68 Richie Fifty

Of the past greats in Knicks history who have been somewhat overshadowed by the championship era, Richie Guerin has been the most outspoken. And, quite frankly, he might have the biggest case.

Guerin was not only a great Knick, but he was one of the game's greatest scorers of his time. The 6'4" guard came in just as Dick McGuire's Knicks career ended and Carl Braun became a player/coach. By his third season, Guerin had established himself as the franchise's next star.

Guerin was a scoring machine through the late 1950s and early 1960s and was among the first NBA players to eclipse the 50-point mark. Guerin did it three times, including a career-high 57 points in a 152–121 rout of the Syracuse Nationals on December 11, 1959. The performance eclipsed Braun's franchise record by 10 points and stood as the all-time mark until Bernard King scored 60 points on Christmas Day 1984.

Guerin would hit the 50-point mark twice more in his Knicks career, and in the 1961–62 season he averaged almost 30 points per game (29.5) on 24.3 shots per game. But Guerin was no gunner; he also distributed the ball for a career-best 6.9 assists per game that season.

The problem was, despite Guerin's individual efforts (he was named to the NBA All-Star team for six straight seasons), the Knicks were never a good team in an era dominated by big men such as Bill Russell and Wilt Chamberlain. And though they had a dominant scoring guard in Guerin, the Knicks could never find a center that could keep the team competitive.

Only once during Guerin's All-Star years did the Knicks have a winning record (1958–59) in his only playoff appearance. But the team was swept. The ultimate indignity came on March 2, 1962, against the Philadelphia Warriors in a game played in Hershey, Pennsylvania. Guerin had 39 points to lead the Knicks, but the Warriors had a player named Chamberlain who more than tripled Guerin's effort that night.

Guerin was traded to the St. Louis Hawks in 1963–64 and played for seven more seasons, including six as a player/coach (in 1967–68 he was named NBA Coach of the Year). He also made eight playoff appearances as a coach.

But all these years later, Guerin is not enshrined in the Basketball Hall of Fame, which is surprising and, to him, frustrating. And despite his standing in the franchise's scoring annals (Guerin is sixth on the all-time scoring list with 10,392 points and is one of only four players on the list with a scoring average of more than 20 per game), his name is nowhere to be found in the rafters at Madison Square Garden.

I asked him in 2009 if he felt forgotten.

"I do, and I don't say that selfishly," he replied. "I say that because if you go into a good number of the arenas around the league and you look at banners or individual numbers or whatever, it's not just for championship players, it's for players they felt dedicated something to an era, and they respected them by retiring a number or something like that. And that's how you create tradition. I don't think they did that here."

It's a gripe many of the players who came before the championship era have carried over the years.

"I hope you don't take this wrong, but let me say something that directly involves me: I had a very good reputation when I played here. The way I played the game, my performances and all of my statistics that lasted for, it seems like, forever," he said. "And yet, that did nothing to get recognition from management on, say, a retirement of a number or anything like that at all. And I'm sure there might have been people before me that might have had something like that in that era...But the era is the world championship era—and don't misunderstand me, you don't ever want to forget that. That's a very important part of a team—but, if you want to have tradition and you want to create something, you have to recognize people that made contributions to your franchise, regardless of how good the team was."

The Knicks finally honored Guerin by naming him the franchise's Player of the Decade for the 1950s. But his No. 9 has not been raised to the rafters. One could argue that if Patrick Ewing, who never won a title during his career, belongs among the players from the championship era, then Guerin should be there, too.

Unfortunately the more time passes, the more Guerin's career fades from memory.

Harry the Horse

In 10 pro seasons, Harry Gallatin never missed a day of work. We don't just mean games. Gallatin never missed a single day of work.

"I never missed a practice, and I never missed a game," he said in an alumni profile on the Knicks program in 2005. "Never. Not once in my entire career."

As a Knick, Gallatin played in 610 consecutive games, a franchise ironman record that stretched from November 20, 1948, to March 13, 1957, and might never be broken.

"There were times when my wife told me I really shouldn't play," Gallatin told D'Agostino in *Garden Glory*. "I did have the flu a few times...I always had some pretty doggone good games when I wasn't feeling that well. I don't know what there is to that, but there must be something there."

What's just as amazing as the streak is that Gallatin also played a very physical game and, at 6'6", was an undersized center going up against much bigger players during his career.

"Harry Gallatin was a real strong, tough guy," former Knicks player and coach Vince Boryla told D'Agostino in *Garden Glory*. "Tough as a horse."

Thus the nickname, Harry the Horse.

He wasn't much of an offensive player; in fact, if Carl Braun had unlimited range on a basketball court, you could say that Gallatin's range stopped beyond layups. But scoring wasn't Gallatin's thing, rebounding was. And if you were going up against the Horse under the glass, you had your hands full.

"Rebounding *was* my forte," Gallatin said in the Knicks interview. "I studied angles, where shots were coming off the board, all kinds of things that would help you board the ball against bigger guys.

"But I scored on a high percentage of my shots because Dicky [McGuire] was my point guard."

For a guy with limited range going up against taller players (he had to match up with 6'10" George Mikan), Gallatin still knew how to finish around the basket. He averaged a double-double in his Knicks career (13 points and 12.1 rebounds per game) and in 1953–54 he averaged a career-high 15.3 rebounds.

Gallatin retired in 1957–58 with the Detroit Pistons and a few years later was a successful coach of the St. Louis Hawks. But in the middle of the 1964–65 season, he returned to the Knicks to take over as head coach to help end a long drought of losing and failures to even make the playoffs in a 10-team league. Gallatin was there at the very beginning of the Knicks turnaround, coaching a young Willis Reed.

Fittingly, it was Reed who would tie one of Gallatin's great records as a Knick: 33 rebounds in a single game.

70 Double-D Lee

During the worst of times, in the dark years of the 2000s, when players came and went with the frequency of a subway turnstile spinning at rush hour, there was one player who generated a source of pride when it was so often hard to be a Knicks fan.

David Lee was a little bit Dave DeBusschere and a little bit Harry Gallatin. Like DeBusschere, Lee could pull opposing big men away from the basket and beat them with a midrange jumper that seemed to get better each season. And like Gallatin, Lee had a knack for rebounding and could read the bounce of the ball better than anyone in the game.

"The most important thing about rebounding," Lee once said, "is you have to *want* to do it."

On selfish Knicks teams that had a lot of guys who wanted to *shoot* rather than do the dirty work, Lee was glad to do it. On a team with shoot-first types such as Stephon Marbury, Jamal Crawford, Quentin Richardson, and a post-up center, Eddy Curry, rebounding was the only way Lee would get to touch the ball.

It was also his way of breaking into the lineup.

Lee was the least heralded of Isiah Thomas' collection of first-round picks on draft night in 2005. Channing Frye was the team's first choice with their lottery pick at No. 8 overall, and Nate Robinson, the 21st overall pick, was snatched up in a trade with the Phoenix Suns, which also brought in Richardson for Kurt Thomas.

Lee was taken at No. 30, a pick acquired from the San Antonio Spurs at the trade deadline along with veteran Malik Rose. He was a 6'9" forward from Florida who was a high-profile star in high school and showed potential at the college level. There were questions about his ability, considering his relatively thin frame, to play power forward at the NBA level. And then there is the fact that he's white.

Thomas these days likes to list Lee as one of his draft-day gems, but truth be told, it was one of Thomas' closest advisors, Brendan Suhr, who encouraged Thomas to make Lee the choice at No. 30.

Lee played sparingly during his rookie season, overshadowed by Frye, who became an All-Rookie team selection, and Robinson, who won the slam-dunk contest that year. But he started to show undeniable ability in his second season, when he averaged a

Nobody questioned David Lee's commitment to the game. Even an elbow to the face couldn't stop him from playing in this matchup.

double-double (10.7 points and 10.4 rebounds per game) to earn some mention among the league's most effective reserve players. He also had quickly become a Garden favorite for his hustle and blue-collar effort (ironic because Lee came from an affluent family and a private-school background).

It wasn't until Mike D'Antoni's arrival in 2008 that Lee's career took off. Once Zach Randolph was traded early in the 2008–09 season, Lee moved into the starting power-forward position for good. Actually, with Curry out of shape and riddled with injuries, Lee became D'Antoni's starting *center* for most of the next two seasons.

Though it was a ridiculous defensive matchup most nights—one time in Phoenix, 350-pound Shaquille O'Neal literally carried Lee right up to the basket—Lee found he could score easily against bigger, slower centers. And in D'Antoni's wide-open, pick-and-roll offense, Lee went from being a blue-collar bench player to the team's leading scorer—and, by 2009–10, he was an All-Star, the team's first since Allan Houston and Latrell Sprewell in the 2000–01 season.

He became a double-double machine and in 2008-09 became the first Knicks player since Patrick Ewing to lead the NBA in double-doubles when he had 65 in 81 games.

Lee had some monster games as a Knick, including 37 points and 21 rebounds in a 138–125 win over Golden State on November 29, 2008 (in that game, Chris Duhon benefited from Lee's ability to finish by recording 22 assists, which broke Richie Guerin's long-standing record). Lee also had his first career triple-double against Golden State the next season, with 37 points, 20 rebounds, and 10 assists, on April 2, 2010. It was the first time an NBA player had recorded a 30–20–10 triple-double since Kareem Abdul-Jabbar did it in 1975–76 (though there was some serious debate about the validity of Lee's 10th assist, a pass to teammate Danilo Gallinari, after which Gallinari took a few dribbles before his shot).

That season, Lee averaged a career-high 20.2 points and 11.7 rebounds per game, but his days as a Knick were dwindling. Lee, at 26, was headed to free agency and openly campaigned about finishing his career in New York. The last significant player to be drafted by the Knicks and play his entire career with them was the last so-called "Great White Hope" the franchise had: Bill Bradley.

But unlike Bradley, Lee was never part of a winning team, and as his star rose, so did the scrutiny. Lee was out of position on a nightly basis as a center, and that led to many defensive issues in the paint. He was also widely criticized for an innocent comment he made late in the 2008–09 season, when the Knicks played (and lost) three hard-fought, entertaining home games against the league's top teams—the Lakers, Cavaliers, and Celtics—and Lee called it "the best 0–3 week I've ever had." Lee was blasted for seeming satisfied with losing. Even former Knicks coach Jeff Van Gundy took him to task on an ABC telecast.

As much as Lee desperately wanted to experience winning in New York (in 498 career games as of the 2011–12 season, Lee has yet to appear in a playoff game), the Knicks were looking for a new beginning in 2010. Once power forward Amar'e Stoudemire signed as a free agent on July 9, 2010, Lee's career in New York was over. The same day Stoudemire arrived, Lee was sent to the Golden State Warriors, a team he torched as a Knick, in a sign-and-trade deal.

There is a saying that they use at the Garden when introducing former greats to the crowd: "Once a Knick, always a Knick." Though he's still in his prime, Lee believes he'll always maintain roots with the franchise.

"I think it applies to me," Lee told me in November 2010. "It's kind of tough [to think that way] when you're still in the league and playing for another team, because at this point I'm a Warrior. But I have great memories from here, and you always remember where you got your start and where you climbed up the ladder."

71 Wat a Pioneer

Sweetwater Clifton played a major role in the breaking of the NBA color barrier in 1950, but there was a player who came along three years earlier who should get the most credit for changing the visual landscape of the all-white league. At least for a few games.

Wataru Misaka was a 5'7" speedster from Ogden, Utah, who captivated the Madison Square Garden crowd in a loss to Kentucky in the 1944 NIT Tournament. He returned with the Utes to win the NCAA Tournament—not as popular at the time—by defeating Dartmouth. In '47 Misaka was back at the Garden again with Utah and this time—by shutting down Adolph Rupp's Kentucky team and great Ralph Beard (held to just one point)—the NIT championship was won.

Hearing New Yorkers chant his name, Ned Irish—who often pushed his assistants, Fred Podesta and John Goldner, to target any college player who had a successful night at the Garden—wanted him on the Knicks. So in the first amateur draft held by the BAA (before it became known as the NBA), the Knicks made Misaka the first of their 10 choices. The Japanese-American became the first player of Asian descent—and the first nonwhite player—in league history.

Misaka attended training camp in upstate Bear Mountain the following season and was given a guaranteed contract of $4,000.

But despite feeling warmth from most of his Knicks teammates—though not all—and acceptance from the Garden crowds, it was still a time of racial intolerance in the United States, especially just a few years removed from World War II.

"Whether real or not, I felt less prejudice against me in New York than I did anywhere else," Misaka said in an NBA.com story from 2001. "Playing for Utah, New Yorkers are great fans of underdogs, and they really backed us up, even against St. John's. When I went back as a Knick, there were people who remembered me from playing for Utah and would say hello on the streets sometimes."

But on the road, things were much different. And Irish eventually decided to release Misaka after just three games. He scored seven points in those three games, which, at the very least, put him in the all-time record books.

What Rivalry?

The mural went up on the side of a building on 34th Avenue and Eighth Avenue in July 2010, and for the entire month, it loomed in the distance over Madison Square Garden.

"Blueprint for Success" is what it said, with the image of hip-hop star Jay-Z and a Russian billionaire named Mikhail Prokhorov. The significance was that Prokhorov was the new owner of the Nets, who moved to Brooklyn for the 2012–13 season. That move will bring the Nets close enough to the Knicks, but this billboard was uncomfortably close.

And the Knicks were annoyed.

Prokhorov took over the Nets in May 2010 and immediately started firing shots across the Hudson River.

"We're going to turn Knicks fans into Nets fans," he boldly said in an interview with ESPN.

Prokhorov, like Jay-Z (who owns a minority stake in the Nets), was at first a Knicks fan. He initially made overtures to buy the franchise—he gave up after realizing the team wasn't for sale as a separate entity from Madison Square Garden and the Rangers—before he turned his attention to the Nets.

And then he set out to destroy what he could not own.

The billboard was only the beginning. Prokhorov's arrival, along with Jay-Z's presence and the anticipation of the Brooklyn move, made the Nets a legitimate player in the chase for LeBron James in 2010. The Nets' meeting with James came immediately after the Knicks sat down with the two-time MVP on that first day of free agency. The two teams literally passed each other in the lobby.

Neither team wound up getting LeBron, but the Knicks came away bigger winners in free agency by locking up Amar'e Stoudemire. They then put up a billboard in Brooklyn, near the construction site of the Nets' arena, which featured Stoudemire and the words, "Brooklyn Represent." Touché.

By August, the competition remained hot, as both teams went from recruiting LeBron to angling for Carmelo Anthony. Though the sense was that Anthony's preferred destination was the Knicks, the Nets tried to sell the Brooklyn-born star on being the center-piece in their historic move.

Three times the Nets seemed to have a trade in place with Anthony's team, the Denver Nuggets, but each time the deal failed to go through. Prokhorov then in late January announced the Nets were no longer pursuing a trade for Anthony, but a week before the trade deadline, when it seemed the Knicks were on the verge of closing the deal, the Nets jumped back into negotiations. Eventually, the Knicks came away with Anthony after a 13-player trade that disrupted the roster, but Prokhorov admitted a method to his madness.

"I think we made a very good tactical decision to force [the] Knicks to pay as much as they can," Prokhorov said in an interview with CNBC. "So it's very good, it's very interesting, it's very competitive."

The Knicks and Nets have played some heated contests, like this one in 2011, but only time will tell if the Nets' move to Brooklyn will create another Subway Series–sized rivalry.

Then a day after the Knicks officially announced the deal, the Nets pulled off a blockbuster that deflected attention away from the Garden: they acquired All-Star point guard Deron Williams.

All of this would be a lot juicier if the teams weren't just competing for players but for a championship. Truth be told, there has never been a real rivalry between the Knicks and Nets since the Nets came to the NBA in the ABA merger.

Real rivalries are formed in the playoffs—the Lakers, Celtics, and Bullets from the early 1970s; the Bulls, Pacers, and Heat in the 1990s—and the Knicks and Nets have met only three times in the playoffs since the Nets joined the league in 1976. The first meeting was in 1983, when Bernard King and company upset the 49-win Nets in a No. 4 vs. No. 5 first-round matchup that resulted in a two-game sweep of the best-of-three series.

It would be another 11 years before they'd meet again, in the first round of the 1994 playoffs. That Finals-bound Knicks team knocked off Chuck Daly's Nets handily.

Ten years later the tables had finally turned. The Nets, led by Jason Kidd, were one of the best teams in the league and had reached the NBA Finals in back-to-back seasons in 2002 and '03. The Knicks, with new addition Stephon Marbury, barely made the playoffs that year, and the divide in talent between the teams was evident in New Jersey's four-game sweep.

But even through that six-year stretch of winning seasons in the 2000s, the best run in franchise history, while the Knicks tumbled into mediocrity, the Nets remained barely a blip on the New York sports scene. The New Jersey name and location at the Meadowlands were detrimental factors, for sure.

The move to Brooklyn, which the Knicks never tried to block (though there are no territorial rights that would give them the power to do so), will be an interesting test of the Knicks' hold on New York.

But there should be enough room for both teams—the city shares the Yankees and Mets and Jets and Giants—and, if they both emerge as league powers one day, it could create a real Subway Series.

Fugazy!

Though the Knicks and Nets have rarely played in meaningful games, the 2004 first-round series did provide some entertaining give-and-take. It is a shame that the series ended in a four-game sweep, if only because it stole the opportunity for more drama.

The Nets completely dominated the Knicks 107–83 in Game 1, and Tim Thomas was knocked out of the series after a flagrant foul by Nets center Jason Collins on a dunk attempt. Thomas went down hard and bruised his back, knee, and ankle. In Game 2, the Nets kept up the physical play and cruised to a 99–81 win.

Thomas was furious.

"My goal is just to get back out there on the court before this series is over so I can go hit somebody. That's it. That's all I'm looking forward to," Thomas said on the off day between Games 2 and 3. "What's been done to me is going to be done to them. It's very simple."

Thomas also called out his own teammates for not answering the Nets' physical play and especially for not trying to avenge the hard hit on him.

"When I was laying on the floor I was expecting somebody to do something, to push, to shove, anybody. But it never happened," Thomas said.

It was a clear sign of the times for those Knicks, who looked nothing like the teams that bullied their way through the 1990s and didn't let anyone touch a teammate without getting a response. Several times in those games, the Knicks looked disinterested. Richard Jefferson took out Stephon Marbury on a fast-break layup; no reaction. Kenyon Martin took a swipe at veteran Dikembe Mutombo, and the strongest response came from the referees, who hit Martin for a technical foul.

But Thomas had plenty to say about the Nets' aggression and targeted the intimidating Martin with a quote that became an instant hit: "Just knowing his character," Thomas said, "he's a *fugazy* guy."

Fugazy: a street term meaning fake.

"He's fugazy as far as the whole tough-guy role," Thomas continued in his rant on Martin. "You get techs and you get fines and that makes you tough? Because your game is wild and crazy, that makes you tough? When a scuffle breaks out, you have 13 guys that can protect you. When it's you and someone else, what happens then?"

Thomas then closed with this: "Somebody call Don King and hook it up for us."

The New York media basked in the juicy controversy. And while Thomas was seething, Martin was amused. He walked into the morning shoot-around practice the next day, before Game 3, with the *Daily News* back page taped to the front of his practice jersey. The headline read, "Whiny Tim."

Martin laughed at Thomas' threats.

"He knows I'm going to be there at 7:00," he said. "He knows where to find me...Lock me and him in a room together and see who comes out."

As for *fugazy*, Martin said, "I think it applies to him more than me."

It also applied to the Knicks that season.

74 The Christmas King

On Christmas Day 1984, Bernard King provided fans with a memorable gift. The dominant scorer, who that season would become the only Knick in franchise history to lead the NBA in scoring, put forth the greatest all-time scoring performance in franchise history, with 60 points against the Nets.

"I still call it the 'Christmas Day Massacre,'" Jeff Turner, the Nets rookie small forward that game, told AOL Fanhouse in 2009. "I think I fouled out before I could break a sweat."

Normally, King would have been facing his brother, Albert, but he missed the game with an injury. Turner picked up three early fouls, and the Nets started throwing everybody at King after that—Micheal Ray Richardson, Kelvin Ramsey, and even Buck Williams. Then coach Stan Albeck sent 6'11" George Johnson to slow him down. It worked, as King missed six of his seven shots in the fourth quarter. Johnson finished with four blocked shots.

But how much credit should go to Johnson? King had 40 at the half and looked exhausted by the end of the game.

"Eventually," Turner said, "he got tired of scoring."

The Knicks, who had led by 17 points, actually wound up losing 120–114. After King, the next two leading scorers for the Knicks were Pat Cummings and Rory Sparrow, who each had 13 points. It certainly took the thrill out of the amazing game.

"I'd rather have scored 10 and we had won the game," King said afterward.

King's 60-point performance stood as a record at Madison Square Garden until February 2, 2009, when Kobe Bryant scored 61 points for the Lakers in a 126–117 win over the Knicks.

King watched the game from his home in Atlanta. When Bryant had 34 at the half, King turned to his 10-year-old daughter, Amina, and said, "Dadum's record is going to be broken tonight."

Other players have had big first-half performances before at the Garden, but there was something about Bryant that only a fellow competitor could recognize.

"I could tell because of that look in his eyes, the way he was moving on the floor," King said. "My record was toast.

"I wore a game face every night, so I know when a guy has that look in his eye. It's over."

And the competitor in him, of course, couldn't resist lamenting the game 25 years before.

"Had I not missed five free throws..." he laughed, pointing out that he went 20-for-25 from the line, while Bryant was a perfect 20-for-20. "...we wouldn't even be talking today."

75 Bernard Battles Boston

Larry Bird paused a moment when I asked him for his thoughts on Bernard King. His was an era of great small forwards, and Bird dominated all of them.

"As far as a basketball player," Bird said, "you couldn't play against a better one."

And in the spring of 1984, when the Celtics set a path for the NBA championship, King was at this best—and the Knicks gave Boston all it could handle.

King and the Knicks had already given Isiah Thomas and the Detroit Pistons more than they could handle in the first round, with a stellar five-game win that saw King average 43.2 points per game and score a league-record 213 points in the best-of-five playoff series.

King's performance against the Pistons had the entire NBA buzzing. And it had Celtics forward Cedric "Cornbread" Maxwell chomping at the bit.

"He ain't getting 40 on us," Maxwell declared before the series. "We're going to stop the bitch!"

Bird recalled the Maxwell quote.

"I think he got like 54," Bird deadpanned.

Actually, the Celtics did manage to contain King for most of the series. The Knicks star had been battling a flu and was playing with dislocated fingers in both hands. He had 26 points in Game 1 and only 13 in Game 2, and the Knicks were in an 0–2 deficit in the best-of-seven series. The Celtics were physical with the Knicks.

"One guy would foul you," King told D'Agostino in *Garden Glory*, "and the foul's already called and then two other guys would hit you."

Rather than have a practice, the team took time to air out its grievances with each other, including coach Hubie Brown. Truck Robinson stood up and made a passionate speech, and the team started to reconnect. Back at Madison Square Garden, before a boisterous crowd, Game 3 opened with Ernie Grunfeld flooring Kevin McHale early in the game.

"After that," Grunfeld told D'Agostino, "the Celtics realized they were in for a battle."

After he scored 24 in Game 3, the "bitch" dropped 43 points on Boston in Game 4, a 118–113 win that evened the series. After the Celtics came up with a blowout win in Game 5 at Boston Garden, the Knicks answered with a wildly thrilling 106–104 win in New York.

The series was physical and nasty. Rory Sparrow, who was taken out by Gerald Henderson, was tossed when he hit Bird in the back of the head going for a hard foul. Aside from Game 7 in

1970, it might have been, at the time, the best playoff atmosphere at the Garden. Bird missed a shot at the end and the crowd stayed around a good half hour afterward just cheering and celebrating.

Oh and the bitch? Forty-four points.

The series ended with a 121–104 loss in Game 7, as Bird, the league's MVP, dominated with 39 points, 10 rebounds, and 12 assists in one of the all-time great playoff performances. King had 24 points.

Bird won that battle with King, but years later he doesn't view it as a head-to-head victory.

"I didn't guard Bernard," Bird said. "I had no chance guarding Bernard."

He then grinned and added, "Maxwell didn't, either, by the way."

76 The Other Garden

Walt Frazier told the *New York Times* in April 2011, "The only green I like is money."

Frazier said he didn't even eat New England clam chowder.

Former Celtic Kevin McHale, now working for NBAtv, was asked to offer some thoughts about the old rivalry between the Knicks and Celtics. He talked about the games and playing in New York. Then he talked about playing in Boston at "the Garden."

He quickly specified, "Not Madison Square Garden. The *real* Garden is Boston Garden."

Now *this* is a rivalry.

Boston Garden was a house of horrors for every opponent, especially in the playoffs (and not just because Red Auerbach would turn off the hot water on cold winter nights, turn up the heat on a warm day, and provide threadbare towels to visiting teams). The Celtics were a dominant team through the 1950s and '60s, when Bill Russell led them to 11 NBA championships, including a dynastic run of eight straight. The tradition continued from there, to Dave Cowens to Larry Bird and then Kevin Garnett. The franchise owns 17 titles and can claim at least one championship in all but one decade (the 1990s) between 1950 and 2010.

The Knicks and Celtics have faced off 13 times in the playoffs over 60 years, most recently in the first round of 2011. That one was hardly a classic, as the Celtics swept the injury-depleted Knicks in four. Despite that, most of the meetings have been memorable battles.

There was a time, though very brief, when the Knicks actually dominated the Celtics. In their first three meetings, the Knicks eliminated Boston in 1951, '52, and '53 on their way to three straight NBA Finals appearances. And Boston Garden, which opened in 1928, was hardly an intimidating building back then. The Knicks won three of their first five playoff games there in those early years.

"We could always beat the Celtics in the playoffs, until Russell came," former Knick Ray Lumpp told D'Agostino in *Garden Glory*. "We could *always* beat Boston. We'd go on and they'd go home. But as time went on, when they got the big guy, Russell, he made all the difference."

By the time Russell arrived, the Knicks were no longer a playoff team. It wouldn't be until 1967 when the teams would meet again. The Celtics' run of consecutive titles ended that year, but not against the Knicks. After a 3–1 series win in the first round—the Knicks' only win in the series came in Boston—the Celtics were defeated by the Philadelphia 76ers in the Eastern Division Finals.

Two years later, Boston sent the Knicks home again after a bitter Game 6 loss at Boston Garden. But that Knicks team knew they were close. The following year, when the Celtics failed to make the playoffs for the first time in two decades, the Knicks won their first championship.

They would meet again in '72, with the Celtics now the young upstart team in the Eastern Conference Finals. The veteran Knicks put them away in five games and won two of three at Boston Garden.

The following year, however, the Celtics were back on top of the NBA. They finished the season with a 68–14 record, and that old Celtic Pride had returned. The Knicks and Celtics met again in the Eastern Conference Finals, and the Knicks won three of the first four games to put the Celtics on the brink of elimination once again. But Boston rallied with a pair of wins—one at home and one in New York—to send the series to a winner-takes-all Game 7 at Boston Garden.

The Celtics looked poised to put away the Knicks. In their storied history, they had never lost a Game 7.

But the Knicks weren't going up against Russell's Celtics. This was a different era.

There would be new history on this night. With John Havlicek limited because of a shoulder injury, Boston was overmatched in a 94–78 win by the Knicks. The Garden mystique was conquered.

A year later, the Celtics finally stopped the Knicks with a five-game win in the Eastern Conference Finals—the third-straight meeting and fourth in six years between the teams—and they went on to win their 12th NBA title.

It would be 10 years until the old rivals would cross paths again in the playoffs, and once again they played to an epic, physical seven-game battle, in which Larry Bird and the Celtics outlasted Bernard King's Knicks and, again, went on to win the championship.

Three years later, rookie coach Rick Pitino had the Knicks back in the playoffs for the first time since '84 and, naturally, their first-round opponent would be those same Celtics. Boston took the young Knicks out in four games but came away lauding the New York team.

"This was as tough a first-round series as we've had in a long time," McHale said after the series-clinching 102–94 win in Game 4 at Madison Square Garden. "The Knicks just wouldn't die."

By 1989–90, the Bird era was on life support but still had enough left for a 52-win season. But that young group Pitino led in '88 had more playoff experience under their belts after reaching the second round in '89. Still, the Celtics won Games 1 and 2 at Boston Garden in easy fashion, including a 157–128 blowout in Game 2 dubbed in the New York press as—what else?—"the Boston Massacre."

There were three days for the embarrassment of that game to simmer before Game 3 at Madison Square Garden, a much better effort. But still, it took a Larry Bird miss at the buzzer to save the season with a 102–99 win. The new life gave the Knicks confidence, and they trounced Boston 135–108 in Game 4 to force a deciding Game 5 at Boston Garden.

Here we go again.

The Knicks had already exorcised the Boston Garden demons in '73, but there was some other history working against them heading into this game: no team in NBA playoff history had ever before come back to win a best-of-five series after trailing 0–2. The Knicks were about to make history on one of the game's most historic courts.

It took a full-time effort from veteran Maurice Cheeks (48 minutes), 17 rebounds from Charles Oakley, and one of the greatest shots in Patrick Ewing's career—a turnaround three-pointer from the corner falling into the Knicks bench as the shot-clock buzzer sounded with two minutes to go—to finally bury the Celtics 121–114.

The win effectively signaled the end of Bird era. It was the first time since Bird arrived in 1979 that the Celtics had failed to advance out of the first round. And the Knicks made Larry Legend look old, especially on a notable play in Game 5, when he missed a reverse-dunk attempt.

Overall, the Knicks and Celtics have played 13 playoff series. After Boston's sweep in 2011, the Celtics have the edge 7–6.

Now *that's* a rivalry.

77 The Most Valuable Franchise

The Knicks don't rank with the Boston Celtics or Los Angeles Lakers when it comes to a championship legacy. But since the 1990s they have been a dynasty in one very important area, at least to the NBA: money.

Forbes magazine publishes an annual ranking of franchise values for each of the major professional sports teams. In January 2012 *Forbes* listed the Knicks as the second most valuable NBA team, at $780 million.

The Knicks haven't won an NBA title since 1973 and haven't been to the NBA Finals since '99. And up until April 2011 they hadn't even appeared in the postseason for seven years. But according to *Forbes*, they were the league's most valuable franchise from 2005 to 2008—and then the world champion Lakers jumped over them in 2009. The Lakers repeated in '10, but still the Knicks, who didn't even make the playoffs, reclaimed their place at No. 1 on the list in 2011. And with MSG upgrades the Knicks will probably be No. 1 again in 2013.

What's that famous saying about the three most important things about real estate?

Location, location, location.

The New York market is certainly this team's greatest asset. The team plays in the second-oldest arena in the league, yet you never hear the team complaining to the city—as we've seen in places such as Sacramento—about the need to build a new one to help generate revenue. The Garden is a revenue-generating machine. And the exposure of the team creates lucrative corporate partnerships (Coca-Cola, American Express, JPMorgan Chase, just to name a few) to fill the coffers.

The anticipation of landing the big prize in the 2010 free-agency sweepstakes, LeBron James, certainly led to a recent boost in investment interest in the team. But even after James was lost to the Miami Heat, the brand remained strong.

"Signing Amar'e Stoudemire has been a big help both on the court and with sponsors," Forbes.com's Mike Ozanian wrote. "The Knicks sold out their full season-ticket inventory for the first time since the 2001–02 season."

NBA commissioner David Stern is often accused of having a bias toward the Knicks, mainly because of the importance of having a successful team in the country's largest market. It's something he regularly downplays, and he has plenty of proof to the contrary. For most of the 2000s, the Knicks were a terrible team that never made the playoffs. Yet the NBA continued to flourish.

"We haven't had a New York team in the Finals for a number of years," Stern said in 2009, "but the league continues to go."

Stern may not show bias, but the source of the league's highest income, broadcast rights, has a different outlook. The NBA is better when the Knicks are good. For instance, when the Knicks, with newly acquired Carmelo Anthony, faced LeBron and the Heat on ESPN on February 27, 2011, the game produced the best preliminary local television rating for a regular-season game on the network. And *that* game went up against the Academy Awards.

"There's buzz in New York now," ESPN president George Bodenheimer told *Newsday*. "It's good for business."

78 The Spirit of '73

After he retired from basketball, Jerry Lucas went on to write a best-selling book about memory development and became one of the world's renowned experts in the field.

This evidence is one example of the unique weapons the Knicks had at their disposal in 1973, when they claimed their second NBA championship. Lucas, a talented center on skill alone, said that by the middle of the season he knew the plays of every single opponent.

"I'd see what they were running," he said at a reunion of the '73 team in 2003, "and I'd be just calling the plays out to the guys."

Imagine how maddening it must have been to play against that Knicks team, which many from the championship era believe to be the best team in franchise history.

As Frazier put it, "We were not the biggest or the fastest. But we were the smartest. And we were the best."

That team had talent. Four—Frazier, Earl Monroe, Willis Reed, and Dave DeBusschere—were later named among the NBA's 50 Greatest Players and six—the aforementioned four, plus Lucas and Bill Bradley (and coach Red Holzman)—have been inducted into the Basketball Hall of Fame.

But it wasn't just the wealth of talent that made this team win. It was the collective IQ of the team, from the stars through to reserves such as Phil Jackson, Henry Bibby, Barnett, and Dean Meminger.

They had stars, they had talented role players, and they had characters, too (for instance, older fans will remember lovable rookie Harthorne Wingo). This was a tight-knit group that, from the 1970 championship, had a collective belief in who they were and what they were. And how to play the right way. They were a coach's dream, the embodiment of Red Holzman's "find the open man" credo.

"Complete unselfishness, hard-nosed defense, and always looking to make the extra pass for the best possible shot," Wingo said at the reunion. "That's what we were about. I was a rookie on that team, and I was in awe. I swear, I'd be watching on the bench, and *weeks* would go by before someone took a shot that wasn't completely open. I've never seen basketball like that before or since."

Teammates Jerry Lucas, Willis Reed, and Bill Bradley celebrate the Knicks championship in style. (Getty Images)

Wingo

Red Auerbach had his trademark victory cigars, but Red Holzman had the human victory cigar in the form of Harthorne Wingo. The 6'6" forward was one of the many beloved characters of the championship era. He played in the Eastern Basketball Association and for the Harlem Wizards before the Knicks signed him as a reserve in 1972. Wingo hardly played but became a fan favorite because when he did get in the game, it usually meant the Knicks were ahead by a lot. For instance, in Game 2 of the '73 Eastern Conference Finals, when the Knicks answered a Game 1 blowout loss with a blowout win over the Celtics, the Garden crowd gleefully chanted, "Wing-go! Wing-go!" until Holzman put him in the game.

Those Knicks owned the city, or maybe it's better put that the city took ownership in them. The way they played, their selfless team-first approach, was widely admired and became a sense of pride.

The one disappointment of that season was that the city couldn't celebrate the championship with the team at Madison Square Garden, as they did in '70. This time, the Knicks were 2,462 miles away in Los Angeles, where, after cruising to a 102–93 win over the Lakers in Game 5 at the Forum, George Kalinsky snapped a famous photo of Lucas, Frazier, Reed, Jackson, and Bradley in a mostly empty locker room, sitting shoulder to shoulder, holding up their fingers to signal who was No. 1.

And there was no ticker-tape parade (though the '69 Mets rode down the Canyon of Heroes, the '70 Knicks team didn't get one, either), just a reception in front of City Hall with mayor John Lindsay.

The franchise is still waiting for its next title and its first parade.

The Hangover

The championship era didn't end slowly; it came to a screeching halt. One by one, the main figures disappeared. Willis Reed's knees caused him to retire early in the 1973–74 season. Dave DeBusschere also called it a day after that season to pursue a front-office career with the ABA's New York Nets (sounds like a Prokhorov move). Bill Bradley's skills diminished swiftly until his retirement after the 1976–77 season. Walt Frazier, who was headed to free agency, was then sent to Cleveland in '77.

And things changed at the Garden.

Ned Irish, who had run the team since it's creation in 1946, retired in 1974. Alan Cohen took over as chief executive officer of the Madison Square Garden Corporation. In 1977 the Garden and both the Knicks and Rangers became corporate-owned, as Gulf & Western paid double the market value for the entire package. All three have been related ever since.

The new corporate involvement—the parent company was known as "Engulf & Devour"—brought new demands. Red Holzman announced his retirement after 1976–77, which saw the third-straight losing season and second-straight without a playoff berth. Cohen, who briefly stayed on as CEO, was once quoted in the *New York Times* as saying he'd rather see the Garden profitable than one of its teams win a championship.

Cohen also previously embarrassed the franchise in 1975 with a ridiculous attempt to sign ABA star George McGinnis, whose NBA rights were owned by the Philadelphia 76ers. The Knicks first attempted to acquire McGinnis from the 76ers by offering Philly legend Earl Monroe, but a deal failed to materialize. So Cohen went ahead and signed McGinnis anyway, and the NBA not only rejected the contract but also punished the Knicks for tampering by stripping them of their 1976 first-round pick. It might have cost them a chance to draft Robert Parish, who went eighth overall that season to the Golden State Warriors.

The Knicks teams of the mid-to-late '70s had talent, such as big men Bob McAdoo and Spencer Haywood, but the talent just didn't mesh the way it did during the championship era. There was suddenly an obvious generation gap that created a divide on a team that once was so close.

"We brought in new people, and when you cross-match that with old people and old ways, things happen," Phil Jackson told D'Agostino in *Garden Glory*. "The new guys would complain that no one took their laundry or that [trainer Danny Whelan's] tape jobs weren't good enough.

"The older guys were used to a Knickerbocker way of doing things. We took our uniforms out and we washed them. There wasn't an equipment man who was doing that. But all these kids had been in these college situations where they'd had everything taken care of for them...It was just a level of responsibility that was expected of a player. If players could come in and rock the boat like that, it made you wonder about whether they had the responsibility to meet what we had established as a basketball team."

Meanwhile, upon Holzman's retirement, Cohen decided he wanted Reed to take over as head coach. The former captain had a little bit of success in his first season as coach in 1977–78, but they were swept in the playoffs that year by the Philadelphia 76ers.

Gulf & Western decided to bring in former New York Jets owner (and Meadowlands developer) Sonny Werblin to run the Garden. The Knicks kept throwing money at free agents, such as Marvin Webster, the latest high-profile big man to come through New York. Reed then was innocently caught up in a war of words in the media with Werblin, who fired his coach 14 games into the 1978–79 season and brought back Holzman.

The Knicks continued to lose, but they finally stopped bringing in high-priced talent and started building with youth. They traded McAdoo to the Celtics for three first-round picks—a deal that was done by Boston's owner and that infuriated Red Auerbach—which eventually added more young talent.

And as the '70s came to an end, the Knicks, seven years removed from their championship era, were starting all over again.

80 The Tragic Story of Ray Williams

Ray Williams was one of the few good stories of the Knicks' transition period after the championship era. The 1977 first-round pick out of the University of Minnesota (by way of that New York basketball hotbed, Mount Vernon) was a dynamo, and when he joined with '78 first-rounder Micheal Ray Richardson the following season, the Knicks believed they had their backcourt of the future.

The younger brother of All-Star Gus Williams, Ray was the perfect complement to the flashy Richardson. Both could score in bunches, and the two terrorized opposing backcourts with their pressure defense. In 1979–80 the tandem averaged 36 points per game and more than five steals per game. The following year, under Red Holzman, they won 50 games and Ray was a team captain.

Young center Bill Cartwright, one of those three first-rounders the Knicks received from Boston in the McAdoo deal, was the team's leading scorer, but there was friction between him and the dazzling backcourt, which played more off each other than off

Cartwright in the post. Williams had two critical flaws in his game: shot selection and turnovers. But effort was never a question.

When Williams' contract was up, the Knicks decided to let him go to the Nets and use his rights to acquire rugged power forward Maurice Lucas to add some veteran experience to the young 50-win team. Meanwhile, Williams flourished in New Jersey, where he averaged 20.4 points per game and scored a career-high 52 points in a game, which remains a franchise record.

After moving Richardson, a backcourt spot opened and the Knicks brought Williams back in 1983–84. He played a big part in that Bernard King–led group that took the Celtics to seven games in the Eastern Conference semifinals.

"Ray Williams was probably the second-most-talented guy on that team," Rory Sparrow told D'Agostino in *Garden Glory*. "He could really score and he sacrificed a lot of what he was as a player to fit into the system."

But when his contract expired at the end of that season, the Knicks decided once again to move on without him. In February 1985, the Celtics signed Williams to back up Dennis Johnson and Danny Ainge. Dave DeBusschere, who had become the Knicks general manager, joked that Williams would help the defending champion Celtics "as long as they keep the ball out of his hands at the end of the game. Otherwise, he'll try taking the last shot instead of Larry Bird."

Williams enjoyed a ride to the NBA Finals with Boston, though the team lost to the Lakers in six games. He then bounced from the Atlanta Hawks to the San Antonio Spurs and then back with the Nets all in the 1985–86 season. The following year, he played 32 games in New Jersey, which were his final in the NBA.

He went into retirement completely unprepared. Back then, unless you were a superstar such as Bird or Magic Johnson, you didn't make a great deal of money. In 10 seasons, Williams made a total of $2.5 million, and he spent a lot of it to buy his mother a house and support his family. He didn't have a college degree and had no idea what to do next. Seven years after his last NBA game, Williams was divorced, in bankruptcy court, and had lost his New Jersey home.

"I was a person who always gave," Williams told *Newsday* on February 10, 2011. "Even when I didn't have money, I would borrow money to help someone else out."

As a result, his life continued to unravel. Williams moved to Florida for a fresh start and borrowed off his NBA pension for a lump sum of $200,000. He worked odd jobs—golf course groundskeeper, maintenance man at an apartment complex, at a warehouse, and also as a girls' high school basketball coach—and continued to borrow money in an attempt to get himself back on his feet. A real-estate deal fell through, however, and it devastated him financially. He was back in bankruptcy court once again.

By the mid-2000s, he was living in his 1997 Chevy Tahoe. When it broke down, he found an abandoned '92 Buick on a back road and made it his home. He would fish for his own food. Gus once in a while would try to help, but he, too, was dealing with his own financial issues.

A story about his plight appeared in the *Boston Globe* on July 2, 2010, and Williams sounded desperate.

"If I didn't have faith, I probably would have done something drastic by now, something I would regret for a long time," he told the *Globe*. "I know what the devil wants me to do, to turn to crime or drugs, or anything to destroy my faith."

"I'm not trying to sit on my butt," he added. "I just need someone to reach out and help me."

When the story appeared, word traveled quickly. Kevin McHale, one of Williams' teammates with the Celtics (and in college at Minnesota) and Bernard King were some of the first to come to his aid. And Williams' hometown, Mount Vernon, offered him a job in the city's recreation department. He now works with kids, teaches basketball, visits his 86-year-old mother, and has even reconnected with his daughters. He also plans to create a foundation to help former athletes in need.

"Life isn't about getting knocked down, it's about getting back up," McHale told *Newsday*. "And Ray is getting back up."

81 The Rebirth of Spree

It had worked once before in franchise history, so why not again? Just before the 1998–99 lockout-shortened season, the Knicks set out to get younger, sleeker, and faster. As the NBA started becoming more of a high-scoring, up-tempo game, the plodding, physical Knicks of the '90s had to change.

Enter Latrell Sprewell.

The Knicks already had a shooting guard in Allan Houston, but the belief was that Houston's perimeter game and Sprewell's ability to slash would make for a dynamic duo. Houston watched video of Walt Frazier and Earl Monroe and bought into the idea.

"They won a championship together," Houston said at the time. "When we watched that tape, my wife and I looked at each other and said, 'You know what? It's the same thing.'"

Not quite. Though like Sprewell, Monroe was on the block because of a dispute with his current team, the Baltimore Bullets. But the Pearl never laid his hands on anyone. Sprewell was notorious for having attacked Warriors coach P.J. Carlesimo after an argument in practice on December 1, 1997. The three-time All-Star, who had previously been involved in physical altercations with teammates during his career, was suspended for the rest of the season and became a reviled icon of this new age of unruliness and disrespect for authority.

(Carlesimo, it should be noted here, was well known for riding players extremely hard and for his over-the-top verbal abuse. It was a perfect storm.)

There was great hesitation by the Knicks. While there was obvious concern about bringing in a controversial player—especially with the New York media ready to prey upon him—there was a greater fear that he would wind up with one of their biggest rivals, the Miami Heat or Indiana Pacers.

A face-to-face meeting with Sprewell at his Wisconsin home in January 1999 convinced them the player was worthy of a second chance. (It also helped that he was one of the league's most explosive scorers and in his prime.) The trade was completed on January 21, 1999 and included sending a beloved fan favorite, John Starks, to Golden State. The fans got over Starks pretty quickly, as Sprewell drew a huge ovation in his Madison Square Garden debut a few weeks later.

He showed a surprisingly gregarious side of him in New York and, after struggling through the regular season battling some injuries, he played a big role in the Knicks' thrilling run to the 1999 NBA Finals. Sprewell's strip on Tim Hardaway in Game 5 against the Heat led to Houston's series-clinching shot in the final seconds. He also poured in 35 points in Game 5 of the Finals against the San Antonio Spurs.

But he also called out his teammates after that Game 5 loss and questioned the collective effort. Some in the New York media felt Sprewell was talking about Houston, who struggled in the series.

Then in the fall he showed up late for training camp—without calling ahead to explain why. He had been in California for a court appearance from an incident that happened before he signed with the Knicks, and he drove cross-country after it was over.

That season, the Knicks reached the Eastern Conference Finals but lost to the Pacers. Sprewell played the last three games with a broken foot. Early in the next season, he spoke openly about how Kings All-Star Chris Webber wanted to be a Knick. Once again, reporters speculated that he wanted to see the Knicks deal Houston for Webber. Sprewell, who, along with Houston, was an All-Star in 2000–01, quietly campaigned all season for Webber. But when camp opened in 2001–02, the Knicks had three new free agents, but, as he said, "It wasn't Chris Webber. That's what I was hoping, but that didn't work out."

The Knicks had given Sprewell a five-year, $65 million contract extension in 2000 but signed Houston a six-year, $100 million extension in 2001. Sprewell started to rebel more and more. He walked out of the annual media training session—along with Marcus Camby—and was fined. Later that season, he blew off a shoot-around in Miami, which drew another fine.

The beginning of the end came when he showed up for training camp in October 2002 with a broken hand. He was hit with a $250,000 fine for not reporting the injury to the team and was suspended by team president Scott Layden and told to not come back until he could make "a positive contribution."

The Knicks finally severed ties with Sprewell in July 2003, when they traded him to Minnesota for pretty much the exact opposite: Keith Van Horn.

Linsanity

This story begins on a couch in Manhattan, where Jeremy Lin slept on February 3, 2012, after the Knicks returned from Boston following another tough loss. Lin played seven minutes in the first half, but did little to inspire an urge within the coaches or most fans to see more of him.

His career was on the verge of another transition; the Knicks were poised to put him on waivers (for the third time in three months) the following night before the passage of a deadline that would fully guarantee his contract for the rest of the season.

Lin crashed on teammate Landry Fields' couch that night and woke the next morning preparing for what could very well be his final game as a Knick. The team hosted the New Jersey Nets that evening and Lin once again came off the bench in the first half.

The Knicks were struggling, six games under .500 and in the process of losing to the Nets. While the Knicks had an All-Star-caliber frontcourt, with Carmelo Anthony, Amar'e Stoudemire, and Tyson Chandler, their offense struggled mightily because of poor point guard play.

Coach Mike D'Antoni was desperate for a spark, but admitted later that he hesitated several times to pluck the undrafted, twice-waived no-name off the bench. D'Antoni was already on the hot seat as it was. How would it look if he went with a guy who had been in the D-League only a few weeks prior?

"We were already in a crisis and I can't be [grasping] at straws," D'Antoni said. "The other players would be looking at me like, 'Are you crazy?'"

Crazy is what happened when Lin re-entered the game in the second half and went head-to-head with All-Star Deron Williams.

Lin poured in 19 of his 25 points in the second half, including 12 in the fourth quarter, to spur a thrilling 99–92 win that sparked a worldwide trend known as "Linsanity."

Lin went on to average 24.6 points and 9.2 assists over a 10-game stretch that saw the Knicks go 8–2, including seven straight wins. Lin started the very next game after the victory over the Nets and had 28 points and eight assists in a win over the Jazz. Two games later, before a national audience on ESPN, Lin dropped 38 points and seven assists against Kobe Bryant and the Lakers. He also hit a game-winning three-pointer over the Raptors on February 14, even drawing roars of approval from the Toronto crowd.

It was the ultimate rags-to-riches story, one that gripped the entire NBA for the month of February.

Lin's Asian heritage—he was the second player of Asian descent in Knicks history, after Wat Misaka—brought him international fame. He was twice on the cover of *Sports Illustrated* and also made the cover of *Time* magazine in Asia. His jersey was the top-seller of all NBA jerseys by the NBA Store from December 2011 to April 2012. He was so hot, even Kim Kardashian's publicity team tried to purport a rumor that the two were dating, though Lin quickly denied it. Yes, it was that surreal.

"I'm not going to sit here and say I knew I was going to do this," Lin said of his sudden fame. "I don't think anyone, including myself, saw this coming."

Overall, Linsanity amounted to 26 games from February 4 to March 24, but it was as wild of a time as anyone could remember in franchise history. Lin's season ended prematurely after a torn meniscus resulted in him sitting out the playoffs after he underwent minor surgery. He sparked some controversy when during the playoffs he labeled himself "85 percent" and yet decided not to play despite the team's desperate need at the point guard position. Here was the beginning of an end no one saw coming.

Lin became a restricted free agent (perhaps one of the reasons why he wouldn't play at less than 100 percent?) when the season ended and one of the teams that had dismissed him only six months earlier, the Rockets, signed him to a three-year, $25.1 million contract. The deal had a whopping $14.9 million payout in the third season, which was labeled a "poison pill" and meant to deter the Knicks from matching because of hefty luxury tax implications that could cost the Knicks upwards of $40 million in that third year. But no one expected the Knicks, one of the NBA's richest franchises, to be deterred by money.

When asked for his opinion, Anthony called it a "ridiculous contract," which fueled existing speculation that Melo didn't want to share the spotlight with the young star. Truth be told, several others within the organization felt Lin betrayed the Knicks by agreeing to a contract that was clearly set up to negatively impact the Knicks.

Compounding the issue is that Lin initially agreed to a four-year deal for the same amount, but the third year had a more manageable $9.3 million payout with the fourth year not guaranteed. The Knicks had every intention of matching that deal, but the Rockets, intent on blowing the big-money franchise out of the water, then went back to Lin with the three-year, fully-guaranteed deal.

And on July 18, just over five months after Linsanity began, the plug was officially pulled when general manager Glen Grunwald called Lin to inform him that the contract would not be matched. Fans were divided in a heated civil war over the decision about this beloved player with such an inspiring story, intriguing potential, and a Tebowesque magnetism.

He said good-bye with a revelation that left Linsaniacs weeping and skeptics sneering.

"Honestly," Lin told *Sports Illustrated* the next day, "I preferred New York."

83 The Night Patrick Hugged the Garden

One player who never cared about media policies or worried about the things he said (or what was said about him) was Patrick Ewing. Throughout most of his career, Ewing often shared a love-hate relationship with the fans of New York: both loved the team but hated each other.

The fans roared when he arrived as a rookie, through the good fortunes—and, perhaps, a strategically chilled envelope—of the NBA's first draft lottery. But early in his first season in New York, when Bernard King was in hermitage and the team was otherwise awful, Ewing was pelted with crumpled-up paper after a bad game. It happened to be Patrick Ewing Poster Night.

In 1996 when the crowd expressed its displeasure with the team, Ewing made the ultimate mistake of saying, "if the fans are going to boo, they should stay home." And by 2000, tired of the media crush that crowded his stall every night and the demanding fans who were constantly on his case about failing to win a championship, Ewing wanted out.

He had been through so much in 15 years. But there was one night in 1994, one moment of catharsis, when it couldn't get any better. It was Game 7 of the Eastern Conference Finals against the Indiana Pacers.

The series was a brutal battle (including the Reggie Miller "chokers" game), but the finale was a classic that went down to the final seconds. The Pacers took a 90–89 lead with 34.5 seconds left after a Dale Davis dunk that Ewing almost blocked while sliding quickly across the lane with help defense. Actually, it could have been a foul on Ewing, but he was spared the whistle, which would have been his fifth foul.

After the ensuing timeout, John Starks and Ewing worked a pick-and-roll. The ball normally would have gone to Ewing, but Starks opted to drive the ball as Miller was caught in the screen. Starks got around Antonio Davis but missed a double-pump layup against the defense of Dale Davis.

No one put a body on Ewing, who crashed into the paint and slammed home the rebound with 27.1 seconds left to give the Knicks a 91–90 lead. It was his 22nd rebound of the game, his playoff career-high, and 11th offensive board.

Miller airballed a contested jumper on one of his trademark curl-and-catch plays with 4.3 seconds left. When Starks caught the inbound pass from Anthony Mason, Miller immediately shoved him to the ground with a foul to stop the clock with 3.2 seconds left. Incredibly, Miller was called for a flagrant foul, which meant the Knicks would retain possession after Starks' free throws. The game was essentially over.

The Garden crowd roared. The NBA Finals were at hand.

Ewing marched up the court along the sideline and, like a wrestler in the WWE, he waved for more. He slapped fives with fans and even bear-hugged one, lifting him right off the ground. Some fans tried to run onto the court to celebrate with him.

Patrick the Great

Patrick Ewing had many big playoff moments throughout his career, but his greatest might have been in a shocking 94–89 win over the defending champion Chicago Bulls in Game 1 of the 1992 Eastern Conference semifinals. Ewing had a monster game, with 34 points, 16 rebounds, and six blocked shots in the win. Chicago won three of the next four to take a 3–2 lead in the series, and in Game 6 the Knicks appeared to be on the cusp of elimination when Ewing went down with a sprained ankle. But he limped back out on the court, welcomed by a roar from the Garden crowd, and put up 27 points, eight rebounds, and three blocks in 42 minutes to lead the Knicks to a 100–86 win to force a Game 7.

For Patrick and the Garden that night, there was nothing but love.

When Haywoode Workman missed a desperation three-pointer at the buzzer, Ewing raised his long arms toward the Garden's famed spoked-wheel ceiling. Teammates hugged him. It was one of the greatest playoff performances of his career, in one of the most important games. Along with the 22 rebounds, he had 25 points, seven assists, and five blocked shots.

And before he left the court, Ewing jumped up on the scorers' table, faced the crowd and outstretched his arms. If it was possible for one man to hug 19,763 people at one time, Ewing did it.

Almost two weeks later, they'd be cheering for him again in yet another playoff performance of the ages. Ewing had 24 points, 12 rebounds, and eight blocked shots (and even hit a three-pointer) to lead the Knicks to a 91–84 win over the Rockets in Game 5 of the NBA Finals at the Garden. Ewing and the Knicks were one game away from a championship.

That would, however, be their last win of the season—and the closest Ewing ever came to the title. A year later, the Garden would fall silent when his finger roll down the lane bounced out at the buzzer and ended the season in the second round. The frustration of failing grew each year until both sides were ready for a divorce.

Absence certainly makes the heart grow fonder, but so does going from a perennial contender to a lottery team. Ewing's departure signaled not only the end of an era but also a missed opportunity. The franchise had one of the game's most dominant centers for 15 years and could not win a title. But that didn't mean his tireless effort and determination year after year should have been taken for granted.

When he returned for the first time wearing the jersey of another team, the Seattle Sonics, years of appreciation showered over him. And when his No. 33 was raised to the Garden rafters on February 28, 2003, Ewing opened his address by thanking the people he realized he missed the most.

"We've had our ups and our downs. Now you know we've had our ups and our downs," he said with a broad smile, which prompted cheers and laughter.

All had been forgiven.

"If I had to do it over again," he said, "I wouldn't want to play nowhere else but in New York."

The O.J. Game

The day started with a memorable celebration, as the New York Rangers cruised down the Canyon of Heroes. The city was celebrating a Stanley Cup championship, the first in 54 years, and with the Knicks in the NBA Finals, everyone believed they would be back at City Hall for another party in a few days.

It was a surreal time at Madison Square Garden that spring of 1994. Both teams had gone on inspiring runs and seemed to alternate games each night, each one increasingly dramatic and exhausting as the New York spring edged toward summer.

Not since 1972 had both teams reached the championship round. (The Rangers lost to the Boston Bruins in the Stanley Cup Finals that year and the Knicks fell to the Los Angeles Lakers in the NBA Finals.) But this year, the Rangers raised the Cup at the Garden in Game 7 over the Vancouver Canucks on June 14 with many of the Knicks players watching on television and some, such as Anthony Mason, in the crowd wearing Rangers jerseys.

The next night, captain Mark Messier brought the Cup back to the Garden and presented it to the basketball crowd during a critical Game 4 for the Knicks, who trailed 2–1 after rookie Sam Cassell's big three-pointer won it for the Houston Rockets in Game 3. Perhaps inspired by the Cup, the Knicks won Game 4 91–82 and were poised to close out the winter season at the Garden with one last cheer. A large television audience tuned in to the national broadcast on NBC to watch what was one of the most competitive NBA Finals in history.

But suddenly, there was something much bigger happening. The broadcast had cut to a developing story in Los Angeles, where earlier in the day, football great O.J. Simpson had been charged with the murder of his wife, Nicole, and her friend, Ronald Goldman. Later in the afternoon, Simpson was said to be a wanted fugitive by the Los Angeles District Attorney.

But by 9:30 PM, Simpson was on the 405 freeway in a white Ford Bronco, driven by friend and former teammate Al Cowlings. And Simpson had a gun.

After a few brief reports from the news desk during stoppages of play, NBC was finally compelled to cut in *during* the game.

"This is Bob Costas. It is our professional obligation to cover the ballgame tonight in what we hope is an appropriate fashion. We are, of course, mindful of the O.J. Simpson situation, and we will apprise you of any developments."

So while Patrick Ewing was having the game of his life (25 points, 12 rebounds, eight blocked shots, and two steals in 43 minutes), hardly anyone was watching. Even people at the Garden went out to the concourse to check out the video of the stunning, bizarre, low-speed chase going on in California. Remember, these were the days when the Internet was in its infancy.

Rather than cut back and forth, NBC showed the game in split-screen with coverage of the Simpson situation in the larger box.

"Bob, we are witnessing tonight a modern tragedy and drama of Shakespearean proportions," NBC anchor Tom Brokaw began.

Almost every market in the country, aside from, of course, New York and Houston, completely cut away from the game and went exclusively with the coverage of the Simpson drama.

Costas was at the Garden and, as he revealed in an August 2000 story in *Playboy*, missed a call from Simpson, who had previously worked with him on NBC's NFL broadcasts.

"I've heard from a couple of people that an audio man answered the phone," Costas told the magazine. "O.J. said, 'Is Bob Costas there?' 'Who's calling?' 'O.J. Simpson.' 'Yeah, right.' And the guy hangs up. The luckiest thing that ever happened to me is that I never received that telephone call."

Very few people saw the Knicks put the finishing touches on a 91–84 win. In fact, the game drew a 7.8 Nielsen rating, which wound up the lowest ever for an NBA Finals game on NBC. Perhaps everyone else was watching CNN.

The series as a whole did rather well, with an aggregate 12.4 Nielsen rating for the seven games. That means a lot of people did see most of the series, including John Starks' 2-for-18 performance in Game 7.

Now *that* was witnessing a modern tragedy and drama of Shakespearean proportions.

85 Bald Heads and Black Sneakers

The NBA has long fancied itself a stylish league (remember Clyde?). Though some might argue that style only entered the league in 1984, when that high-flying guard from North Carolina came on the scene with his wagging tongue and two-toned sneakers. And he, as everyone knows, introduced the league to baggy shorts.

Michigan's Fab Five took that to another level, or should we say, a longer length. The Fab Five also added black sneakers with black socks to their look.

"Straight solidarity," Jalen Rose said in a March 2011 interview with Complex.com.

That's what Charles Oakley had in mind late in the 1993–94 season, when he started pushing an idea on his teammates that soon became a Knicks playoff tradition.

Part of it, actually, started in 1992. Up until the dawn of the Air Jordans (which at first were banned by the NBA), every team aside from the Celtics wore white sneakers. The Celtics tradition of wearing black sneakers wasn't a fashion statement as much as it was Red Auerbach being cheap. As legend has it, Auerbach had his team wear black because it hid the scuff marks and wear-and-tear. Therefore, they didn't have to be replaced as often as white sneakers.

The Knicks wore black sneakers in the 1992 playoffs, which opened with a five-game win over the Detroit Pistons. The idea came not from Oakley or Patrick Ewing or John Starks. It came from a reserve player named Kennard Winchester, who played just 15 games that season (and saw just 11 minutes of action in the playoffs).

"We wanted to show we were unified, more than anything else," reserve center Tim McCormick told the *New York Times* that year. "And now Kiki Vandeweghe has some formal shoes he can wear."

By '94 black sneakers in the playoffs were a given. But Oakley had something new he wanted to add. Something that really would be a show of solidarity.

In involved an electric razor.

Only four other players joined Oakley on his mission: Derek Harper, Greg Anthony, Herb Williams, and Charles Smith.

"I thought it would be a good gesture on my part, to let the guys know that we're not going to care about how we look," Smith told the *Times* that year. "If we look silly, stupid, it doesn't matter. It's a thing of coming together."

The 32-year-old Harper, who kept his moustache, already had a receding hairline to begin with.

"I hope mine comes back," he said.

Of course, Pat Riley, with his trademark thick, slicked-back coif, wasn't going to take a seat in Oakley's barber chair.

"I don't think they'd want me to do that," Riley said. "It would be such a shocker that they wouldn't be able to play. If I had to look like that, I'd scare the hell out of everybody. I know it won't be unanimous, because I know Patrick won't do it."

Truth. "I like my high-top," Ewing said of his square fade.

While Ewing would resist each year—coincidentally, he now wears the little bit he has left tight to his skull—Oakley, Harper, and the others would shave it clean before the playoffs began. It became the equivalent of the playoff beard, which is a hockey tradition.

It took Allan Houston three years before he decided to go with the flow for the 1999 playoffs. He then hit the biggest shot of his career, in Game 5 against the Miami Heat.

The long playoff drought in the 2000s created a separation from the playoff era, and when the Knicks returned to the postseason in 2011 for the first time in seven years, black sneakers had become a regular part of every team's road uniform. As for shaved heads? Only Chauncey Billups and Anthony Carter had that look, but that had more to do with genetics than solidarity.

86 Mase and the Messages

Anthony Mason didn't join his other teammates in the head-shaving rites of spring, which Charles Oakley tried to make an annual playoff tradition. Mason had his own trademark tradition.

Before the current generation of NBA players started wearing their thoughts and inspirations on their skin with tattoo ink, Mason made his skull a living billboard.

The burly 6'8" forward from Queens was a discovery of longtime Knicks scout Fuzzy Levane, who saw Mason playing for the Long Island Surf in the United States Basketball League, a summer circuit that, at the time, gave peripheral players a chance to be seen by NBA scouts and perhaps earn invites to training camp.

Mason wasn't exactly an unknown. He was selected by the Portland Trail Blazers in the third round (53rd overall) of the 1988 NBA Draft but didn't make the roster after training camp. He played overseas in Turkey and Venezuela and then bounced around the Continental Basketball Association, where he met a guy named John Starks.

The NBA called occasionally, but he didn't stick. There were 21 games late in the 1989–90 season with an awful Nets team that finished 17–65 and then three games in a brief stint with an equally bad Denver Nuggets team in 1990–91. Mason joined the Surf in the summer of '91 when Levane had Ernie Grunfeld come out to take a look at this powerful yet skilled forward who was averaging 27 points per game. He earned an invite to camp, where he reunited with Starks.

"I knew of Mason back when he'd been a star in the CBA playing for the Tulsa Fastbreakers," Starks wrote in his autobiography, *My Life*. "Mase used to be the man in Tulsa and he'd be the first person to tell you. He liked Tulsa. Mase was originally from Queens, but he'd come back down to Tulsa in the summertime even when the CBA season was over. Tulsa has a way of charming people...Mase got his nickname, 'the Beast' in Tulsa."

Mason and Starks became two of Pat Riley's favorite workers, and yet both of them drove him mad. By his third season, Mason had crossed the line with Riley when he had a war of words with the coach that led to a suspension late in the regular season. Riley had benched Mason and Charles Smith in the second half of a loss to the Hawks, and Mason was furious. It led to him publicly disagreeing with the coach's decisions and saying that Riley "defines offense different than I define it."

But Mason played a big role in Riley's rotation, and his toughness fit perfectly with that rugged team. In the 1994–95 season, he was named the NBA's Sixth Man of the Year. The award earned him a six-year, $25 million contract.

When Don Nelson replaced the departed Riley, he was determined to use Mason in the role of "point-forward" in his up-tempo offensive system. Nelson's intention was to feature Mason in an offense that would put less emphasis on Patrick Ewing's methodical post-up game. As a result, Mason played 3,457 minutes that season, which still stands as a franchise record in his first season with the Hornets.

Not everyone was impressed with the CBA/USBL refugee. Dennis Rodman, in his book, *Bad As I Wanna Be*, named Mason along with Indiana's Dale Davis and New Jersey's Derrick Coleman in his criticism of some big contracts that existed in the NBA. "I see injustice," Rodman wrote. "Who buys a ticket to see those guys play?"

Mason shot back in a 1996 story in the *New York Times*, saying of the future Hall of Famer, "What does the guy do, other than rebound?"

In the summer of '96 the Knicks brass seemed to agree with Rodman. In a busy summer in which the Knicks added high-level talent to put around Ewing (he had been reestablished as the focal point once Jeff Van Gundy replaced Nelson), Mason was dealt to the Charlotte Hornets for Larry Johnson. Mason was named third-team All-NBA and second-team All-Defensive in his first season with the Hornets.

Fans today might remember Mason for his head almost as much as his game, and we're not talking about basketball IQ.

There was a barber in Jamaica, Queens, named Freddie Avila who worked his artistry into Mason's hairstyles. It started with simple things, such as the Knicks logo and a skyline of Manhattan.

Then Mason had the name, "Dogg Pound," which was a reference to the Knicks bench players. By the NBA Finals, the message was simple: "In God's Hands."

Harp

Charles Oakley may have been the toughest, Anthony Mason may have been the meanest, and John Starks may have been the wildest, but in the 1994 playoffs, it was one of the newest—and oldest—Knicks who engaged in one of the wildest brawls in Knicks playoff history. And it was one that would forever change the league mainly because of where it happened and, most of all, who had a front-row seat.

The Knicks and Bulls met in the playoffs for a fourth-straight year and fift time in six years. By that point, these two rivals were sick of each other. But Derek Harper was new to this. So was Jo Jo English, a 24-year-old, second-year guard who barely played.

But things happen when the playoffs come around. And after Harper's hard foul on B.J. Armstrong in Game 2 at Madison Square Garden, Phil Jackson called for his team to "fight fire with fire."

The Jordanless Bulls, down 0–2 in the best-of-seven Eastern Conference semifinal series, came out a grittier team in Game 3 at Chicago Stadium, where the atmosphere was always intense whenever the Knicks came to town. English was in the game late in the second quarter and playing Harper tough, with a great deal of hand-checking that started to annoy the veteran point guard.

With 2:41 left in the half, Horace Grant was called for a foul. But as the play came to a stop, English and Harper were suddenly face-to-face. And English had plenty to say.

English shoved Harper in the chest, and the two went at it. Before anyone could react, the two were wrestling into the backcourt until Harper got a hold on English and body slammed him into the first row.

A melee ensued as the two grappled while stunned spectators fled. Bulls center Scott Williams then did something idiotic: he dove into the fray. That set off Patrick Ewing, who went after Williams, while Pat Riley jumped into the pile and pulled Harper away.

It was literally a bench-clearing brawl, one that old Chicago Stadium had seen plenty of times before—but for hockey, not basketball.

As the players pushed and shoved—and John Starks was getting double-teamed by arena security—there was one onlooker about 10 rows above them who stood and watched with a horrified expression.

His name was David Stern.

Harper and English were both ejected from the game, a trade-off the Bulls, who led by 10 points at the time, would gladly take. They opened up a 22-point lead in the third quarter but needed a buzzer-beater by Toni Kukoc to escape with a 104–102 win.

Stern levied hefty fines and suspended Harper for two games and English for one. (The fight would resonate three years later, after the ugly ending to Game 5 in Miami, when Stern hit the Knicks with even harsher penalties just for leaving the bench during an altercation, a rule that was borne from the Harper-English incident.)

Without Harper, the Knicks lost Game 4 but rallied to win Game 5 87–86, thanks to a pair of Hubert Davis free throws (and a Hue Hollins whistle).

Harper was at his best in the NBA Finals that year, with huge performances in the three games at Madison Square Garden, including 21 points, with five three-pointers, five assists, and two steals in the critical Game 4 victory.

Harper became a Knick that year in an in-season blockbuster trade with the Dallas Mavericks after the team's starting point guard, Doc Rivers, blew out his knee and was lost for the rest of the season. Harper played well and for three seasons was a rock at the point-guard position until he was let go as a free agent in 1996.

A Return to Defense

As we've already discussed, defense had been the foundation of the championship era of this franchise. It was the identity of the teams led by Patrick Ewing in the 1990s, when the Knicks went to two NBA Finals and reached the Eastern Conference Finals four times.

But after Ewing's departure following the 1999–2000 season, that defensive mindset slipped away. The reputation of the Knicks as a rugged, hardworking team that thrived on shutting you down disappeared by the mid-2000s. And by 2010, the Knicks were viewed in a much different light.

"The thing that is thought about here is that they don't play defense," Tyson Chandler said on the day he became a Knick.

This is why Chandler was acquired in a three-team, five-player transaction on December 10, 2011. Glen Grunwald, who was interim general manager at the time, pulled off the sign-and-trade to fill what had been a gaping hole at the center position—and the defensive side of the ball—since Ewing left.

And Chandler, an athletic, hardworking 7'1" center with long arms and a championship ring from his time with the Dallas Mavericks, embraced his role from day one.

"That's my first goal, is to get everybody thinking defense," he said. "We know you can play offense…but defensively, I want us to buckle down."

The stunning move came at somewhat of a price, as the Knicks used their amnesty clause, which was the result of a new collective bargaining agreement, to waive veteran point guard Chauncey Billups, who was acquired in the Carmelo Anthony trade.

But while it left a deficiency at the point guard position for most of the season—though Jeremy Lin's emergence helped fill the void—Chandler's impact was immediately felt. He led the revival of that old defensive mentality at Madison Square Garden and the Knicks saw vast improvements as a team.

The Knicks were sixth in the NBA in defensive efficiency in Chandler's first season, a year after the team was the ninth-lowest in that category. They also improved from 27th in the NBA in points allowed (105.7) to 11th (94.7) in Chandler's first season and became a better rebounding team, from 25th in 2010–11 (47.7) to 12th in 2011–12 (51.1).

Chandler did not put up gaudy defensive statistics (he was top 15 in rebounding and top 25 in blocked shots), but his unquestionable impact on the team's improvement earned him the coveted NBA Defensive Player of the Year award for the 2011–12 season.

"He changed that team around defensively," said Miami Heat forward Shane Battier, who, himself, knows a thing or two about defense.

Though Chandler also had a solid reputation as a defensive-minded center, it was the first time he won the award in his career.

Perhaps more notably, despite the Knicks' history with defensive-focused teams, Chandler was the team's first ever Defensive Player of the Year winner since the award began in 1982–83.

However, Chandler wasn't just a defensive stopper in his first season in New York. He also led the NBA in field goal percentage—mainly thanks to lob dunks and put-backs—with a franchise-record 67.9 percent clip, which was the third-highest in NBA history.

Flanked by Anthony and Amar'e Stoudemire, Chandler's presence creates a potentially dominant frontline for the Knicks that was built to make a run at a championship.

"I think when you talk about building a championship team," coach Mike Woodson said, "it starts in the middle."

89 50/50 Vision

There have been only six players in franchise history who have hit the 50-point mark in a game. Richie Guerin did it first. Jamal Crawford did it last. Bernard King did it most.

And on consecutive nights in Texas during the 1983–84 season, King did it twice.

He had just appeared in the All-Star Game in Denver, in which he scored 18 points in 22 minutes. The first stop for the Knicks was San Antonio, against a middling Spurs team and an aging George Gervin.

The Iceman could still fill it up, however, and after the first quarter, he matched King shot-for-shot as the two each had 16 points. It looked, as Rory Sparrow would joke to Trent Tucker, "like a shootout at the O.K. Corral."

King just kept firing away and hitting his target with devastating accuracy. "It was almost like an unconscious feeling," he would tell writer Bruce Newman in a story about his amazing trip in the February 13, 1984, issue of *Sports Illustrated*.

Gervin ran out of bullets at 41 points. King hit 50 on the nose to lead the Knicks to a 117–113 win.

The Knicks headed right to Dallas for a game the following night against the Mavericks, who were a solid team—with, incidentally, a rookie named Derek Harper and a high-scoring small forward of their own, Mark Aguirre.

King told Newman that he wasn't normally superstitious, but coming off the 50-point game he decided to follow the same routine as the day before. He called room service and ordered a turkey-breast sandwich with a vanilla milkshake and hit the court for his pregame warmup exactly 10 minutes before the pregame meeting.

The Knicks cruised to a 105–98 win. As Sparrow went to dribble out the clock, his teammates on the bench were screaming for him to pass the ball to King.

"I didn't realize he had 50," Sparrow told Newman. "In San Antonio, Bernard scored points in mass quantities. But in the Dallas game it was more a matter of grinding out 50 points. That is, if you can grind out 50."

King caught the ball and drilled a 20-footer for his 50th point.

"I just said to myself, 'I'm not missing this one,'" he told Newman.

It was a shot that made history. He was the first player to record back-to-back 50-point games since Rick Barry did it almost two decades before. And he was the first to do it on consecutive nights since Wilt Chamberlain in 1963–64.

Since King, there have been four players in the NBA to record back-to-back 50-point games, including, of course, Michael Jordan, who is the only player to ever do it in the playoffs. The others are Antawn Jamison, Allen Iverson, and Kobe Bryant.

Guerin had three 50-point games as a Knick, and Willis Reed became the second Knick to hit 50 with 53 points in a 129–113 win over the Lakers at the Forum.

Ewing had two 50-point games in his career: 51 (plus 18 rebounds) in a 115–110 loss to the Boston Celtics on March 24, 1990, and 50 (and 15 rebounds) in a 113–96 win over the Charlotte Hornets on December 1, 1990.

In the 2002–03 season, Allan Houston twice went for 50, but those games were a month apart. He had 53 points in a 117–110 win over the Lakers (Kobe had 40) on February 16 and then had 50 points in a 120–111 win over the Bucks on March 16.

On January 26, 2007, Crawford had 52 points in a 116–96 win over the Miami Heat, which is the last time a Knick has hit the 50-point mark to date.

90 The Minutemen

The Knicks were so good, so deep, in the 1969–70 season that one joke around the league was that if you wanted to balance the talent in the NBA, break up the Knicks bench.

Red Holzman's reserves were too good to be merely known as super subs. There were collegiate All-Americans in this group, players who in any other situation would be starters. *New York Post* writer Leonard Lewin dubbed them "the Minutemen" for their ability to step into a game for as little as one minute and make an impact.

That year, Cazzie Russell and Mike Riordan were the lead Minutemen, with major contributions from Dave "the Rave" Stallworth and Nate Bowman. Russell had lost his starting role to

Bill Bradley after he broke his ankle during the 1968–69 season but was unquestionably the league's most talented reserve player.

Cazzie came up big on many occasions that season, such as 25 points against the Celtics in a 102–96 win and 18 points when Bradley left the game early with an ankle injury in a blowout win over Detroit.

He and Riordan, a rugged defensive stopper and native New Yorker, took the reserve thing to a whole new level that season, too. March, just before the playoffs began, brought the start of the U.S. Postal Service workers strike. President Richard Nixon called on the National Guard to step in and handle the mail-distribution duties.

These days, the only way a postal strike would impact a pro athlete is when fan mail or—heaven forbid—a paycheck would arrive late. But in the 1960s, before the abolition of the military draft in 1973, most athletes would enlist in the National Guard to fulfill their military obligations.

So when Tricky Dick (no, not McGuire) needed someone to deliver, two of Holzman's best reservists turned in their Knicks jersey for the uniform of a postal worker. Russell spent a few days working at an armory in Kingsbridge (the Bronx), while Riordan delivered mail through suburban neighborhoods on Long Island.

Riordan then switched back to his Knicks jersey and scored 11 of his 13 points in the fourth quarter of Game 2, a 106–99 win over the Baltimore Bullets.

Russell came up big again in the playoffs with 18 points in 25 minutes in a critical Game 4 win over Lew Alcindor and the young Milwaukee Bucks, to give the Knicks a 3–1 lead in the best-of-seven Eastern Division Finals. The Knicks would close it out the next game and advance to the Finals.

Then Russell and Riordan both made major contributions in the first game of the NBA Finals against the Lakers, a 124–112 win.

And that critical Game 5 that saw Willis Reed go down with the thigh injury? Dave DeBusschere gets most of the credit for battling Wilt Chamberlain, but Russell and Stallworth combined for 32 points off the bench in that pivotal win.

Stallworth was a success story just being on the court. It was late in his second NBA season when the 6'7" former first-round pick started feeling "twinges" in his chest. Then, during a game against the Warriors in Fresno, California, he had what tests later revealed to be a heart attack. Amazingly, he played the next night. He was cleared by a doctor in San Francisco before results of a cardiogram showed that the 25-year-old in fact did suffer a heart attack.

Initially, there were concerns that his career was over. "The manner in which he responds to treatment," general manager Eddie Donovan said at the time, "will determine his future in basketball."

He missed the next two seasons but managed to return to full health in time for training camp in 1969–70. He went on to play six more seasons in the NBA and retired as a Knick in 1974–75.

Stallworth, along with Riordan, was also part of one of the biggest trades in Knicks history. Early in the 1971–72 season the Knicks sent the two valuable Minutemen to the Bullets for Earl Monroe.

"I had a feeling about the trade all week," Stallworth told reporters in Baltimore. "We'd get into a particular situation, and Red wouldn't use me."

It was a welcomed move for both, mainly because it provided the opportunity to become starting players. Russell was also moved that year to acquire center Jerry Lucas, who, with Phil Jackson and first-round pick Dean "the Dream" Meminger, carried on the Minutemen tradition through the 1973 championship season.

But not everyone was thrilled to be Minutemen. Don May, a 6'4" forward who was a third-round pick in 1968, blasted Holzman and the Knicks after he was picked up by the Buffalo Braves in the 1970 expansion draft.

"I felt inadequate last year," May told Phil Berger. "The other guys were the stars of New York, and I was just filling a uniform. And a lot of 'em last year were on their own ego trips."

May might not have felt like he was a part of the Minutemen, but the players had their own nickname for him: "the Phantom," because you never really noticed him. Ouch.

91 The Greatest Comeback

Every championship season has a little magic in it, something that tells you it has the potential to be special. For the 1973 team, that came early in the season, on a night that at first looked like it would be a total disaster.

The Milwaukee Bucks were no longer that young team the Knicks had overwhelmed in the 1970 Eastern Division Finals. This team, with the overwhelmingly versatile Oscar Robertson and the dominant Kareem Abdul-Jabbar, won the NBA title a year after that loss to the Knicks (and Lew Alcindor changed his name the next day). They were now among the league's elite.

And they were really putting it on the Knicks on November 18, 1972, at Madison Square Garden. Milwaukee led by as many as 20 points late in the third quarter and had an 86–68 lead with 5:50 left in the game. Up 18 with less than six minutes to go usually means, as Marv Albert would say, extensive *gar-bahhhge* time.

Oh it was—for the Bucks.

"Things didn't look good, but I wasn't rattled, knowing from experience that anything could happen in basketball," Red Holzman wrote in *Red on Red*. "Besides, I wasn't going anyplace anyway. I knew if we kept the pressure on the Bucks and got some breaks, we would have a chance. We had won other games that year with last-minute rallies, and we would win a lot more coming back from what looked like knockouts.

"That was a special thing about my teams then. Like thoroughbreds, they had the capacity to rise to the occasion no matter what other teams did. They always had the ability and the heart to come back. I called time and in the huddle thought to myself that all we had to do was score 19 points and hold the Bucks scoreless and we would be able to win."

Seriously, Red?

"It was wishful thinking," he added, "but not crazy."

After an Earl Monroe three-point play with 4:52 left, the deficit was 15 and the Garden crowd picked up the "De-fense!" chant. A Walt Frazier steal and layup cut it to 13. Shortly thereafter, a Frazier jumper brought the Knicks within 11. The Garden was rocking.

Robertson missed a lazy turnaround jumper over Frazier and Abdul-Jabbar somehow blew the put-back. Monroe then scored twice, closing the gap to seven. Another Kareem miss and then Dave DeBusschere scored on a jumper off a handoff from Monroe. There was 2:20 left in the game, and the Knicks were down only five.

"They're going to bring the house down in a minute, Bob," Knicks broadcaster Cal Ramsey noted to play-by-play man Bob Wolff.

Monroe was dazzling. He had 11 points in that final stretch, including a fast-break layup that cut it to three. More misses by the

Bucks stars and then Frazier was fouled. Two free throws, swish. The Bucks were clinging to a one-point lead.

Bucks coach Larry Costello had already called two timeouts. His team was caught in a tornado.

But he had Lucius Allen at the line to ice it. Allen, in his fourth season, was a capable free-throw shooter (76.4 percent in the season before). This, however, was just one of those nights. Allen missed both. The Garden roar reached a deafening level.

Willis Reed snatched the rebound, and the Knicks headed up the court. With 36 seconds left, Monroe buried a jumper from the left elbow, and the Knicks had the lead.

The roof almost blew off at that point.

"The building," Holzman wrote, "actually shook."

When Abdul-Jabbar missed an off-balance skyhook against strong defense from Reed with 27 seconds left, DeBusschere aggressively tore down the rebound. Bill Bradley then dribbled out the clock but curiously never took a shot. The 24-second shot clock expired, and the Bucks had one last chance with an inbound to Abdul-Jabbar with three seconds left.

He airballed a long, corkscrew fling, the MVP's fifth-straight miss. Frazier caught the ball and, as the Garden screamed with delight, ran off the court.

Knicks 87, Bucks 86.

Wolff called it "one of the most fantastic victories of all time." Officially, it was a 19–0 run in the final 5:11.

Monroe finished with 22 points and Frazier added 17.

Abdul-Jabbar had 32 points in the game, but Reed, who returned to the game after getting injured earlier, held him to two points in the final 8:10.

"It seemed like an impossible accomplishment," Red wrote, "and we had some breaks along the way. But it was our system that had made it possible for our players to operate almost instinctively. We played as a team and we won as a team. It was our discipline, our unselfishness and our confidence in our ability that won it for us."

92 The Streak

Comebacks, as Red Holzman said, were a trademark of his teams during the championship era. And it took one late in a game against the Cincinnati Royals on November 28, 1969, to set a franchise record (and, at the time, an NBA record) with 18 straight wins.

The Knicks opened the season with a 5–0 mark but dropped a 112–109 loss to the San Francisco Warriors at the Garden on October 23. The next night, they went to Detroit and took a 116–92 win. They played a third game in three nights back at the Garden against the Bullets and enjoyed a 128–99 blowout.

And the Knicks just kept winning after that.

Down went the Hawks (128–104), San Diego Rockets (123–110), and the Bucks twice (112–108 and 109–103). The team headed west for a four-game road trip and just barnstormed, with wins at Phoenix (116–99), San Diego (129–111), Los Angeles (112–102), and San Francisco (116–103). It was getting ridiculous.

"The fourth quarters, the starters were on the bench," Frazier said in a *New York Post* article in November 2009. "We were blowing people out."

The streak reached 11 when the Knicks came home to beat the Bulls 114–99 and then the defending-champion Celtics 113–98.

The league's record for consecutive wins of 17, held by the 1959–60 Celtics and 1946–47 Washington Capitols, was nearing.

Down went the Cincinnati Royals 112–94, and then came a nail-biter, a 98–94 win at Philadelphia on a Friday night. The team's record was 20–1 after a 128–114 win over the Suns at the Garden, followed by another home win over the Lakers, 103–96. The Knicks then took a trip to Atlanta before Thanksgiving to play the Hawks. Atlanta, where the Hawks moved in 1968, is Frazier's hometown and, as such, a place where family takes up most of his time.

He was all over the floor that night, in a 138–108 win. "I remember I stole the ball so many times," Frazier told D'Agostino in *Garden Glory*. "I told the [Hawks players] to hold onto the ball, I'm tired."

The Knicks tied the NBA record with 17 consecutive wins. The day after Thanksgiving, they were in Cleveland, Ohio, to play the Cincinnati Royals at the old Cleveland Arena. Oscar Robertson was his usual dominant self with 33 points, but he fouled out with 1:49 left on a questionable call while going for a loose ball.

Bob Cousy, then a player/coach, checked himself into the game for Robertson. His free throws with 27 seconds left gave Cincinnati a 105–100 lead that should have all but iced the win and ended the Knicks' chances at the record.

Cousy, it should be pointed out, was a member of that Celtics team in 1959–60 that tied the mark (that team's bid for 18, coincidentally, ended against this same Royals franchise).

Willis Reed drew a foul and made both free throws to cut it to a three-point deficit, and Cousy called timeout and set up a play. But the guy he had inbound the ball—it happened to be himself—made a mistake, and the pass was picked off by Dave DeBusschere, who took it in for an uncontested layup to bring the Knicks to within 105–104.

"I threw the game away," Cousy would say after the game. "All I had to do was throw the ball in bounds, and we would have won."

Incredibly, the Knicks came up with yet another steal, this time by Reed, to pull off the miracle. Reed hit Frazier, who was fouled by Tom Van Arsdale. Frazier hit both free throws with two seconds left for the 106–105 win.

The streak ended the very next night at the Garden against the Pistons in a 110–98 loss.

The record was eclipsed the very next season, when the Bucks ran off 20 straight wins. That one didn't last long, either, as the Lakers posted an amazing 33 straight wins that, to this day, remains an NBA record. Since then, five other teams have either matched or surpassed the Knicks' run of 18 straight wins, but it is a mark that remains unmatched in franchise history.

93 Kobe vs. Jordan

The NBA is a stars' league, and one thing David Stern has often done is take care of the game's biggest stars. When Stern announced that New York City and Madison Square Garden would host the 1998 All-Star Game, it was not only a nod to the basketball mecca, it was a chance for Patrick Ewing to be the centerpiece of what is always a fun weekend.

It was the fourth time the All-Star Game had been played in New York but only the first since 1968, when the league came to the spanking-new Garden on Seventh Avenue.

There was already great anticipation for that season in New York, especially after the frustration of how '97 ended against Miami. But the team opened the season with a middling 15–10 record and headed to Milwaukee on a Saturday night, in the second game of a back-to-back series. A frustrating 98–78 loss was compounded, literally, when Ewing went up for a pass and was pushed from behind by Bucks center Andrew Lang. It caused Ewing to fall awkwardly and, as he braced himself, a bone in his wrist popped right through the skin.

Forget the All-Star Game; there were serious concerns about Ewing's career at that point.

When the All-Star break arrived, the Knicks were 25–21 and already knew they'd be without their star center for the rest of the season. Ewing had been voted by the fans as a starter—with Shaquille O'Neal's move to the Lakers, Ewing became the top center in the East once again—but obviously couldn't play. He was replaced by one of his Georgetown disciples, Dikembe Mutombo. No other Knicks players were selected as reserves, so the only Knicks representation in the game was the Garden itself.

But thanks to Michael Jordan and a dazzling teenage protégé, there was still plenty of buzz about the NBA's big show that weekend.

Kobe Bryant, a high school phenom who was a lottery pick by the Charlotte Hornets (and then forced a trade to the Lakers), was an instant fan favorite for a league that was in need of some new faces to replace the fading stars of the 1980s and '90s. (One of them, Larry Bird, was actually coaching the game, representing the Indiana Pacers as the head coach of the East All-Stars.)

It was also billed to be Jordan's swan song, as rumors abounded about the impending end of the Chicago Bulls dynasty. It was already known that Phil Jackson would not return as coach, and Jordan was sniping with team executive Jerry Krause about it. Jordan said he had no plans to play for another coach, and he was expected to retire after that season. And this time he meant retire *for good*, not go play baseball for a couple of years and return.

So this was being billed as his final All-Star Game (though of course it wasn't; he would make two more appearances as a member of the Washington Wizards in 2002 and '03) and there was an anticipation of a torch-passing between the 34-year-old Jordan and the 19-year-old Bryant, who was giddy, to say the least.

"I can't believe it," Bryant was quoted as saying in the days leading up to the game. "Nineteen and I'm going up against Michael Jordan in the All-Star Game. I might sit here and say I'm not looking forward to it and I need to concentrate on the next game. But deep down I can't wait. Going to New York is a dream come true."

Bryant, who was voted by the fans as a starter, came out firing with enthusiasm and a ubiquitous smile, going one-on-one with his hero.

The league, for the first (and only) time since All-Star Saturday was introduced, decided to not have a Slam Dunk contest, because after Jordan and Dominique Wilkins stopped putting on a show, it was no longer a spectacle. But Bryant came into the league as a Jordanesque dunker, and since he didn't have the contest to enter, he turned the game into his own chance to soar for the cameras.

On an early fast break, Bryant took off from the dotted circle in the paint and spun for a spectacular one-handed, 360-degree slam. Later, another young star, Kevin Garnett, lobbed an alley-oop to Bryant for a high-flying tomahawk jam that brought the Garden crowd to its feet.

Jordan's game at that point in his career was starting to show the effects of gravity, but he was still an unstoppable force. He posted up the skinny Bryant for trademark fadeaway jumpers that splashed the net.

By the end, the East dominated with a 135–114 win, and Jordan finished with 23 points and eight assists to claim his third All-Star MVP. He took his last free throw with his eyes closed, just because Nick Van Exel wanted to see him do it.

"I love this place," Jordan later told Mike Lupica of the *Daily News*. "I love this arena...It's a great, fitting place to finish up."

Bryant had 18 points (on 16 shots), including one amazing behind-the-back fake pass into a back-to-front crossover between his legs (trust me, YouTube it) that he finished with a wild runner. It was a defining moment for the next generation. West coach George Karl, however, opted to keep the young gun on the bench for the fourth quarter, leaving the game to the elders.

"It's like looking in the mirror," Jordan would tell his pal, Ahmad Rashad, the NBC host. "This is how I was in my first All-Star."

It had been 20 years since the Garden hosted an All-Star Game and has been 13 years and counting since. With a major transformation under way, which is set to be completed in 2014, there is reason to believe the NBA will come back again.

Will Bryant be there, too? Will he be the one watching with a grin as the next phenom attempts to steal the show?

We can only hope.

94 Meet a Knick

Before the days of the megabucks contracts, when professional athletes often had to work during the off-season to keep up with he bills, they were more accessible, more tangible, to the average Joe. The Brooklyn Dodgers, for instance, were so beloved because they were literally part of the neighborhood; many of them lived there throughout the entire year and raised their families there.

When the Knicks were created, many of the players were from the New York area, such as Rockaway natives Frank and Al McGuire, so there was a similar situation, though not nearly as concentrated as the borough of Brooklyn. But even the beloved teams from the championship era still had somewhat of a personal connection with the people of New York because so many of them embraced the city. You didn't find them scattered deep in the suburbs. Many of them were right in Manhattan, spending the season at a luxury hotel, walking the streets, riding the subways and, of course, enjoying the nightlife.

And for a quick autograph, you could easily spot Willis Reed stepping out of the old Garden on 49th Street, perhaps to grab a Nedick's or maybe even to check on his own eatery, which survived for a brief time. Or there was also the opportunity you might find a miserable Bill Bradley on the E train as he headed off to practice at the Lost Battalion Hall in Rego Park, Queens.

That old facility was originally built in 1939 and converted into a basketball gym in 1960. The Knicks, who didn't have their own practice facility, would use it on occasion, which made the players miserable. Not only was it an old building, but the court was small and the locker room was even smaller.

As they became popular, the players would notice an unsettling amount of kids who would show up to watch the team practice during the week. And the location and accessibility allowed for one youngster named Mike Saunders to work his way onto the court, rebounding for the players. He would eventually become the team's longtime trainer after the legendary Danny Whelan retired.

When the Knicks designated the gym at SUNY-Purchase their official practice facility in the 1980s, there was no longer a reason to live in the city, nor did anyone want to live there during an era when New York was dirty and crime-ridden. At Purchase, you couldn't get into the gym to watch practice, but you could attempt to get an autograph if you had a car and ventured the 40 minutes up to the Westchester campus and had the time to stake out the parking lot outside the gym.

That all ended in 2002, when the team opened its private training center in an industrial park in Greenburgh (slightly farther from the city than Purchase) and the players now had their own private lot, locked by a motorized gate. Most of the players choose to live in Westchester because of its proximity to the facility, where the team spends most of its time and the gym is always available to them. Nate Robinson, for instance, was notorious for calling up a trainer to meet him for a late-evening shooting session.

The arrival of Amar'e Stoudemire, however, brought a reconnection to Manhattan, as he preferred to live in the city rather than in the 'burbs. Stoudemire purchased a penthouse in the West Village. Carmelo Anthony followed suit, with an Upper West Side penthouse duplex. It has been a while since the Knicks had stars that lived right there in the city.

So where can you experience a chance encounter? Aside from frequenting the tony Manhattan neighborhoods, a better plan would be to wander the White Plains City Center mall on a winter afternoon. You're almost certain to find a player or two, especially rookies, out shopping.

Take a Ride in the Clydemobile

If only you could.

The aura of cool that surrounded Walt Frazier was accentuated by the style he lavished upon himself during his playing career. We told you about the Borsalino hat, the impulsive purchase he made while shopping in Baltimore that created the Legend of Clyde.

Frazier had the suits, the muttonchops, and the ridiculously luxurious $5,000 mink that made his dates so jealous they would ask him not to wear it.

Frazier, shown here in 1974, shows off the Clydemobile and his signature style.

His first major purchase, however, was a maroon Cadillac El Dorado. It was the original Clydemobile. But really there was only one true Clydemobile, and in 1970 he bought it literally on the spot at a dealership on Third Avenue: a $35,000 Silver Shadow Cloud III Rolls-Royce.

"Before buying it, I liked the lines but not the stodgy black or gray colors," Frazier wrote in the re-release of his classic book, *Rockin' Steady*. "I had it painted with some flair—burgundy and antelope (a shade of beige). But it still wasn't right. Needed more pizzazz.

"Then I had them put on those gangster whitewall tires. I said, 'Now you're talkin.' The Clydemobile."

He drove it to games, even though he lived in Manhattan. He took it everywhere, and quickly it became as much his trademark as the hat.

"If I were a player today and making what they're making—$10, $20, $30 million a year—I'd have that Rolls, but I wouldn't drive it," he wrote. "I'd have a full-time chauffeur."

Coincidentally, Frazier said there were a few times in the 1970s when people mistakenly took him as the chauffeur. He told the story of a time when he was out with a female friend and stopped at a store to pick up something. When he returned, the girl said a kid came up to the car and said, "I've seen rich people before, lady, but no one like you who can afford Clyde Frazier for a chauffeur!"

He originally had a vanity license plate that read CLYDE, but being easily identified wasn't the best move. The plates were often stolen, so the CLYDE tags were replaced with less conspicuous ones. It was worth a Google just to see if someone had attempted to sell them on eBay years later to make a little money off a collector's item. Nothing turned up.

The Clydemobile went with him to Cleveland after his trade, but neither really looked like they fit in the Rust Belt. After he retired, Frazier took the Rolls-Royce to his hometown of Atlanta

Read *Rockin' Steady*

Walt "Clyde" Frazier has been a sports icon for over 40 years. You might say he could write the book on style and cool for the modern athlete.

Actually, he already did.

Frazier teamed up with sportswriter Ira Berkow in 1974 to pen the popular book, *Rockin' Steady: A Guide to Basketball and Cool.* The initial plan was to come up with a basketball instructional book, one that could teach the fundamentals of the game from various aspects: the physical, the mental, and the emotional. And while the book still includes some wonderful tutorials about the basics of the game, after spending time talking with Frazier, Berkow quickly realized that there was more to Clyde than just fundamentals.

So the book also delves into the life of a pro basketball player, from the travel to rest to diet and, yes, even night life. ("I've met girls on the coast but I know I won't be back for another year, so why communicate all the time? I just throw the numbers away and start fresh next season.")

There is also an anecdote that lends to Frazier's legendary defensive prowess, when he was talking to kids at his basketball camp one summer and snatched *two* pestering flies out of mid-air. And he matter-of-factly explains how to do it.

The book was a hit in the '70's—a pre-teen President Barack Obama had it on his shelf—and was reintroduced by Triumph Books in 2010 with an update by Frazier on the style and cool of today's NBA stars.

Almost 40 years later, Frazier's cool has expanded beyond style and basketball and now involves one of his post-career passions: vocabulary. As an analyst for Knicks broadcasts for MSG Network, Frazier once again discovered a unique coolness, with phrases such as "dishin' and swishin'" and "splendor off the glass."

"Some people liked it, some people didn't," he says of his vocal stylings in the revised edition of the book. "But as I tell kids, 'Be different. Don't follow the crowd. Leave your own footprint.'"

That is the consistent message throughout the book, which, like this one, is a must-read for all Knicks fans.

and found himself using it less and less. In 2001 he sold it to a Knicks fan, who still owns it today.

"That was a tough decision, man," Frazier told D'Agostino in *Garden Glory.* "Thirty years. That car was like my wife. And I wasn't there when he took it. I just couldn't see it go. I just told him where it was and that was it."

96 Feel Right at Home on the Road

Seeing the Knicks at Madison Square Garden is the ultimate experience for any Knicks fan, but where can you go to enjoy a little home cooking on the road?

There are several NBA cities where the Knicks are received well, almost to the point where the home team feels like the visitor.

Of course the best one used to be in New Jersey, just a skip across the Hudson River. Even during the Nets' best years, when Jason Kidd led them to consecutive NBA Finals runs (and embarrassed the Knicks in a four-game sweep in 2004), Knicks fans still outnumbered Nets fans at the Meadowlands. In the 1994 first-round playoffs, the arena (known then as Brendan Byrne Arena) was also loaded with Knicks fans, which made for a wild atmosphere in a 93–92 overtime loss that came down to a John Starks miss before the buzzer.

In 2010–11 the Nets moved to a temporary location at the Prudential Center in Newark, which only made it more convenient—and, in many cases, cheaper—for Knicks fans to catch the game. While the Meadowlands is often a traffic nightmare, the Rock, as it's called, was an easy train ride under the Hudson from Midtown Manhattan.

And when Carmelo Anthony appeared in his first game in New Jersey after the trade that sent him to the Knicks (remember, the Nets were in hot pursuit all season long), he couldn't believe how loud the building sounded each time he scored and the sing-song chants of "Meh-low! Meh-low!" rang out.

"I'm not used to that, getting cheers on the road," Carmelo said.

Amar'e Stoudemire, who missed the game with a sprained ankle, drew a loud ovation just for coming out to sit on the bench for the second half. When he and Carmelo exchanged glances, Stoudemire raised his eyebrows and said, "I told you."

The Nets are moving to Brooklyn beginning in the 2012–13 season, which should be interesting since that basketball-rich borough contains not only the game's most passionate followers in the city but some of the most loyal Knicks fans, too.

Philadelphia, because of proximity (and recent disinterest in the team since the Allen Iverson era has ended), has started to become a more Knicks-friendly crowd. But perhaps the most notorious warm welcome the Knicks receive outside of the New York area can be found in Atlanta, where the Hawks struggle to draw large crowds, though Philips Arena is often filled when the Knicks come to town. When the Knicks swept the Hawks in the '99 Eastern Conference semifinals, they were using the cavernous Georgia Dome as a home facility while a new arena was being built. It might as well have been a neutral site.

Stoudemire and Anthony again were overwhelmed by the response they received there, as well. In a hotly contested game on March 6, 2011, the Philips Arena crowd was actually booing the Hawks when they went to the foul line. The Hawks players were furious. Josh Smith was fined for making an obscene gesture to the crowd—*in his own building*—after he hit a free throw.

"It felt like a home game," Stoudemire said afterward. "It was great."

You'll find yourself in the company of many Knicks fans if you attend a Knicks-Heat game in Miami, where snowbirds flock to see the team of their childhood. During those heated playoff battles in the '90s, the Knicks enjoyed a biased home crowd while the Heat had to settle for a 50-50 split. And yes, there were cheers when Allan Houston made that series-clinching shot in 1999.

Even with the arrival of LeBron James to join fellow superstar Dwyane Wade, there were still loud chants of "De-fense!" late in the February 27, 2011, win at American Airlines Arena *when the Heat had the ball.*

And Amar'e heard loud chants of, "MVP!" from crowds at the Verizon Center in Washington, D.C., early in the season.

Though the Lakers have been the league's most dominant franchise in the last 15 years, you'll still hear loud cheers for the Knicks when they play at the Staples Center. And, of course, the celebrities you usually see at the Garden will often make the trip, as well.

The Lakers return the favor, however, when they come to New York.

97 Lapchick Set the Standard

Officially, Neil Cohalan was the first coach in franchise history, but he was really holding the space for Ned Irish's top choice, the popular and successful St. John's University coach, Joe Lapchick.

The 6'5" son of Czech immigrants, Lapchick was already somewhat of a legend, not only by winning back-to-back NIT championships with the Redmen in 1943 and '44 but as a member of the dominant "Original Celtics" teams from the 1920s.

When Irish agreed to join the BAA and form the Knicks in 1946, he immediately targeted Lapchick, who had one year left on his contract with St. John's but privately agreed to make the jump to the pro game. By his fourth season with the Knicks, Lapchick had the Knicks playing an up-tempo style that carried them to three consecutive NBA Finals appearances.

"He was the kind of fellow that you'd go through a brick wall for," Harry Gallatin told D'Agostino in *Garden Glory*. "He was just that nice of a guy, and he didn't put too much pressure on you at all."

Lapchick also had a stipulation in his contract that some coaches today probably wish they could have: no player could earn more than his $4,000 annual salary.

And while he treated his players well, Lapchick often was fiery on the sidelines and took out his frustrations on referees. One trick he often did was flip coins onto the court toward a ref who made a questionable call. As told in the terrific book, *Lapchick*, written by former St. John's player Gus Alfieri, referee Sid Borgia wondered what the coin-tossing meant.

A plainclothes officer assigned to the referee's room suggested it might be a reference to an organ grinder, who had a monkey pick up coins thrown to him as he walked the streets. The suggestion was that Borgia, like the organ grinder, had poor eyesight.

Lapchick would often suffer from the internal stress he harbored over his decisions and the potential ramifications that would come from them. Three straight Finals appearances did not result in a single championship, which had Irish grumbling and Lapchick fearing for his job.

The stress finally got to him, and Lapchick left the Knicks during the 1955–56 season and eventually returned to St. John's. The Knicks were 26–25 at the time he stepped down and finished 35–37, under .500 for the first time. His 326 wins still rank second all-time in franchise history.

98 The Next-Best Thing

In that deliriously fun Spring of '94, when the Knicks and Rangers had simultaneous runs to the Finals in their respective sports, it seemed like every single night one of them had a game. Tickets into the Garden were, obviously, tough to come by, especially when you were a 23-year-old like me with not much more than a few bucks and some lint in your pockets.

But while you couldn't get inside the building, there was always somewhere to go near the Garden to immerse yourself in the exciting playoff atmosphere. One place back then was literally in the Garden, five floors below the court (or ice), called Charley O's. It wasn't much for food—your basic chain-restaurant fare—but it was, at the very least, right *there*.

You almost have to be there, or as close as possible, if you're a die-hard fan. One of the best things about the Garden being right in the heart of the city—unlike so many of these new buildings that are off somewhere in the suburbs or on the outskirts of town—is that when the game ends and the fans burst out the doors, the party is only just beginning.

So if you can't get into the Garden (or if the Knicks are on the road) the best plan to get the most out of your experience is to watch the game with other fans. Cheering is far more enjoyable when it's done with a choir.

So while you may have a great television at home, you probably can't pack your living room with a few hundred people who are as passionate about the Knicks as you are (and your parents, spouse, roommate, or neighbors may not appreciate it). Before you die, hit one of these places and experience a Knicks game from a whole knew perspective.

Clyde's Wine & Dine: It's a must for Knicks fans who want to make a jaunt into the city for a game the complete experience. Head to Clyde's, which is a short walk from the Garden on 10th Avenue between 37th and 38th Streets. The place is dedicated to its owner, with large portraits of Clyde from his playing days and also in several of his most famous suits. In fact, the ceiling is tiled with cutouts of his trademark suits. The bar is flanked with countless flat-screen televisions, which play every sporting event you can imagine—including, of course, the Knicks' broadcast on game nights. The food is great (may I recommend the Clyde Burger?) and after home games there is a great chance you might get to meet and greet the living legend himself, as he is a very hands-on owner who regularly mingles with his guests. Oh, and there's a room with a basketball hoop if you want to try a little dishing and swishing, too.

Stout NYC: Located on 33rd Street, just a short walk across Seventh Avenue from the famous Garden marquee and the lobby, this traditional New York–style pub has countless flat-screen HD TVs above the bar, so you won't miss a second of the action (or a replay). Over 20 beers on tap and well over 100 selections by the bottle, plus a full menu. And when the game ends, you're a quick sprint to the epicenter to join in the revelry and perhaps catch a few of the players driving out of the Garden ramp. Or better yet, the opposing team's bus. (Also a good spot, if Stout is too crowded, is Blarney Rock, which is located right next door.)

Café 31 Sports Bar & Grill: Literally across from the Garden on 31st Street, this is a perfect place for pregame, during game, or postgame. Large TVs on the wall are almost exclusively tuned in to MSG Network, friendly hosts John and Paul know all the latest team gossip and, on occasion, you may even see a Knicks legend or three pop in for a late meal. (When the brick oven is still on, my advice is to go for the thin-crust pizza.) True story: it was where I met Patrick Ewing for the first time. Truer story: Charles Oakley held his farewell press conference here with the

New York media after he was traded to the Raptors for Marcus Camby in July 1998.

If you're into barbeque and noise, just down the street is Brother Jimmy's, which has two levels, usually a loud atmosphere and, well, ribs.

On those warm spring nights, when the team is deep in the playoffs, another great spot would be Local West, a bar located on the other side of the Garden on 33rd Street and Eighth Avenue. The second-floor open-air deck bar overlooks the Garden and is a great spot to pregame. They also have TVs if you decide to stay and just the right ratio of men and women if you're in the mood to focus on other games.

If you're looking to rub shoulders with a few Knicks players after the game (or some visiting NBA stars the night before), and your wallet still has a little weight left in it after the game, head down to where Chelsea ends and the Meatpacking District begins to a swanky joint called 1Oak. It's not cheap, but what would you pay for the chance to raise your glass to Amar'e Stoudemire?

99 Engage in Some Knickerblogging

In 2006, during my career as a sportswriter, *Newsday* assigned me to the Knicks beat. I have to admit I left my cozy assignment covering the NHL and the New York Islanders with great apprehension. Don't get me wrong, I spent most of my early years in the business—as a part-time phone clerk...the glamorous life, indeed—pining for the chance to cover my favorite basketball team.

But I had a great deal of concern about going up against the competition at the other newspapers, some of whom had been on the beat for over a decade. How could I possibly measure up? How could I get my voice heard when fans for so many years had been trained to go to the same sources for their Knicks coverage?

It was then that my blog, The Knicks Fix, was introduced. Blogging was still relatively new to the mainstream media, and most of us didn't know what to do with it. We already wrote stories for the newspaper. What was the blog for? In my case, I tried to turn it into a public forum for opinion, insight, and breaking news. The comments area became almost like a chat room, where fans interacted with each other—and me—and a community was born. The blog has since moved from Newsday.com to my new employers at MSG.com, but like Led Zepplin, the song remains the same.

At this point, every beat writer has a blog, and you'll find news, insight, and anecdotes that may not make the cut for the copy that goes to print. (Kids, you do realize that newspapers still actually *print* stories each day, right?)

And what has been proven over time—led by sudden superstars such as Bill Simmons and Henry Abbott—is that you don't need to be in the mainstream media to develop a credible voice and a following on the Internet. All you need is a blog, some form of social media to promote it (i.e. Twitter), and, of course, some intelligent, logical insight. Or just be insanely funny.

In other words, don't just accept what we're saying about your favorite team (but do keep in mind that we're still the only ones with actual access to the players—so there).

Though Mavericks owner Mark Cuban (an avid blogger) has suddenly turned on his own by dismissing the value of sports bloggers, and Cavaliers owner Dan Gilbert once dubbed internet media as "bloggisists," the Knicks have been open to giving media access to anyone who can make the case that they have a legitimate website.

And speaking of breaking through the mainstream barriers, let me tell you about Anthony Donohue, who has his own Internet radio show at Blogtalkradio.com/theknicksblog. Donohue, a former producer on a New York sports radio station, doesn't just rant and rave, he regularly has current and former Knicks players on, plus celebrity Knicks fans. He's kind of like this generation's Marv Albert, who you know got his start in the 1950s as president of the Knicks Fan Club and by announcing games into a tape recorder.

Some of the best blogs that aren't affiliated with a major newspaper include one of the oldest, Knickerblogger.net, which offers a great deal of statistical analysis and historical references. If its game analysis you need, then it's TheKnicksBlog.com, which not only sifts through all of the stories written by the mainstream media and filters out the news but also breaks down the game like a scouting service. Among fans with voices to be heard—and to hold us mainstream guys accountable—it's KnicksFan.net, BucketsOverBroadway.com, and the hilarious PostingandToasting.com, which is, of course, an homage to Walt Frazier's rhyming styles.

Some players have attempted to get into the blog game, too, but no one has come close to matching the popularity (and entertainment value) that Gilbert Arenas had going a few years ago. When you look back, it's too bad there weren't blogs during the championship era. You have to believe that thinkers and characters such as Bill Bradley, Phil Jackson, Frazier, and Dick Barnett (darlin') would have come up with some great copy.

Then again, in a way they did. And a few of the beat writers back then made some money off of it with a few coauthor book deals.

Damn.

100 Go on a Knicks-Themed Landmark Scavenger Hunt

Now that we've reached the end, you should, at this point, have everything you need to know and do before you die. The best part is, we're both still alive.

So now let's have some fun. In the summer, while you're waiting for the next season, the next chance to get that third title, the next opportunity to sit among your brethren under the famous copper ceiling, where the banners billow when the applause is just right, go on a scavenger hunt of Knicks landmarks. Take photos at each stop, then create your own Knicks blog and post them there or at my Facebook page, facebook.com/Knicksfix or send it to me via Twitter at my account @alanhahn.

We'll start in Yonkers, at Oakland Cemetery, where you'll find the grave of coach Joe Lapchick. Pay homage to a legend and a standard-setter.

From there, stay in Yonkers and head over to wash the dirt off your tires and undercarriage at Charles Oakley's Car Wash on Central Avenue. While your ride is getting detailed, submerge yourself in Knicks nostalgia, which Oak has all around the waiting room. Bonus: photos of the rugged power forward and many of his teammates, memorabilia and, if he happens to be around, great stories.

Oh, and be sure to get the VIP special, which comes with a 48-hour guarantee. After this is over, you're going to need that free wash.

With your whip now squeaky-clean, type 711 Old Saw Mill River Road in Greenburgh into your GPS. You'll see an unmarked facility nestled in a row of trees. On the street, near the motorized gate, is where Larry Brown used to rebel against the team's media policy and speak to reporters in June 2006, the days leading up to his firing. Bonus points if it's raining, which it was many times back then.

Then, around the building, where the main entrance is located (don't try to go inside, it's private property), you'll see the parking lot where Latrell Sprewell also held his own private chat with reporters in October 2002, when he was suspended for showing up for training camp with a broken hand. Those double-doors are the ones Stephon Marbury stormed through as a Knick for the very last time, just after he agreed to a buyout in March 2009.

Okay, let's improve the mood and drive west about seven miles to the campus of Purchase College (formerly known as SUNY-Purchase). Find Stevenson Gymnasium and, if you can, go inside. It is here where John Starks tried to dunk on Patrick Ewing, who slammed him down so hard he injured his knee and, as a result, couldn't be cut. Which of course wound up a blessing. Those memorable Knicks teams of the 1990s practiced here. An unassuming, unpretentious young assistant coach with no NBA experience started his career chasing rebounds in this gym. Within five years, he became the head coach. It is also here that Pat Riley closed the doors to the media, which meant a lot of middle-aged men loitering around a college gym lobby on a daily basis. Creepy. Let's get out of here before someone calls security.

The next stop should be East Orange, New Jersey, to Upsala College, where the team practiced for years before they came to Purchase in the late 1980s. It is there where Bernard King made his comeback from that 1985 knee injury. But considering the gas prices these days and taking into consideration traffic, let's pass and instead head south and cross the Throgs Neck Bridge to Long Island. Trust me.

Find the town in Nassau County called Cedarhurst and get to the corner of Central and Cedarhurst Avenues. There you will find a 12-foot cast-iron clock. This is not just some village décor propped up to make the streets look vintage. This is a monument. In April 2002 this clock was dedicated to the great Red Holzman. Legend has it, Holzman used to keep an old pocket watch on him, and he'd calmly pull it out for obvious display whenever a player would arrive late for practice. There needn't be a word spoken. The player knew once he saw the watch, a fine was coming.

Cedarhurst is a special town because it is where Holzman and his wife, Selma, lived for over 40 years. When he left the Garden on May

The 69th Regiment Armory was host to many Knicks games over the years—and not just when the circus came to town. It still stands today.

8, 1970, the season complete with the franchise's first NBA championship, Red went home to Cedarhurst. Where the clock now stands is where Red and Selma would often go for a stroll or out to eat.

Their home was nearby on Oceanpoint Avenue, which is your next destination. No, not the house, just the road, which has been renamed Red Holzman Way. It's kind of more than a name, isn't it? It's a methodology that coaches today still try to follow.

Jump back on the Long Island Expressway and head west into Rego Park in the borough of Queens and locate the Lost Battalion Hall at 93-29 Queens Boulevard. Though the fortresslike red brick building, or just the very thought of going there, caused misery for most of the Knicks players at the time, it did serve as a regular practice gym for the championship-era teams. The facility has gone through some updates since then—Bill Bradley and company used to shoot on wooden backboards, which are now glass—but the building itself still has some history.

Now it's time to head through the Midtown Tunnel and into the heart of the Big Apple. Head south on Lexington Avenue to 25th Street to the 69th Regiment Armory. If I have to explain too much here, that means you didn't read the book. And if that's the case, pull over, put the car in park, and get to reading.

The Armory is one living time capsule in Knicks history. Whenever the old Garden wasn't available, the Knicks would play their games here on that exact court you see there in the middle of the main floor. And take a look up at one end of this historic building and you'll see an old analog clock, which ticked off the final seconds of Game 5 of the 1953 NBA Finals, when George Mikan terrorized poor Lapchick again for the championship. And below that is the sign, NEXT HOME GAME, which for a while seemed to serve as a threat. At least until the team became important enough to earn choice scheduling at the Garden.

Let's head across town to Eighth Avenue and up to 49th Street, where the World Wide Plaza now stands. I'm told there's a McDonald's nearby that has a small homage to the old Garden in a hallway near the bathrooms. It's the only remaining acknowledgement of the three decades of history that took place there. If you find yourself craving a Nedick's, you're now starting to get it.

The final trip follows the same route the team took when the old Garden closed, down Seventh Avenue and between 31st and 33rd Streets. Before you go in, however, stop on the plaza and find, to the right of the entrance, a pedestal with a large stone eagle with its wings spread proudly.

That is one of three eagle statues that were preserved from the old Pennsylvania Station, which was demolished in 1963—in the midst of heavy criticism—to make way for the new Garden.

Then take in the area a moment. Look at the dated roof of the Penn Station entrance and the rectangular marquee, which, in comparison to the one that used to sparkle over 49th Street, looks so ordinary. All of this will, in time, be replaced, too.

Acknowledgments

I have to thank Scott Rowan of Triumph Books for one of the greatest challenges, and adventures, of my career.

Along the way I had Triumph's Adam Motin and Jesse Jordan keeping me motivated and optimistic that we would meet deadline. And editor Katy Sprinkel's red pen worked its magic to complete the effort. Thanks also to Patricia Frey and Ken Samelson for their crucial assists.

I owe a great deal of thanks to Dennis D'Agostino, the Knicks' official historian and a great mentor in the art and effort of book writing. I reference Dennis throughout the book with quotes he collected over many years writing about the team, especially for his wonderful oral history of the Knicks, *Garden Glory*. If you don't own it, then the 101st thing a Knicks fan must do before they die is to get that book and read it.

Also from the Knicks, a thank you to the team's media relations staff, led by vice president of media relations Jonathan Supranowitz, and the many players, coaches, scouts, and team executives who I covered over the years and provided the stories and anecdotes I was able to share with you. A special thanks to Donnie Walsh, whose brief tenure not only resulted in the rebirth of the franchise, but also served as a wonderful education in basketball for me personally.

Of course, a special thank you to my family; especially my children, Emma, Zachary, and Gracie, who understood why Daddy had to spend more time at the keyboard than the swing set. With the knowledge that I had 100 chapters to write, each day they'd ask, "How many chapters are you up to?" They were my own daily pep rally.

And most of all, to my wife, Stephanie, the greatest teammate a man could ever have. Like everything in my house, this book doesn't get done without her.

About the Author

Alan Hahn is a studio analyst for the MSG Network for all New York Knicks broadcasts. Before he made the move to television, Hahn spent five seasons as the Knicks beat writer and NBA columnist for *Newsday*, where he worked for more than 15 years also covering the New York Islanders and the NHL. Hahn also does occasional work as a host for ESPN Radio in New York City and writes the "Knicks Fix" blog on the MSG Network website. He is the author of *The New York Knicks: An Illustrated History, Birth of a Dynasty: The 1980 New York Islanders, Fish Sticks: The Fall and Rise of the New York Islanders,* and *Bruin Redemption: The Stanley Cup Returns to Boston.* The New York native, and former college basketball benchwarmer, currently resides on Long Island, New York.